Shadows into Light

SHADOWS INTO LIGHT

*A Generation of Former Child
Soldiers Comes of Age*

Theresa S. Betancourt

Harvard University Press

Cambridge, Massachusetts
London, England
2025

First printing

Library of Congress Cataloging-in-Publication Data

Names: Betancourt, Theresa S., author.
Title: Shadows into light : a generation of former child soldiers comes of age /
Theresa S. Betancourt.
Description: Cambridge, Massachusetts ; London, England : Harvard University Press,
2025. | Includes bibliographical references and index.
Identifiers: LCCN 2024008849 | ISBN 9780674251052 (cloth)
Subjects: LCSH: Child soldiers—Sierra Leone—Case studies. | Children and
war—Sierra Leone—Case studies. | Posttraumatic growth—Sierra Leone—Case
studies. | Girls—Violence against—Sierra Leone—Case studies. | Resocialization—
Sierra Leone—Case studies. | Sierra Leone—History—Civil War, 1991–2002—
Participation, Juvenile—Case studies.
Classification: LCC BF723.W3 B48 2025 | DDC 303.6/6083—dc23/eng/20240621
LC record available at https://lccn.loc.gov/2024008849

For the true Sahr and Isatu:
Thank you for letting me tell your stories.

Contents

Contents

Foreword

MOSES ZOMBO

As Sierra Leone's brutal civil conflict raged, one big question was on everyone's mind. What would the post-conflict future look like? A people known for tolerance and peace had suddenly become perpetrators of some of the worst acts of violence in a war that tended to elude all explanation. The rebels of the Revolutionary United Front (RUF) routinely abducted entire communities, subjecting the women and girls to a life of sexual servitude and the boys to forced combat duty. The atrocious tactics of the rebel group meant that young boys and girls were groomed to a life without conscience.

As the conflict dragged on, it became obvious that an entire generation of young people was growing up knowing no other life but one of violence and crime. Many young ones among the ranks of the RUF had witnessed the butchering of their loved ones and the massacring of their communities. Afterward, they were required to subject others to the same treatment they had endured. Senseless brutality was glorified and rewarded. A BBC article aptly described the situation as "barbarism beyond belief." As the nation looked on in horror, we asked ourselves over and over again: what future awaited us after the war ended? Would these young people ever make a transition to responsible adulthood? What could the rest of us do to make the situation better, or avoid making it worse? There was just no telling. This was uncharted territory.

It was in this climate of uncertainty, as the guns finally fell silent in 2001, that I met Theresa Stichick Betancourt, a research scholar from Harvard. Theresa was studying, for her doctoral degree, the effects of traumatic family separation and exposure to violence on human development. Sierra Leone's child soldiers were returning home, and Theresa sought local partnership to study risks and protective factors in their psychosocial adjustment and social reintegration. It was an attractive, if challenging, prospect. The conflict had barely ended, and venturing deep into the interior regions of the country was not without its own risks. A group of United Nations peacekeepers had just been taken hostage by the rebels in the very area where the study participants were concentrated. But the woman whose ideas inspired the study was not one to shy from a challenge. Theresa's belief and enthusiasm were infectious.

Our social science team had no prior experience in research. A diverse collection of people of widely varying ages and backgrounds was united only by a strong knowledge of the local languages and culture. Far from seeing this as a weakness, Theresa seemed to relish the idea of minting fresh research assistants in the mold that suited the work at hand. She set the standard from the first hour of the crash-course training that she led in preparation for the start of data collection: *bad data is worse than no data.* It has remained the mantra of the study.

This was some twenty years ago. The study subjects grew up. They formed relationships and started families. They dealt with the challenges of jobs and livelihoods. Throughout it all, the study kept going. The longitudinal study has become an intergenerational study. The succeeding generation has come to be an important part of the research as the team investigates the effects of war exposure on subsequent relationships and family life. Other facets of the study have examined questions such as the role of emotional self-regulation in employability and professional performance of youth. Scores of academic papers have been written during the course of the research conducted. The insights provided have gone beyond the immediate post-conflict landscape and matured into profound insights about long-term development.

At the center of it all has been one formidable woman. Theresa is not one to rest on her laurels. Well before one phase of investigations was complete, she was already preparing for the next challenge. She wanted to make an impact on as many fields and professions as possible, in developing nations like Sierra Leone as well as in the developed world. It was this vision of reaching the broadest possible audience that gave birth to the idea of a single concise book. *Shadows into Light* is a story that cuts across cultures and walks of life, a story that, despite its author's origins, is first and foremost a Sierra Leonean book. The study is certainly relevant globally, but the Sierra Leonean language and culture have been at the heart of all investigation.

All truly great works are driven by passion. Theresa's passion for the cause she pursues is unmistakable. She is completely immersed. In her professional circle, she is the exacting academic, pushing everyone to the limits of their potential. In the community, including especially the communities of Sierra Leone, she is all patience and understanding. When she feels a piece of work has been inadequately executed, she is rather ruthless on the question of whether to discard it, and just as ruthless at discarding her own views when the evidence seems to be to the contrary. But with family and friends, she is the anxious mother, worrying if her children are empathetic enough in dealing with less fortunate peers. On one occasion, I had just returned with her kids and mine from a trip to a children's home in the capital of Sierra

Leone. Theresa was nervously asking how her children had fared alongside those of the children's home. It was amusing that she showed any nervous concern. Both children were perfectly respectful and empathetic. This is a side of Theresa that is not always on display in work circles.

At another time, I learned that a teenage boy among the study's participants had passed away. We had been following his case with a sense of trepidation, given the red flags that the case presented. I was face to face with Theresa when I broke the news. How her emotions poured out! At that moment, not an eye remained dry in the office. It was moments like this that strengthened her bond with the rest of the team in my country.

If you want someone telling your story, it had better be someone with a heart. As one of the participants in our study said: you can be the most skilled surgeon, but it is the value that you put on the humblest people that actually saves lives.

Abbreviations

AFRC	Armed Forces Revolutionary Council
BEIP	Bucharest Early Intervention Program
CAAFAG	children associated with armed forces and armed groups
CDF	Civilian Defense Forces
DDR	disarmament, demobilization, and reintegration
EVD	Ebola virus disease
GIZ	Deutsche Gesellschaft für Internationale Zusammenarbeit (German Corporation for International Cooperation)
ICC	interim care center
ICER	incremental cost-effectiveness ratio
IRC	International Rescue Committee
MHPSS	mental health and psychosocial support
NET	Narrative Exposure Therapy
NGO	nongovernmental organization
NIMH	National Institute of Mental Health (United States)
PTSD	post-traumatic stress disorder
QALY	quality-adjusted life year
RUF	Revolutionary United Front
UNAMSIL	United Nations Mission of Sierra Leone
UNCRC	United Nations Convention on the Rights of the Child
YRI	Youth Readiness Intervention

PART I

War's Impact

———————

1

War's Children

Sahr

It was a bright, clear morning in Kono District. Sahr clutched his grandmother's wrinkled hand as they stepped softly through the lush jungle. The air was still fresh before the afternoon heat. Light filtered through a brilliant green canopy above, the trunks of tall palm trees twisted with jungle vines. Soft orange-brown dirt dusted Sahr's toddler feet and the edges of his grandmother's flowered wrap skirt. Suddenly, a branch snapped and an explosion of voices erupted from the deep foliage. A small group of rebel fighters burst through the bush, surrounding the pair. The old woman scooped Sahr protectively into her thin arms as the band of men in tattered fatigues, their eyes bloodshot and wild, waved their guns aggressively, commanding her to give up the boy.

She begged them not to take him. "Take anything else that I have," she cried. "What would you want with a little boy like this?"[1]

They shoved a gun barrel to her head in response. When she screamed, they pushed her to the ground and dragged the terrified boy away, threatening to kill her in front of him if she continued to cry out.

The rebel commander took Sahr to be raised by his "bush wife," a young woman who herself had been abducted and forced into a relationship with him. As Sahr's uncle later explained, "one of the men said his wife did not have a child and the boy would make her a fine son." Sahr's life would change forever.[2]

During the four years of his childhood spent with the rebel group, Sahr was forced to see and participate in the horrors of armed conflict daily. He bore witness to countless massacres and killings. Eventually, as he grew, he was pressed into new and more dangerous roles. He was ordered to help the older boys carry out reconnaissance missions: they would spend time in a village, sometimes befriending its inhabitants and studying its layout in order to help the rebels plan their attacks. As one such remote community after another was leveled by bloody raids and brutal killings, a growing group of abducted children trudged along with the rebels, forced to haul the loot they confiscated. Their emaciated arms lugged the spoils of war: dusty loads of machetes, bags of rice, dried fish, and cooking oil, and treasures like wrist-watches and transistor radios.

To calm their nerves and inure them to violence, commanders would force the frightened children to drink intoxicating palm wine or smoke marijuana. The cruelest carved their initials into the skin of abducted children to brand them as their own. In Sahr's case, his captors carved "AFRC" across his chest, to mark him as property of the Armed Forces Revolutionary Council, a branch of the Sierra Leonean army that had joined forces with the main rebel group fighting against the government, the Revolutionary United Front (RUF). On occasion, rebels would press gunpowder or drugs into the bleeding wounds. They told the children that this practice conferred special powers of protection, that the treatment would help them run with great speed—even outrun gunfire.

As the days stretched on, hope for escape quickly faded. The abducted children buried their memories of home deep, for safekeeping. What emerged in place of vulnerability was a primal drive for survival. Each day was a test. Food was scarce, and commanders meted out horrific punishments for the smallest infractions. Children who tried to escape would be beaten to death in front of the others.

New horrors emerged daily. "I was afraid because they killed people in front of me and they gave me a gun during battles," recalled Fatmata, a girl abducted at age ten and held by the RUF for four years. "They used us as human shields, so we stood in front with our guns."

The events that small children witnessed on a daily basis would be hard for most people to endure. Joseph, who had been abducted at age thirteen, reflected on his experience several years later: "All of a sudden I started to see dead bodies, wounded people, blood, people with guns, people fighting and hearing gunshots. . . . You know it affected me so much as a kid."

The children turned to each other for companionship, support, and survival. Persevering meant a daily struggle to secure a meal, find a safe place to sleep, and avoid harm. Repeatedly, children witnessed the torture and abuse of others. "I saw what they did to other children they captured," Fatmata recalled. "They raped and devirginated them—and at times even killed them."

Quiet obedience was a means of survival. To resist or complain could mean violent beatings and even death. Days faded into nights. Weeks blurred into months. Home became a distant past. New families and alliances formed to counter hunger and the physical and sexual violence of their vicious, unpredictable captors. Captivity under the RUF was a living nightmare, one that stretched on for years. Each young person who made it out alive had brutal stories of survival.

Isatu

Isatu had always been a bright girl and a dedicated student. The day the rebels attacked her village, she was a motivated twelve-year-old taking her exams. Her tight braids were bound with colored rubber bands and dangled at her shoulders. She wore a well-pressed blue school uniform with pink detail at the seams. She had prepared well for the exams that day, and she felt confident as she made her way through the questions on the test, soft light filtering through the high windows of the school building.

Without warning, a loud popping noise erupted in the compound. Children cried out. The acrid smell of gunpowder filled the air. Everyone bolted for cover. Children began to hide behind doors and under desks. Screams came from the hallway. Within seconds, rebel fighters burst through the classroom door. People scattered, running for their lives. In an instant, school books and exams were a thing of the past.

"They attacked our village, and everybody ran," Isatu recalls. She couldn't keep up with the others. Everyone was running, panicked, into the dense jungle that surrounded the school building. She fell behind and was quickly captured. She soon realized that the rebels who had grabbed her were boys about her age. Her heart pounded.

Isatu was marched back to the RUF jungle camp at gunpoint. A boy dressed in ragged camouflage shorts and a torn T-shirt featuring the image of American rapper Tupac screamed at her to sit with the other children. As Isatu cowered in terror, her eyes locked on the frightened face of her younger sister, Amina, huddling among a group of small children also rounded up in the village raid. Isatu was filled with relief, but also devastation. She had hoped that Amina had escaped.

Isatu and Amina spent two years with the rebels. "We were obedient and did everything they asked us to do," Isatu later recalled. "If you did the wrong thing or disrespected the women, they would beat you to death." She witnessed terrifying events, which made her constantly fear for her own safety. "The rebels used to rape people, burn houses, and capture people to carry their loads . . . I was unhappy and cried because I saw them do terrible things to other children and I was afraid that they would do the same to me."

The deep connection and protectiveness the sisters felt for each other was their lifeline. Isatu recalls how having the responsibility to look out for Amina helped her through the darkest of times. "I think that was even my strength. I considered that whatever I was doing I had to look out for somebody." Their devotion carried them through many terrors. Sisterhood, love, and sacrifice were their salvation. Each would have given her life for the other in a second. Luckily, that moment never came.

Sahr and Isatu were both torn from their families under the most frightening of circumstances. And for both of them, their eventual homecomings were marked by intense struggles to reconnect with their lives. In the aftermath of captivity, both Isatu and Sahr experienced community tensions, interpersonal difficulties, and intense emotions that were hard to manage. Over the years, though, their life paths have taken very different directions. The forces shaping such divergent paths are at the heart of this story.

2

The Global Face of Conflict

In 2024, it was estimated, that one in every five children in the world—some 468 million children or more globally—live in an active conflict zone.[1] The numbers are even higher when we include regions that are recovering from the devastation of earlier wars: damaged infrastructure, weak economies, under-resourced schools and health systems. War is not only a threat to children's immediate safety and survival; it also disrupts their relationships to family members, peers, and communities, as well as access to future opportunities and livelihoods. The echoes of war, both socially and biologically, resonate for generations.

The global face of conflict is ever-changing. The protracted civil wars in Sudan, Somalia, and the Democratic Republic of Congo have no apparent end in sight. Russia's 2022 invasion of Ukraine and the ensuing combat have displaced two-thirds of the children in the region.[2] As the war in Ukraine dragged into a second deadly year, brutal attacks by Hamas in 2023 and Israel's bloody retaliation kicked off a fresh and horrific new phase of conflict in the area, with thousands of Palestinian civilians again caught in the crossfire. In mid 2024, the United Nations estimated that over 17,000 children had been killed in the conflict.[3] Meanwhile, the abduction or forced participation of children associated with armed forces and armed groups—a group often known by the abbreviation CAAFAG—remains a common theme for conflicts as far-flung as northern Nigeria, Yemen, and Colombia.

It has been easy for many to assume that children who face the extreme trauma of war are simply "lost generations." But what if that's not true? What factors can help young people recover from their wartime experiences? What if changing our ways of thinking and reconsidering our approach to bridging the humanitarian, peacebuilding, and development nexus might allow many of these young people to not just recover, but thrive? These questions form the core of the study, now ongoing for more than twenty-two years, that informs this book.

Our study was meant to build on prior research on children whose lives were disrupted by war and help fill gaps that had been identified. As a doctoral student in public health and psychiatric epidemiology, I found the questions of how individuals and societies overcome adversity and violence particularly compelling. I had grown up in a remote part of Alaska, a region haunted by cultural loss and collective trauma that often manifested in high rates of suicide, family violence, and squandered human capital. I wanted to know more about what helped people fight their way back from trauma and begin to rebuild their lives. That's what encouraged me to accept the invitation from the International Rescue Committee (IRC) to go to Sierra Leone and understand how children had been affected by the civil war that ravaged that country from 1991 to 2002.

The causes of Sierra Leone's war are complex. They are rooted both in the legacy of its colonial past and also in the subsequent corruption and exploitation of its rich resources. After gaining independence from the British in 1961, Sierra Leone struggled to launch its fledgling democracy. By the time its second president, Joseph Momoh, took office, the economy had quickly deteriorated. Power and wealth rested mainly in the hands of a few Freetown-based elites linked to political "big men" who lined their own pockets rather than attending to the desire of citizens to have access to education and health care. At first, the RUF rebel movement, led by Foday Sankoh, even had some popular support. However, with financial backing and weapons from dictator Charles Taylor of Liberia, the RUF quickly turned its back on its promises and moved to take control of Sierra Leone's rich alluvial diamond mines.

The conflict quickly deteriorated into corrupt and brutal action on all sides. The RUF were well known for their practice of using machetes to cut off hands or arms of the civilians they sought to terrorize, leaving behind over 10,000 amputees in the aftermath.[4] Another infamous feature of Sierra Leone's civil war was the estimated 15,000 to 22,000 children who were associated with armed forces and armed groups.[5] Before the war's end, all sides in the conflict—from the RUF rebels to the Sierra Leone Army to the paramilitary Civilian Defense Forces (CDF)—had involved children in their fighting forces. The National Committee for Disarmament, Demobilization, and Reintegration (DDR) estimates that nearly 4,600 children were formally demobilized, but many others returned home without formal support.[6]

In the conflict, the RUF often made deliberate attempts to sever ties between young people and their families and communities. As villages were raided and children and youth rounded up, it was not uncommon for a young person to be ordered to kill friends, relatives, or neighbors under threat of being killed themselves. This practice not only contributed to horrific collective trauma but was intended to make it impossible for a young person to feel that they could ever again be accepted back home, thus, it was thought, keeping them from running away from their captors.

Several scholars on children involved in Sierra Leone's conflict and other wars of this nature have underscored the theory that children were taken because they were seen as more easily manipulated and more likely to perform horrific acts with obedience.[7] In addition, the proliferation of small arms in the region meant that weapons could be easily operated by a child.[8] In some cases, children also joined willingly as a means of securing food and protection.

When Sierra Leone's civil conflict finally ended with the signing of peace accords in 2002, waves of children were released from fighting forces. Local leaders and development experts debated what should happen next. Could these children return home, despite deliberate efforts to sever ties between young people and their communities? Would they be accepted? What was in the best interests of these children? What was in the best interests of the communities that had been horribly scarred by conflict themselves?

In the end, the Sierra Leone government and its international policy partners at United Nations agencies decided that CAAFAG, or more colloquially "former child soldiers," should return to their families and communities if at all possible.

Communities and international stakeholders went to work. To facilitate this process, interim care centers (ICCs) were set up around the country by nongovernmental organizations (NGOs) with oversight from the government. ICCs attended to the initial needs of children who came out of fighting forces quite traumatized. They provided medical care, food, and shelter, as well as recreational activities like soccer and art. Informal learning opportunities and some support from social workers at the ICCs were also arranged.

As ICC staff began to develop relationships with children, they would ask about their backgrounds. Where had they come from? Who had they last lived with? How did they become involved with the armed groups? Did they have living family members back home? What were their thoughts about returning home?

These interviews were part of a practice called "family tracing," a process of information-gathering essential to reuniting separated children with their families or extended kinship networks. Once the tracing interview was as complete as possible, a social worker armed with this information would go to communities identified in the interview and try to make a match.

Yet the moment of returning home was only the beginning of the journey. By what means could children so violently separated from their families and subjected to such extreme and prolonged trauma reintegrate into their communities? What leverage points might lead to better life outcomes? How could naturally occurring community processes be supported by outside programs and policies? To explore such questions, my local team and I launched a longitudinal study of war-affected youth— LSWAY for short. Our intent was to follow several hundred young people over the course of their lives, following reintegration. In particular, we wanted to understand the pathway from those early moments at the end of the war into adulthood and beyond.

At the core of our study is a cohort of boys and girls who had come through the doors of an ICC serving five of Sierra Leone's then-fourteen districts, administrative units that function much like states do in the United States. (Since then, the country has been reorganized into sixteen districts.) In an ICC office in Kono District without electricity or running water, we had been given a list of names of all the children served by that ICC during its most active eight months of reintegration activities. We invited these young people and their families to be a part of our study.

Initially, we also hoped to compare the life experiences of children who had been involved in armed groups with those who had not. But our attempt to identify a comparison group of children and youth who had absolutely no involvement with armed forces and armed groups proved futile, because the main ICC lists used for study recruitment came from regions where there had been both heavy RUF abduction and also strong counter-resistance from the CDF—an expansion of the traditional hunting societies known as *kamajors* among the Mende people. Over the course of the war, the CDF had expanded, coming to dwarf the RUF and Sierra Leone armed forces. Ishmael Beah's famous book *A Long Way Gone* describes his experience in the war as a boy involved with the CDF.[9]

It would not have been appropriate or ethical for us to go randomly door to door and ask if there were any children there who had or had not been involved with armed forces and armed groups. We hoped that by discreetly inquiring later about such involvement we might get a sizable comparison group. But in the end, of the 529 children who we enrolled in our study, only thirty-six of them said that they'd had absolutely no involvement in any of the fighting forces. Nonetheless, we decided, a longitudinal study of over five hundred war-affected youth who were mostly CAAFAG—128 girls and 401 boys, ages ten to seventeen at our initial contact in 2002—would still be a useful contribution to understanding the life course impact of severe trauma and loss, and the factors that might shape more resilient outcomes over time.

The research presented in these pages summarizes experiences arising from over twenty-two years of this research project, a true labor of love. We have observed some surprising findings in this work, such as the way that girls faced heightened risks immediately after the conflict in terms of stigma and poor mental health, but over time actually appeared to do a lot better than boys as they moved into young adulthood. We also observed how the social context offers various opportunities, or leverage points, that can be modified in order to shape more positive outcomes for youth. And above all, everything we have learned about resilience in the face of extreme risk has helped us to develop and test group mental health interventions for youth, as well as family-based preventive interventions to break cycles of violence across generations.

With time, Sierra Leone has witnessed significant progress. The country rose from a history of horrible trauma to hold democratic elections, shepherding a fragile yet optimistic post-conflict era. Since those early days, this small but mighty nation has been visited by additional adversities, including a historic outbreak of Ebola virus disease (EVD), discussed later in this book, as well as the consequences of the global COVID-19 pandemic. However, throughout all of its ups and downs, Sierra Leone remains a place of beauty and joy with great wisdom to share. The lessons that it has taught us have value for anyone working with war-affected children and families around the world today.

3

Children, War, and Trauma

For many children around the globe, exposure to war is a fact of daily life. Even in higher-income and more developed countries, such as the United States, young people are exposed to violence in many forms. Due to ongoing crises in the Middle East, Horn of Africa, Central America, and Ukraine, the world today faces the largest humanitarian crisis since World War II. In the aftermath of the global COVID-19 pandemic, fragility has only deepened.

Does exposure to war lead to irreparable harm for children? Without question, war has both direct and indirect effects on children's lives. Not only are there threats to their physical health and even their survival, but the mental health consequences of exposure to violence and loss have also been well-documented in war zones. In addition to these threats to physical and mental health, the indirect effects of war may include disruption of social networks and neighborhood functioning, and interruptions in access to health care as well as educational and occupational opportunities.[1]

My team's research aims to uncover factors that influence who does better or worse over time that can be leveraged by policies and programs. Ultimately, bringing an end to war is the true solution. Unfortunately, war remains a reality in the lives of millions of children around the world.[2] Although the trauma that children have experienced in war zones cannot be undone, the good news is that we can do a lot to shape the support that children, youth, and families receive in settings of active conflict and to build back mental health social services in post-conflict settings. At present, these are opportunities that remain significantly overlooked.

For those children who have come through their experiences in ways that might be termed "resilient," we want to know what might have helped them—what resources or opportunities may have been at play? Similarly, for those whose lives seemed irreparably harmed by their experiences, we also want to understand the cascade of risk factors that may have led to lost potential or even young lives lost far too early.

There is a growing body of evidence showing that the consequences of violence are propagated across generations. When children experience extreme violence in war, they face profound negative effects. These effects linger beyond those directly exposed to violence—they ripple into the subsequent generations. The intergenerational cascade of violence has immediate relevance to our understanding of modern warfare as well as post-conflict fragility. Until recently, most of our knowledge on the intergenerational impact of war came from studies of European Holocaust survivors and generations of refugees from wars in Asia.[3]

Scholars and scientists have described in detail the ways in which trauma experienced by one generation affects subsequent generations. Natan Kellermann, a psychotherapist who worked closely with Holocaust survivors, proposed four major patterns representing the common processes involved in trauma's cascading effects across generations.[4] The first theoretical orientation focused on the unconscious and indirect effects of parental trauma on children. These theories, or models, posit that emotions that were unable to be expressed by traumatized parents are passed down to later generations.[5] Research with children of Vietnam veterans described various ways in which parents had trouble containing emotions and were observed to resort to projecting their anxieties and concerns onto their children through parenting behaviors. As a result, severe emotions such as persecution, aggression, shame, and guilt are split and projected onto their children, leading to higher levels of mental health distress and interpersonal difficulty.

A second pattern illuminated in Kellermann's work relates to how parents "socialize" their children. Drawing from theories such as the work of Albert Bandura, researchers have emphasized that children learn by imitating their parents, thus, parental behavior affected by trauma can be passed on and replicated in the next generation.[6] These models focus on direct and observable behaviors and interactions, such as expressing strong reactivity and emotion in response to stressful events, or doing the reverse and tuning out when stressors arise.

A third model pertains to biological and genetic mechanisms by which the effects of parental trauma may travel across generations. A body of convincing evidence is emerging that trauma leaves a biological mark that can be carried by one's descendants. For instance, physician Rachel Yehuda and her colleagues at Mt. Sinai Medical Center studied parents with and without posttraumatic stress disorder (PTSD) and their children. They found that adult survivors of the Holocaust had lower levels of the stress hormone cortisol, as did their offspring, and that lower cortisol was significantly associated with both PTSD in Holocaust survivors and lifetime risk of PTSD in their offspring. This pattern was not observed in parents who had no other psychiatric conditions apart from PTSD. In addition, Yehuda and her colleagues have also observed methylation of DNA, a process affecting how genes are expressed, among trauma survivors. Yehuda published a study indicating that trauma survivors demonstrate such changes in the glucocorticoid receptor gene, which has a negative effect on gene expression years after the exposure to traumas.[7]

A fourth model examined by Kellermann and colleagues pertains to family systems and communication models.[8] In these models, families where a caregiver has suffered significant trauma operate as isolated communities with little outside interaction. In these situations, very intense and circular dynamics can exist between a traumatized parent and their children whereby both direct and indirect processes are at play, which can increase the likelihood that the trauma of the parent also impacts the mental health and functioning of the children. For instance, Kellermann writes, children can feel it necessary to overachieve as a response to the attempted extermination of their ancestors.[9] Behaviors such as parental hypervigilance, as well as overprotective parenting, have also been observed.[10] In relation to such dynamics, research on multigenerational samples has been carried out by Yael Danieli, who has interviewed children whose parents are Holocaust survivors. Her work puts forth adaptational styles, similar to the Kellermann typology, that include "victim, numb, and fighter post-trauma adaptational styles."[11]

Research from wars in Europe dominates the literature; when it comes to sub-Saharan Africa, the research evidence is far less developed, despite the numerous conflicts that have raged on the continent. In Rwanda, where I have worked since 2006, some very important research has been led by local scholars following the 1994 genocide against the Tutsi.[12] Like those who have worked with survivors of the Holocaust, local researchers in Rwanda, in collaboration with European peers, have investigated both biological and social dynamics.

The evidence for intergenerational transmission of trauma related to war experiences in Rwanda is compelling. A study by

Celestin Mutuyimana at the University of Rwanda and his colleagues followed three different groups of study participants: First,
those who were in-country during the genocide against the Tutsi
and directly targeted; second, those who were refugees out of
the country from 1959 but may have had family members in-
country who were targeted; and third, people who were living in
Rwanda during the 1994 genocide against the Tutsi but were not
themselves directly targeted by the perpetrators. The researchers
observed different rates of PTSD among all of these groups. Individuals who experienced direct trauma as a result of being targeted by the genocide demonstrated the highest rates of PTSD,
as did their offspring.[13]

A subsequent study then set out to investigate the processes at
play that may have explained their research findings. First of all,
the team conducted in-depth interviews with a group of women
survivors of genocide who scored high on the study's PTSD
screening tool and their children. When Mutuyimana and his
colleagues read the interviews with these mothers, the levels of
trauma they reported were staggering. Furthermore, the violence
and deaths often led directly to economic hardship. For many
of these women and their children, not only had the war brought
terrible trauma and loss, including witnessing violent deaths of
those they loved, the events of the genocide had plunged the
families into social and economic hardship in a manner that was
difficult to overcome.

Like those who survived the Holocaust in Europe, survivors
of the genocide against the Tutsi in Rwanda showed distinct patterns of response. For example, a common pattern was for genocide survivors to feel grief and longing for those who had been
lost. Survivors hungered for a connection to their loved ones who
had been killed. Similarly, for children, they desired to know
about the lost person. A second theme pertained to a sense of
emptiness. In Rwandan culture, it is typical for a parent to raise

children in an extended family who assist and provide advice and care for young children along with the biological parents. During the genocide, many elder family members were killed, leading to feelings of emptiness in the homestead both for parents and their children. Family members spoke about becoming increasingly aware of the reduced nature of their family. A third dynamic pertained to the theme of "heart wounds," by which children were observed to internalize the trauma of their parents. These children felt compelled to help their parents navigate their psychological pain. In this manner, subsequent generations took on the suffering of their parents.

Importantly, we know that the effects of war can vary across individuals, even when levels of trauma and loss are comparable. Despite some of the worst horrors imaginable, some survivors manage to live on with more or less typical functioning and interpersonal relationships. In fact, some individuals are so propelled by their past that they go on to demonstrate great compassion and empathy for others and become wonderful caregivers and helping professionals. Substantial past exposure to trauma, loss, and violence *does not* prescribe a doomed future.

Deepening our understanding of the potential mechanisms by which emotional and behavioral disruptions due to war may march across generations remains critical. There is concern for how future generations of war-affected youth will fare.[14] Will untreated trauma and problems with anger and hopelessness doom interpersonal relationships and life outcomes? For many war-affected youth, the aftereffects of loss and trauma can result in a paradox: even when given a life opportunity, it may be carelessly squandered. Many NGO programs have lamented low attendance in youth employment and education programs in conflict zones. Astute observers have noticed that in the aftermath of conflict, even after weeks of well-intentioned training and NGO-issued tool kits, program materials have appeared for sale on the black market; sewing machines abandoned for quick money and carpentry kits promptly traded off. The mindset after so many years of predictability was oriented to just living for the present. A young person might think "the future is unpredictable; best to live in the moment." In this manner, what can look like immature behavior is actually a response to trauma. Thus, seemingly selfish actions should not be taken at face value as illustrations of laziness, but rather as manifestations of the mental health consequences of war.

Numerous studies of war-affected youth remind us of the consequences of exposure to "toxic stress"—repeated, high levels of violence and fear that jolt the body's fight-or-flight response so frequently that the bodily stress response becomes recalibrated. For most, a traumatic event causes the heart to race. Children with repeated trauma exposure may demonstrate patterns of stress physiology that are quite different from children without such exposures.[15] When some children are exposed to repeated traumatic events, they may eventually show a more blunted response. Children and adolescents exposed to frequent and repeated trauma may also demonstrate a foreshortened sense of the future, living in the "now" rather than engaging in present-moment trade-offs, like investing time in school or work, in hope of a brighter future.[16] This sort of "survive for the moment" perspective can lead a young person to sell the very tools given to them with the intention of promoting self-sufficiency.

As Ann Masten describes in her book *Ordinary Magic,* resilience research has experienced four major phases.[17] Early efforts focused on description: defining, assessing, and documenting the process of "good function or outcomes in the context of risk or adversity."[18] Studies of the individual traits and characteristics of children deemed as resilient emerged from research on children living with serious mental illness to children who survived war and extreme poverty. Following this, a second phase of resilience science began to unpack the question of *how* resilience might occur. Much like the study documented in this book, this phase involved the investigation not just of resilience, but also of modifiable risk and protective factors shaping that process to understand how resilient outcomes might emerge. Building off of this orientation, a third phase of resilience science has worked to harness identified mechanisms to envision, create, and evaluate the impact of interventions to promote resilience itself. The old adage applies here: if you want to truly understand something, try to change it.

Recent advancements in our understanding of the neurological and genetic features of child development and toxic stress gave rise to the fourth phase, which is characterized by dynamic, systems-oriented approaches that, in particular, focus on interactions between genes and experience, and the person and family within a larger context. In this era, the sort of research questions that dominate have parallels to those that arise in precision medicine—questions such as "what works for whom, and under what circumstances?" Relatedly, this phase of research has begun to explore questions of differential susceptibility and how intervention models might be refined to move beyond a "one size fits all" approach to have greater and more sustainable impact. In this manner, the study of resilience has matured from early moments of documentation to an understanding of processes involving protective, promotive, and preventive influences, including genetic and biological influences to risk and protective factors in operation across systems that extend from neurons to neighborhoods: families, peer groups, one's larger social network, and even the larger cultural, political, and historical context.

COVID-19 has extended the reach of adversity and loss to nearly every corner of the world. By mid-March 2020, our public schools and businesses had shuttered. My university teaching, along with that of others, moved online, and international travel was canceled.

As the days of "social distancing" dragged on and blurred, office work turned into endless Zoom meetings while we also became homeschool leaders who managed our energetic children, struggling to learn online. I was contacted by journalists writing about stress and adversity to comment on the situation for children and families. For children in the United States suffering under the lockdowns and anxiety of a global disruption, I advocated for the same rights and interventions that we propose in refugee displacements: routines, predictability, and relationships. One of the hardest things to witness was the immense difficulty of online learning and the isolation of children craving peer interaction and teacher guidance. What was difficult for many was impossible for those children already facing inequitable access to the internet and digital tools, or without the family support that would make online learning possible.

Even in my own household, it was nearly impossible to ensure that everyone got online, that assignments and meals were all prepared on time while navigating an at-home workday. I couldn't imagine the challenges households might face that were more crowded and had fewer resources. Indeed, we heard from our partners in Maine that Somali Bantu refugee parents had encountered problems with Child Protective Services, as their inability to navigate supports for online learning was considered child neglect.

As I reviewed the literature in preparation for calls with journalists, I stumbled upon a book published in 1999 called *The Children of the Great Depression*.[19] The author was a professor emeritus at the University of North Carolina at Chapel Hill, Glen Elder. I read the book voraciously, underlining sections; it seemed to be written for times like these.

The world has witnessed many moments of great adversity. Under the shock of the Great Depression launched by the 1929 stock market crash, infant mortality rates that had been falling were soon climbing again by 1933 for the first time since such data had been collected in the United States. By 1932, 23 percent of the breadwinners in households were unemployed.[20]

Many families that had been in the middle class during the 1920s slipped into poverty, contributing to rising incidences of hunger and malnutrition affecting children and adolescents, much like we see in Sierra Leone today. School districts ran out of money, classrooms became more crowded, school years were shortened, and many young people dropped out of school to seek work.[21] During the Great Depression, cash-strapped business owners and parents ignored or intentionally violated existing child labor laws. Franklin D. Roosevelt warned that one-third of America's citizens were "ill-housed, ill-clad, ill-nourished."[22] Of those, the majority were children. The extreme economic fallout of the Great Depression took a psychological as well as physical toll on children and families.

Elder's research on children during the Great Depression led to his development of the Family Stress Model.[23] Elder observed that individual-level economic hardship increases marital conflict and mental health problems, which in turn increase negative parenting practices (increased harsh / aggressive parenting behaviors; reduced warmth / closeness between parents and children), which result in increased child behavior problems. In the United States and elsewhere, similar dynamics were observed again in the Great Recession of 2008, initiated by the high-risk mortgage market collapse. Studies of families during this time observed increased risk of child abuse and men's controlling behavior toward romantic partners.[24] These findings are a reminder that cataclysmic events, such as the terrible trauma and loss perpetuated in times of war, have cascading effects on how society and families function in the aftermath. In this manner, development actors, practitioners, civil society, and governments have to attend to the ripple effects— the detrimental conditions that continue to perpetuate the effects of war continue long after the ink on the peace treaty has dried. Oftentimes the subsequent tsunami of economic and social stressors can extend for generations.

Even today, the impact of the global COVID-19 pandemic reverberates, mixed with growing anxiety about the realities of climate change, all in a world dominated by racial and political tensions fueled by a toxic social media culture. The mental health needs of children and adolescents are reaching staggering new extremes. By some estimates, rates of anxiety and depression in children rose by 27 percent and 24 percent respectively between 2016 and 2019, and 25 percent and 20 percent during the COVID-19 pandemic.[25] Soon after the COVID-19 pandemic reached its peak, a report by Vivek Murthy, the US Surgeon General, detailed how the exponential rise of child and adolescent depression and anxiety collided with the very moment that health care was in a tailspin. What resulted was a global mental health crisis and an increasing chasm in access to evidence-based services, often filling emergency mental health beds in psychiatric facilities and emergency rooms with people much younger than would normally be expected.[26]

We face difficult times. However, the message of history is that it is the nature of humankind to encounter suffering, but also to overcome it. Despite all of the challenges we face in the world today, until our inability to care for our planet leaves it uninhabitable, the human species will continue to persevere, to face hardships, but also to find a way forward. The shape of this journey in Sierra Leone, passing through the darkest of times and slowly emerging into light, is what we will explore next.

4

Jellybeans in Darkness

Koidu Town, the capital of Kono District, was shrouded in darkness. The power grid had sparked, choked, and fallen silent. The night sky resembled a blanket studded in spots by a smattering of stars. The war had ended earlier that year, and the crusty cement buildings standing in tight corridors along the main market were still pocked with bullet holes and deep machete wounds. Their pastel paint, in green, yellow, and pink, was peeled and chipped. Corrugated tin rooftops had been hurriedly stripped for scrap metal.

The United Nations Mission of Sierra Leone (UNAMSIL) had installed itself in one of the only solid buildings left in Koidu Town—the local school. A school session had not been called for over a year, much to the despair of children and their weary parents. All sides had fought bitterly to control Kono, a diamond-laden district that had become the last rebel holdout in the war's waning years. In the heyday of diamond mining, hopeful locals and exhausted indentured workers had plundered every inch of soil in search of treasure. As a result, most houses there teetered above a rabbit's warren of tunnels carved desperately in the red dirt.

On this trip in 2002, I took it all in: Koidu Town lay in devastation. Outside of the UNAMSIL compound, children rambled in search of activity. When our white four-wheel-drive Jeep bumped and jostled into the UNAMSIL compound, they crowded around the vehicle, squealing with curiosity and shoving their friends aside. They pressed their hands to the windows, clamoring to look at the "Lebanese" people inside, as white folks were often referred to. Perhaps the appearance of an NGO vehicle might herald a school reopening?

To the children's disappointment as well as my own, our meetings confirmed what we had heard from others. The school would remain shuttered for some time. There were no teachers, no supplies—not a book to be found.

That evening, the local staff and I shared a meal in silence. We had neither tables nor chairs, so we sat on the floor as dusk settled in, soaping our hands in a colorful blue-and-green plastic basin purchased at the local market. The cook positioned a large, flat tin plate in the middle of our group. She had heaped the plate with steaming locally grown rice and dried fish in palm oil sauce, laced with cassava greens. The sauce gleamed black in the dim light. We each dug into the dish, politely but hungrily, our spoons clacking at its metal base. Darkness deepened the rich fatty flavor of palm oil and the smoky chunks of dried fish.

Although we came from dramatically different backgrounds, those differences felt less stark as we sat on the floor together in the dark. We were all aid workers trying our best to develop programming for children whose lives had been violently interrupted by war. After a day of speaking with stakeholders and meeting parents, children, and community members, we were hungry and ready for sleep, desperate for a hot meal after a long day.

I was finishing my doctoral work in Maternal and Child Health and Psychiatric Epidemiology at Harvard, and this was my third trip with the International Rescue Committee (IRC). The IRC is a well-respected organization, launched at the behest of Albert Einstein following World War II to realize the lofty humanitarian mission of tending to those made vulnerable by war and humanitarian emergencies. Work with refugees and children in war-torn settings is its specialty. It has country programs spread across most continents and a strong focus on gathering evidence about how to help war-affected children, youth, and families.

Since my very first days of fieldwork with the IRC, first in Albania for the Kosovo crisis, and later on at the Ethiopia-Eritrea border, working on education programs for Kunama refugees, I had learned to bring "local gifts" to share with partners in new settings. Back in the January cold of Cambridge, Massachusetts, my rushed shopping trip through the snow-covered red brick streets of Harvard Square had brought me to the Harvard bookstore.

Hurriedly, I had grabbed handfuls of white and crimson pens and small notebooks emblazoned with the university insignia in gold letters. Harvard's name was sure to channel some gravitas, even in a place several continents away. While I was standing at the checkout counter, though, my eyes had landed on a brightly-colored rack of candies lined up for impulse purchases. At the last minute, I slung a box of Jelly Belly miniature jelly beans across the counter onto the pile of pens and notebooks. A small cellophane window on the box revealed a chaotic range of colors, and a label boasted "Over fifty different flavors!" Now, in the smoky darkness of Koidu Town, I reflected on the genius of this purchase. Guessing jelly bean flavors was an ideal activity for a night without electricity, a perfect ice-breaker.

Moses Zombo was immediately my favorite among the group. A tall, thin man with a broad face and deep brown skin, he spoke with a faraway gaze, scratching thoughtfully at the growth of beard at his neck with one long pinky fingernail when he made a critical observation. He had a delightful laugh and a booming voice that he could squeeze into a very high pitch when lingering on a point. I loved how he pronounced my name as "Tereeza," like a British aristocrat. Moses is an intellectual and gifted story-teller. He studied linguistics and worked as a teacher for many years at the illustrious Prince of Wales School, one of the best-known boys' schools in Sierra Leone.

After dinner, we all sat on the floor in the middle of the living room. I began to dole out the jelly beans. The light was dim, and our eyes could make nothing of the colors as we tried to guess each flavor. Without the benefit of vision, our full attention turned to savoring and reflecting on each flavor. Everyone spoke English, but the American candy flavors were foreign. We held up a scuffed hiking headlamp to squint at the legend emblazoned on the white carton. Some fruits were familiar and easy to confirm even in the dark—guesses of "banana!" and "orange!" came easily. Other flavors, like "toasted marshmallow" and "peach," simply didn't register. Had these jelly beans come from Sierra Leone, they would have celebrated flavors like mango, soursop, and ginger. The Krio language, the lingua franca of Sierra Leone, has roots in English, but its terms can trip the unwary. To this day, I am unsure how to speak about a pear, given that *pear* means "avocado" in Krio. Perhaps pears do not exist in Sierra Leone?

Moses and I had spent a long day discussing the beginnings of a research project. It was a wild idea we had cooked up with the IRC's director of the Child Protection Unit, the indefatigable Marie de la Soudière, who had developed the methodology for child tracing still used to this day.

I had first met Marie at the IRC headquarters in New York City. I come from a small village in Alaska, with no recognizable street grid nor even paved roads; city navigation has never been my strong suit. I remember feeling like a character in a movie as

I popped out at Grand Central Station and found myself wowed by the looming skyscrapers and grand entrances of midtown Manhattan. The IRC headquarters are in a building also housing several newspapers. A bronze statue of Atlas carrying the world on his back gazes down from the main entrance.

"We have a range of programs to help children reintegrate," Marie had explained to me, "but we really don't know much about how these children fare over time." She went on in her lilting French accent, her ice-blue eyes glinting: "No one has really looked at that."

So on that first bright morning in Koidu Town, Moses and I pored over the registries of the several hundred children who had passed through the IRC interim care center. A friend of mine, a biostatistics PhD candidate at Harvard, had sent me a random numbers table to help with our sampling. However, the more we had discussed it over email, the clearer his statistical advice became: with such small numbers, there was no reason to take a random sample. We'd just need to invite every one of them to participate.

The next morning, Moses and I laid out our plan to Marie: we would invite all those from the roster who were under eighteen, the typical definition of a "child" according to international law and the United Nations Convention on the Rights of the Child.[1] This sample would capture those passing through the reintegration center during its most active period of reintegration. We would talk with their families, too. And we would make this a longitudinal study, meaning that we would then come back routinely to learn what their lives were like. We didn't realize then the rich journey we had just begun.

5

Swit Salone

Sierra Leone, or *Salone* in Krio, is a place of staggering natural beauty. Locals speak of it as *swit Salone*—sweet Salone. The country sits like a round emerald jewel on the West African coast. Sierra Leone's bustling capital, Freetown, in the Western Area, contains nearly a third of the population. The rest of Sierra Leone comprises more rural districts, some entirely off the grid of cell phones and electricity. Sierra Leone's rich red soil, rolling verdant hills, and turquoise sea offer a banquet of sights, tastes, and unforgettable experiences. Freetown has one of the deepest saltwater ports in all of Africa. The country has tremendous mineral wealth: bauxite, iron ore, and, of course, diamonds.

The spectacular natural resources of Sierra Leone, including its vibrant and creative people, have historically been fodder for horrific abuse and exploitation. Dating back to the twelfth century, busy trade routes facilitated the flow of gems, minerals, and timber from the region to other parts of Africa. With the arrival of Portuguese explorers in the 1500s, a vicious trade in human beings erupted.[1] The slave trade in Sierra Leone also manipulated ethnic conflicts among tribes, who, at times, would help to abduct and sell members of warring parties into servitude.

For such a small country, a disproportionate number of African Americans can trace their ethnic heritage to Sierra Leone.[2]

The famous story of the Cuban schooner *La Amistad* features the valiant revolt of captured slaves from Sierra Leone and other parts of West Africa, who rose up to demand freedom from their captors. After they took control of the vessel and demanded that it sail back to Africa, the slave traders pretended to head in that direction, but at night they would redirect the vessel once more to the northwest.[3] It was eventually captured in American waters and a legal battle ensued. The historic trial witnessed the testimony of Sengbe Pieh, a young man from the Sierra Leone city of Kenema, who cried out, "Give us free!" John Quincy Adams joined the legal team, taking the case of *United States v. The Amistad* all the way to the US Supreme Court. With only one dissent, the justices ruled in favor of the kidnapped Sierra Leoneans.[4] In 1841, the remaining *Amistad* captives were returned to Africa.[5]

The colonial presence of the British in Sierra Leone lasted over two hundred years. During that time, the British took copious amounts of human and natural resources from the region for the gain of the Empire. This violence still echoes today in Sierra Leone. In the two centuries of British control in the region, health systems in particular were ignored, and the well-being of the local population was of little consideration. Over the course of British rule in Sierra Leone, no schools of medicine or nursing were established.[6] Mental health in Sierra Leone was even more neglected than physical health. The Kissy Lunatic Asylum, established in 1820, was the first colonial asylum in sub-Saharan Africa. As colonial reach expanded in West Africa, it soon became the psychiatric asylum for all of the British West African colonies. It was only after 2018, with the establishment of the Kissy Psychiatric and Teaching Hospital, that appropriate psychotropic medications were made available to its patients and the widespread practice of chaining patients to their beds was largely eliminated.[7]

The race to exploit and plunder Sierra Leone's richness left behind not just families torn asunder but a system of governance often criticized for corruption. Too often, the region is known for the narrow-minded advancement of big men pursuing their own interests at all costs. These dynamics were horribly exemplified during the response to the 2014–2016 Ebola outbreak, in which millions of dollars that were intended to save the lives of the very poor were mismanaged or went missing.[8]

It is a strange source of pride for me that in all of my years of work in Sierra Leone, I have never paid a bribe. To do this has cost me many painful hours, as it goes counter to what scholars of Sierra Leone have described as a "postindependence history of political corruption."[9] I remember many sweet visits dampened by a last-minute shakedown at the airport. After one particularly upbeat period of fieldwork, for example, I had celebrated with a quick trip to buy gifts at Freetown's Big Market (which infamously had once been used for the selling of humans during the height of West Africa's slave trade). Tucked into the center of Freetown, this massive, crumbling yellow concrete building features endless hallways of kiosks staffed by energetic local sellers. There's not a single working electric socket in the building; natural light filters in, illuminating piles of carved wooden masks and woven baskets. On the second floor of the Big Market, women energetically hawk striking indigo batiks and country cloth wall hangings. Local artisans compete with sellers of everyday household objects, from plastic washing tubs to soup ladles.

I had bought beaded headbands and a handcrafted slingshot for my children. I was smiling to myself, reflecting on the wonderful trip I had just finished, as I cleared the airport luggage security check. I was roused from my musings when I realized that the security guard rifling through my bag was beckoning to me in a low voice.

She tapped the threadbare army duffel bag between us and asked, "What's in here?" She ignored the fact that she had strewn most of the contents of my bag onto the aluminum table between us.

"Oh, these are gifts for my family," I said, distracted.

She paused for a moment. Leaning in, she gestured to me to come close. In a hoarse and low voice, she asked, "How about a gift for me?" Her hands were firmly planted on the top of my bag, unyielding. It was clear that passing a quick $20 bill would help me avoid further delay.

Instead, I looked at her blankly. I've learned a technique over time that I call the "loud and confused" approach, and I took a deep breath as I prepared to use it. "A gift for you? I'm not sure what you mean!" I said as loudly as I could. The flustered guard quickly waved me through, not wanting to call any further attention to us.

The frustrating part of corruption in Sierra Leone is that too often it is seen as an acceptable practice. More often than not, officials will give it a try, hoping for a weak moment and eventually backing down once futility becomes obvious. But taking part in this dance robs everyone of time and faith in others. I know NGOs that have set aside thousands of dollars for bribes. They explain that it's just the cost of doing business, but this sort of business continues to hold the country back. With some small resistance, I find that people always yield. We must all resist in order to create change.

On another occasion, we were stopped just one hour into what was to be a six-hour drive to Kono District for data collection and dissemination. We had left behind the Barmoi, my favorite hotel in Freetown, that morning. I usually stay at the Barmoi with my dear friend and colleague Adeyinka ("Yinka")

Akinsulure-Smith. She grew up in Sierra Leone in the town of Njala. Her father, a psychologist, lectured at what later became Njala University; her mother rose to become its chief librarian. Her mother and several other family members had survived the Siege of Freetown in January 1998. Yinka had grown up hearing stories about how the family and neighbors had hidden in their homes during the battle.

This morning, our trip stalled at a vehicle checkpoint. A young man in worn camouflage leaned jauntily on a wooden post to which a tattered rope was tied, blocking the road ahead. An energetic collection of boys dressed in shorts and old T-shirts lingered behind him, poking sticks in the dirt and at each other. It looked like a scene from news coverage during the war; young boys manning checkpoints was not a good memory. Yinka and I both sighed. *This could take a while.*

The officer approached our car. He looked hungry and likely had not been paid for months. He leaned against the Jeep, tapping the window angrily. He asked for our vehicle registration. Dikoh, our driver, shuffled nervously for paperwork in the glove compartment. The officer grabbed the papers and frowned as he flipped through them, only looking up from time to time to scowl. Dikoh was anxious. He remembered those checkpoints from the past even more intensely than all of us. His fear was electric. We all leapt when the officer tapped the window glass again.

He handed back the papers with disgust. Dikoh's license was soon to expire. The hungry young officer saw an opportunity. He leaned his full weight on two hands, planted on Dikoh's car door. He now looked past Dikoh directly at me and Yinka and crooned, "Oose to blame?"

We looked back at him steadily. *Who's to blame?* When the officer was not looking, Yinka and I rolled our eyes at each other. She had attended Freetown's prestigious Annie Walsh Memorial

School for Girls as a child until 1979, when her father died suddenly. After her mother took a leadership role as head of documentation with the Economic Community of West African States, Yinka completed her schooling in the United Kingdom and Canada, and finished a PhD in the United States. She's a true New Yorker. But she understands the local context, and both of us knew that all we could do in this circumstance was to be patient.

The dance continued for well over forty-five minutes, with the officer only returning to tap on her window and ask again, "oose to blame?" We would look back at him blankly, sometimes shrugging our shoulders. It became clear that he was looking to wear us down. A quick payment would drop the rope and let us go on our way, but our hearts knew this was the wrong thing to do. Every bribe paid lays the path for the next shakedown. With no one around to hear my "loud and confused" approach, we had to wait it out. The officer paced around the Jeep, inspecting it furtively. Yinka and I sat, resigned. Dikoh looked like he was awaiting a death sentence.

At one point, Yinka demanded in Krio that the officer explain the wait, but he persisted, continuing to shake his head and ask, "oose to blame?" Another hour later, he finally caved in and dropped the rope. Relieved, Dikoh took us back to Hotel Barmoi for some much-needed relaxation.

Dynamics of corruption have propagated in Sierra Leone, especially in the times immediately following the war; it remains a major stumbling block to advancement in the region. There has been a long tradition of payoffs for everything from building contracts to good grades in school. The dominance of a "big man" culture and society also means that women and girls are oftentimes the casualties of these dynamics. A legal scholar I know recounted going to speak with a minister many years ago about sexual and gender-based violence facing women and girls after the war, only to see a young girl involved in the commercial sex trade exit the minister's office; he opened the door while still fastening the belt on his pants. Peace Corps volunteers in rural areas report being encouraged by fellow teachers to sleep with students—sometimes seen as one of the benefits of being a teacher. Yinka has told me horrific stories about young women being extorted for sex in order to improve their grades in school, especially at the university level.

I remember a series of conversations with my good friend, the boy genius of Sierra Leone, Dr. David Sengeh. David is the son of a colleague, Paul Sengeh, who used to be the head of monitoring and evaluation at UNICEF Sierra Leone. David was a UNICEF youth ambassador and a gifted student. Like Yinka, he graduated from one of Sierra Leone's prestigious exam schools, the Prince of Wales School, located in Bo district. His talents eventually took him to Harvard University, where he completed his undergraduate degree in engineering, and then to the Massachusetts Institute of Technology for a PhD in robotics. After working at mobile tech companies such as IBM and declining recruitment offers from Google X, he was asked by the newly elected president of Sierra Leone, Julius Maada Bio, to join his administration as its first chief innovation officer. He introduced new technology and data science techniques as a way to help strengthen governmental reforms.

Evidence-based interventions and policies began to gain traction within the new government. While still in his thirties, David was appointed Minister of Basic and Senior Secondary Education. A role model and leader, passionate about the potential of education to transform the country, he brought new ideas and improved digital systems to help shore up the government's meager education budget.

One of the biggest hurdles he faced was massive corruption in the system. Teachers, for example, continued to draw salaries even though they did not show up to their posts. Angry, burned-out, and underpaid, some had not received a paycheck in months. David moved quickly to modernize the system for tracking and monitoring the quality of teaching across the country and to implement more robust proctoring of national grade completion exams.

With the Maada Bio government re-elected in July of 2023, the dream of a meritocracy for Sierra Leone remains. The new cabinet has exceeded its goal of ensuring that women represent at least 30 percent of the cabinet positions. David Sengeh is now Chief Minister, a role in which he will oversee all the ministries of government and pull them together toward a shared vision. Change is slow, but change is indeed coming.

6

The Embodiment of War

Trauma gets under the skin. It is well documented that exposure to frequent and repeated neglect and physical or emotional abuse can considerably increase risks of physical and mental disorders.[1] Understanding the impact of toxic stress early in life and across the life course has been a central focus of a great deal of research related to early trauma and neglect resilience.

Not all stress is bad stress. In fact, some degree of stress in life is normal and helps children learn necessary coping skills.[2] Even when stress manifests in more significant forms, like a frightening accident or event in the school or community—including the devastating impact of the recent COVID-19 pandemic—caring adults play a critical role in helping children manage stressors. In some cases, however, loving caregivers are not available to the child or are so impaired that they are unable to provide the needed soothing or protection when such events occur. In the worst cases, adults and other caregivers are themselves responsible for the abuse and neglect.

The situation of child soldiers embodies the definition of toxic stress: repeat activation of the bodily stress response from innumerable traumatic events without the presence of caring loved ones who might otherwise help the young person to navigate frightening experiences. Research shared by the Harvard Center on the Developing Child reveals that such toxic stress experiences disrupt and alter the architecture of the developing brain in ways that can lead to difficulties across the life span, with lasting consequences for behavior, health, and learning.[3]

Toxic stress is most damaging when it occurs early and repeatedly. However, growing up within an armed group can look quite different from one case to another. For children born into a rebel group, for instance, if their mother was loved, cared for, and protected by her commander "husband," it may well be the case that they had access to a nourishing and somewhat safe environment, despite the situation.

Many of the children and adolescents abducted into armed groups during Sierra Leone's civil war, meanwhile, were on more or less normal developmental trajectories up until their moment of capture. For these children, the traumatic experiences came suddenly into what had otherwise been ordinary Sierra Leonean childhoods. Although Sierra Leone remains one of the poorest countries on earth, with very limited health care and access to educational opportunity, many of the children in our study had strong and healthy attachments to committed caregivers before their abduction, which may, in many cases, have laid the groundwork for resilient outcomes despite the exposure to trauma. In particular, these more or less normal early beginnings may have provided a critical foundation for navigating the consequences of trauma exposure, especially if the naturally occurring sources of protection were reinvigorated following reintegration.

For other children, abduction may have worsened an already challenging developmental context, especially for those children living with ongoing poverty and violence prior to their involvement with armed forces and armed groups.[4] After all, the war in Sierra Leone was not a sudden event. It was a long and drawn-out process that dragged the country into economic and political instability for years. These years of chaos were characterized by interruptions in educational access, food production, health care, and inconsistent governance and protection. When children who have grown up in the context of a broken economy, poor educational opportunities, and insecure governance then face trauma due to violent and brutal abduction and captivity, the risks to their development intensify. Similarly, when an already vulnerable young person returns from captivity and encounters family and community rejection and stigma, the stage is set for lasting difficulties.

An increasing body of research on the epigenetics of stress has illuminated several mechanisms by which the types of toxic stress common in former child soldiers (i.e., traumatic death of loved ones, repeat sexual violence, being forced to participate in injuring or killing others) can disrupt the biological processes that operate in relation to DNA. Epigenetic changes do not change the DNA, but they do alter how the instructions contained in DNA operate. Both behaviors and the environment can change the way that our genes work, switching on and off how our body "reads" the instructions buried deep in our immutable DNA. Chemical processes unleashed during the body's stress response have been linked to epigenetic changes such as the unraveling of telomeres, the ends of DNA strands that encode our unique genetic blueprint. As genes and the environment interact, genetic predispositions buried deep in the DNA lie waiting for the chemical triggers of distress to activate them, thus switching on disease processes, including risks for mental health difficulties.

But the fact that effects of trauma can echo across generations does not mean all is lost. When we envision mitigation measures, we cannot underestimate how much family, community, and the broader societal and cultural context can influence individual outcomes. Legendary child developmental theorist Urie Bronfenbrenner coined the term "social ecology" to capture these layers of influence.[5] While toxic stress can lead to lasting damage, protective factors can serve as a soft cushion, blunting some of the hardest knocks.

Bronfenbrenner's ecological systems theory envisions child development as a complex system of relationships influenced in an interrelated way by multiple levels of the surrounding environment. Like waves surrounding a pebble thrown into still water, these layers—from the immediate settings of family and school to broader influences of cultural values, policies, and customs— surround the individual child. Thus, to understand any one child's development and mental health, one must look not only at the child and her immediate environment, but also at the interaction of that setting and those broader influences as well.

Bronfenbrenner divided the environment of the developing child into five different systems: the microsystem, the mesosystem, the ecosystem, the macrosystem, and the chronosystem.[6] Of these, he underscored that the microsystem is the most influential level of ecological systems theory.[7] This is the most immediate setting of the child's development. It contains the developing child and their primary attachment figures. Each microsystem containing the child also includes the actors with whom they have direct contact, such as parents, siblings, peers, and teachers. Most critical in the microsystem are attachment relationships, especially attachments to loving and nurturing caregivers. As Bronfenbrenner famously quipped, "Every child needs at least one adult who is irrationally crazy about [them]."[8] Such love can be transformative, an elixir against stress.

Returning to the image of the pebble falling into a still pool, many concentric circles beyond the microsystem shimmer around the young person, holding them at the center—a metaphor for the multilevel processes that can lead to more resilient outcomes despite tremendous trauma. To kick off this process, certainly individual factors matter, like the child's own sense of will and determination. However, once this process is initiated, it can build into what psychiatrist Stevan Hobfoll termed protective "resource caravans."[9]

Resources, as they emerge, beget additional resources. They interact with the child's individual agency and grow in magnitude and breadth, rippling out across the many layers of life, from family to peers to even larger societal relationships. The mesosystem refers to interactions beyond this immediate microsystem, such as those between the child's family and the school environment. The ecosystem contains formal and informal structures that do not immediately contain the child but impact the microsystems in which the child participates—for example, settings such as the parents' workplace and their extended community. At an even broader level of influence, the macrosystem refers to the established cultural, political, and historical context in which the microsystems and ecosystems are embedded. It is within the macrosystem where culture, customs, and social norms come into play. Affecting all of these levels is the chronosystem, a timeline of major events along the course of a child's development. In war-affected children and youth, the chronosystem includes major historical events and trauma events. In a setting like Sierra Leone, it also includes transitions into the post-conflict period.

As many children in our cohort demonstrated, just having loving family members can be a salve, but stigma and family rejection can deal a mortal blow. In the cohort of 529 war-affected youth we've followed since 2002, we have seen the full bell curve of outcomes—a fully fleshed-out statistical distribution. Some of the young people in our sample died in horrible moments of violence, such as a young man who was involved in criminal ganglike activity and was eventually murdered by his peers. Others lived lives marked by social isolation. Yet there have been others whose individual perseverance was matched with and catalyzed by supportive families and communities, opening opportunities for a brighter future, including several young people who have turned their lives toward becoming healers.

Patterns emerge when we unpack each story. The risks are real, but so are the resources. Our interviews with Isatu, the twelve-year-old girl kidnapped while taking her school exams, tell of the horrors she has seen. She was sure her parents had been killed when their village was attacked, and that she was on her own. However, her prospects changed when she arrived at the rebel camp and saw her sister, Amina, with the other terrified children. Amina became her touchpoint, a key attachment figure and source of love and soothing through harrowing years with the rebels.

When the RUF was disbanding toward the end of the war, both Isatu and Amina escaped and were transported by the International Rescue Committee to an interim care center, where they awaited a foster home placement. A desire to return to school smoldered in Isatu's heart. It defined her existence, a beacon beckoning her forward and leaving behind the dark memories of all she had lost. In those long months at the ICC, she was paralyzed by the fear that she might never return to school.

Finally, a foster home was found that would take both girls. Their new foster family had several grown children, with only their youngest child, an eleven-year-old boy, at home. The foster mother channeled her religious faith and commitment to caring for others into her treatment of the girls. She knew they had been through a lot. She loved them through the difficult times, she told us, "the way I take care of my own children." In the early days, Isatu and Amina's behavior could be stubborn and feisty. As the foster mother described it, the girls gave her and her husband some trouble, albeit "minor trouble." However, Isatu remained fiercely focused on her education. Resources were limited, but the girls were loved boundlessly.

It was soon clear to everyone in the family that Isatu had incredible drive. Isatu's foster mother and father often discussed how to help her. When interviewed, her foster mother called Isatu "very intelligent." Her natural intellectual ability, perseverance, and resourcefulness drew people in. Isatu's drive engaged a broad team of people all invested in this smart, determined young girl. Her helpers all wanted her to succeed, and they were rewarded in turn by the fierce effort Isatu put into every opportunity sent her way.

Isatu's perseverance generated additional ripples of support, soon to become a self-fulfilling virtuous cycle. Before long, she had a team of supporters all doing what they could to help, and she was knocking down the challenges in front of her, left and right. She told me about one particularly committed local UNICEF staff member who passed a basket to collect small change and contributions to help Isatu cover her school fees. Isatu's initiative and the response it elicited in others was synergistic. Wave by wave, this energy propelled Isatu all the way to the top of her class.

In the face of staggering trauma, we see how a relatively small ripple of personal agency and determination can set off a series of reinforcing efforts when met with the efforts of others. This is the resource caravan, about which Hobfoll wrote, "As individuals strive to obtain, retrain, and protect personal, social, and material resources for the self, they create social structures that necessarily support this primary motivation."[10] Kind guidance and a listening ear can be a balm to the pain of years of trauma and loss. Donated resources can deliver promise to a young person determined to do better.

The great physician and social justice leader Albert Schweitzer was quoted as saying, "In everyone's life, at some time, our inner fire goes out." But he also reminded us to attend to the moments when "that inner spark is then burst into flame by an encounter with another human being."[11] In this way, small opportunities can fuel a roaring fire, fanned by self-efficacy and determination. Resilience is about kicking off these unstoppable chain reactions and keeping the virtuous cycle alive.

7

Without Family

My memories of the Koidu ICC differ from the joyful images the children there painted. A favorite painting of mine by a talented child artist used thick tempera paint to portray a bright yellow ICC building backed by a brilliant blue sky and a scene of children happily playing soccer in the courtyard. The in-person reality was very different. The walls of the ICC were a dirty mustard color and pocked with damage from shelling. The walls were worn with use, one layer of plaster giving way to the jagged edges of crumbling concrete beneath. It was hot. Dust filtered through the air.

The day I arrived at the ICC, three boys eagerly greeted me on the porch sporting outfits common among many poorer children in sub-Saharan Africa—tattered secondhand T-shirts from the United States. These hand-me-down shirts that the children wore were often emblazoned with Western logos and perky phrases. From working with former child soldiers both in northern Uganda and this ICC in Koidu Town, it was not the first time that I had seen a child survivor of extreme trauma in a shirt sporting upbeat references to a very different life. Smudged with dirt and full of holes, the T-shirts recalled sunny summer getaways far away from conflict zones, like *Cape Cod Little League*

1998, or junior pajama tops festooned with the grinning faces of Mickey Mouse or the Teenage Mutant Ninja Turtles. The pop culture image always jarringly contrasted with the reality its wearer faced.

That first stifling afternoon in Koidu Town, the boys on the porch were silent, looking at me with soulful gazes. I was an oddity in these parts. Another rare "Lebanese lady"—not to be trusted. The boys looked to be about age eight or nine, but an ICC staffer told me that they were all well into their teens. One boy was so thin that an angular shoulder poked through the frayed neck of his oversized T-shirt.

These children were the lucky ones. They were safe. But even so, these were far from luxurious conditions. In fact, each time I visited the ICC, I was bothered by the dingy, windowless sleeping quarters. A single room could be crowded with more than two dozen children. The once bright-yellow foam mattresses they slept on were now graying, pitted, and discolored from use. The young boys slept in one large wing of rooms off the quad. The ICC was full of mainly boys. The few girls were packed into smaller rooms in a separate area.

Not all of the children's art was upbeat and hopeful. Their images also documented horrific memories of war and loss. There were paintings of families loading all of their worldly belongings into dugout canoes to escape village raids, a large fabric bundle balancing precariously over the water. Others depicted soldiers in fatigues with bombs falling from the sky. I remembered similar paintings from northern Uganda, showing captives held by rebels with their bleeding hands tied behind their backs. Some of the drawings portrayed what might happen if someone tried to escape. The frightened figures were painted bloody and wounded. The message was clear: to make a move to escape meant a horrific death by torture.

For children, their early days in captivity were certainly frightening, characterized by raw efforts to survive. There were moments of flight, hiding, negotiation, and painful separations. Phatimah, one of our interviewees, shared a particularly heartbreaking story:

> We used to move, hiding, from one place to the other. Then they shot my father, and we ran away, but I was later captured . . . in a village, because when the rebels said they were going to kill us, my mother ran, leaving me behind. So the rebels captured me. The rebel who captured me was a woman, and my mother was later captured and brought to the same village where I stayed. My mother got sick and moved to another village with my brothers, who died eventually of *kwashiorkor,* a malnutrition disease.

Later, we also had the chance to interview Phatimah's mother, Kadiatu. She still remembers those days of flight in terrifying detail:

> It was on a day like this. I had just given birth to Phatimah's young brother. One week after his birth, they told us that the war was heading in our direction and it was very serious. We had no food, no money . . . I was nursing a week-old baby. We later left and entered into the bush. I had three male children, and they all died during this time. On that solemn Thursday, which I will never forget, rebels captured us, killed my husband, and left me alone with Phatimah and my baby.

During capture, Kadiatu said, she was injured severely. She still suffers pain from that day many years ago:

> They killed one man in our presence. In shock I said, "There is no God but Allah and Muhammad is his messenger," and at once a man struck me with the edge of his gun. I

sustained a deep wound into which my finger could enter. Throughout my time in the bush I had that wound, and pain and blood ran through my nostrils. Even now, when the pain starts occasionally, they have to lay a stone on my head.

The injury to her head and skull, Kadiatu told us, makes it impossible for her to have her hair braided. "That is why when plaiting my hair I do not allow it to be overstretched, because I still feel the pain."

Phatimah and her nursing baby brother were all that Kadiatu had left. However, Phatimah too would soon be taken away from her. Kadiatu recalls,

I resorted to sleeping out with my children. I said we would manage even if we were to sleep outside as long as my children survived . . . If we were going to die then that was it. . . . I spent the whole day feeling no hunger, though I was a suckling mother. As we reached the village . . . the rebels were coming from all directions . . . One of the rebels by the name of Jeneba took Phatimah as her own daughter. She was very small at that time and I pleaded that the rebels not take her away from me. I told her that she was all I had as her father and three brothers were no more . . . Phatimah was carried away, and she was very small, just like the age of small girls who fetch water. I was left crying for my dead husband and children and Phatimah, who I thought I'd never see again.

Kadiatu's feelings of helplessness were accentuated by the horrific sounds of beatings of the abducted children—Phatimah among them—while she and others hid in the bush to avoid being captured themselves. The rebels "went with those they captured to a very big house . . . and threatened to kill them," she recalls. The sounds of abuse filled the night air as the children's family members huddled together in terror, hoping some of the children might escape. "They continuously beat them while we were in the bush . . . for over three days. How could we come out, when we were there hearing the cries of those they captured? Some even died as a result of that."

Kadiatu's story reminds us that parents who survived the war also lived through horrific suffering, loss, and deprivation. Like their abducted children, they had to persevere in the face of extreme trauma. Kadiatu, with her nursing son, was facing starvation as she hid in the jungle with a few other survivors:

We were there for three months, and at the end we had no source to get fire. Therefore, we resorted to eating raw cassava. After spending the day, when it was approaching dusk, we would then go and uproot cassava to chew for that day.

In our survey, we had included a long list of items about war-related trauma and loss. It had always been perplexing that clothing deprivation was one of the items *most* strongly associated with traumatic stress reactions. However, as Kadiatu's story reveals, to be without clothes was a marker of an extreme form of deprivation:

I became clothesless. I had only a head tie and a *lappa* [wrapper] to carry my baby on my back, and I also had three underpants on, so I was not totally lacking in underpants, as I used to launder the used one every day.

After Kadiatu recovered from the illness that killed many of her children, she persisted with the small group of villagers who had been moved from the rebel encampment due to their sickness. As with many family members who experienced traumatic separation from their children, however, their own journey toward survival would be marked by many more difficult moments:

> We continued traveling in the bush until fortune smiled at us and we heard that soldiers were at Matru Jong and decided to find a road to Nemgbe. We traveled in that bush until we reached Nemgbe. I saw another child whom I asked for Phatimah . . . I was told that he didn't know the direction they took. I concluded that Phatimah would be dead by then—except by the grace of God. The boy comforted me and told me to take courage and said that as long as God says so, I would see Phatimah again. She will one day come.

That glimmer of hope soon darkened for Kadiatu, who said, "We passed two nights in Nemgbe and on the third day, the soldiers and the rebels engaged in combat . . . They killed many people in our presence." Kadiatu remembers "lying on top of my child." She recalls, "People who they shot were falling on me and their blood spilling on our clothes; my child and I were all soiled with blood . . . this continued for a very long period. The moon shone on that day, and I want to believe it will never shine so again." Eventually, after more than three harrowing months, Kadiatu made it to safety. However, she and her daughter remained separated.

For Phatimah, the years of captivity were a blur of pure terror. She explained it as a numbed memory of survival: "When I was captured, I got injured, but I did not feel any pain." Dissociation and numbing of experiences are known elements of traumatic stress reactions and a core set of symptoms of PTSD.[1] For children surviving terror on a daily basis, dissociating and numbing of the pain can serve as an important coping mechanism. However, as Judith Lewis Herman outlines in her book *Trauma and Recovery,* this sense of numbing can persist and cause challenges in later intimate relationships.[2]

Phatimah also faced physical injuries. She described what happened in this way: "I was chased by the rebels and the civil defense force . . . I fell in a hole and fractured my foot." Without treatment, Phatimah's injury healed badly. She was only nine years old.

For Phatimah and other abducted children, the years of terror in captivity also meant years of yearning for family. She spent six years with the rebels. Horrible physical and sexual abuse was rampant. Every day was a fight for survival. Medical care was nonexistent. Injuries often healed poorly, without opportunities to wash wounds or set broken bones.

Phatimah had become a teenager by the time the war began to wane. She described in vivid detail what reunification looked like:

The UN took us from Kailahun. They announced that those children who were captured from their parents during the war should come forward so that they could trace their families. . . . So, the UN took us to a camp in Daru, and we were given supplies, then interviewed. They interviewed me about my village and family and used the document to trace my village and family.

After some time, a contact was made. "When we went to Bo . . . my family was traced, so they took me to them."

Kadiatu told how she was reunited with Phatimah:

My sister had gone to the farm; she mentioned Phatimah's name, and it was said that they were coming with them and that they were around Kailahun. In addition, they came up to me and asked if the rebels abducted my child, and they asked me for her name and I said "Phatimah."

Kadiatu had not lost hope. She had been consulting traditional healers for help:

> Anytime I went to consult sorcerers, they told me that my daughter was alive . . . I performed all the sacrifices they asked me to perform. Soon after consulting a traditional healer, there was a breakthrough: On that day, they brought Phatimah into this town. I was in the farm bush when they sent for me. . . . Upon hearing the news, I kept on moving until I reached the town. She came now, matured though deformed a bit as she sustained that injury. When she came, she could not lift one of her legs while walking but had to drag it.

The family had been a bit cautious when she first returned home. Kadiatu also remained hesitant. Phatimah remembers that Kadiatu "was afraid of me but I was not afraid of her . . . she said I am a rebel." Phatimah did her best to fit in and to be helpful. She wanted to show everyone how thankful she was to be home. But a horrible accident contributed to everyone's suspicions that the girl was somehow haunted by her past. One early morning, Phatimah was sent to help with cooking. Moving about was hard, given her injury, and as she poured out a pot of boiling water in the darkness, she did not see that her uncle was resting nearby:

> My uncle was sitting beside the fireplace in the kitchen, and I was sent to remove boiling water from the fire, when some spilled on him and he got a serious scald all over his body. . . .

It was by mistake because when I was pouring the water, I was not aware that it would splash on him because it was at night and the place was very dark.

The family borrowed money to pay for his hospital bills, but as Phatimah explained, "Up until now they have not finished paying the woman." The accident was a source of tension in the family. "My uncle was still hurt when he died," she said.

Today, Phatimah perseveres despite her injury and the many difficult events she has experienced. Her relationship with Kadiatu has improved, but she has a persistent limp, as well as pain and swelling in her foot where the injury occurred. Kadiatu remarks, "If she walks for long, her foot pains her for more than two days."

After the war, Kadiatu ensured that Phatimah was back in school, but the girl's attention quickly turned to more social interests. As her mother described it, "She nicely started schooling for some time, but due to the size of the bed we had, which cannot accommodate more than two people, she slept with her peers." Phatimah was pulled into new social circles. "They went to dances at night when we were asleep," Kadiatu explained. Soon she noticed a change: "One morning after observing her, I accused her of being deflowered and impregnated . . . due to the size of her breasts. She was finally exposed."

With Phatimah's father dead, Kadiatu didn't have the resources to support Phatimah's new baby along with the expenses related to her schooling. "I gave her advice to take her studies seriously for her future because she is fatherless, and maybe the people who sent her to school will help her," Kadiatu said. By the time Phatimah was to have the baby, her relationship with her mother was very strained. Kadiatu recalls, "she confessed that she was afraid of us and actually afraid of me. In fact, she delivered in another village, as the nurse here could not help her bleeding predicament and advised us to go . . . she bled until she lost the pregnancy."

One upside of Phatimah's pregnancy was that it tested her relationship with the baby's father. He remained by her side, speeding her to the nurse in the next village when her bleeding became too intense. Phatimah and her partner have stayed together. They now have several children.

From my Western perspective, I saw Phatimah's story as a tale of a young girl who was forced to drop out of school and foisted on her partner because of a mother who could not afford the costs of her education. Yet, after discussing her story with Moses and Musu, our research team lead, I began to see Phatimah's life in a different way. Moses concedes that even compared to many other young people in our study, the destitution experienced by Phatimah and her husband was extreme. When he visited her household, Moses was struck by the level of poverty. Phatimah was welcoming and polite, but her clothing was threadbare and she was wearing only a bra as her top. Musu remembers her simple earthen hut and its thatched roof, which would certainly not fare well during one of Sierra Leone's intense downpours. Musu also recalled that on the day she last interviewed Phatimah, the girl was eating cut cassava dipped in salt. To Moses, that is a true indicator of poverty, as both items are very inexpensive but not at all nutritious.

Yet both Moses and Musu saw Phatimah's story as one of success, an example of survival in the face of extreme odds. They mentioned that despite the family tensions and the multiple traumas endured, including the accident that led to her disability, Phatimah is accepted and well-liked in her community. In addition, they emphasized, her husband has been devoted to her. She lives in a committed and loving relationship with a man who treats her well. Moses underscored that, for a woman in this part of Sierra Leone, Phatimah's life today is quite "normal." Despite all that she had been through and the horrors of her time with the RUF, Phatimah's life now was indistinguishable from other women in her village.

Musu concurred, pointing out how Phatimah's community problems have dissipated. She is now well-integrated into her village. In fact, given her health challenges, many of her neighbors were worried when she became pregnant again. Some feared that the smallest birth complication could be fatal. Even Musu had been worried after interviewing her and seeing the level of poverty the family faced.

Several months later, Musu received a call on her cell phone. It was Phatimah. She wanted to share the news that her baby had been born healthy, and the birth had gone well. Phatimah had triumphed.

8

Touchstones

In the study of trauma, the close and nurturing relationship between child and caregiver plays a major role as a resource for healing. While the study of attachment has focused on mother-infant relationships, our research indicates important elements of attachment relationships relevant to larger social groups as well. The return home of abducted children was a true test of the power of these different attachment relationships. In Sierra Leone, this test involved not only the children's families, but their entire communities.

Although little had been written on attachment relationships in the Sierra Leone context prior to the war, the broader study of attachment, parenting, and child-rearing across cultures has a long and rich history. Although cultures vary in their orientation toward collectivity or the primacy of the mother-child dyad, the early bonding between infants, mothers, and other caregivers has been shown to lay a foundation critical to the course of later development. Key early attachment relationships create the scaffolding that will help children to navigate later life challenges, for better or for worse.

The profound importance of attachment relationships and family-based care cannot be overstated. The global child development field has shifted from a focus on viewing the child in isolation, such as a concern for "vulnerable children" de-contextualized from their family and social networks, to understanding the critical role of attachment relationships and the importance of family-based care. The groundbreaking work of Nathan Fox, Charlie Zeanah, and Chuck Nelson in the Bucharest Early Intervention Program (BEIP) has been tremendously influential in this regard.[1]

The BEIP research began in Romania in 2000 in the shadow of the Nicolae Ceauşescu regime. Ceauşescu had pushed population growth as a pathway to economic growth. To that end, the regime banned both contraception and abortion. What ensued was a booming population of children born into extreme poverty. High birth rates also led to high rates of children abandoned to orphanages. Under-stimulation and neglect became a common experience for even the smallest of babies. Physical and sexual abuse were common in institutional care, as was the practice of drugging children to control behavior. It was a man-made disaster for a generation of children.

Post-Ceauşescu government options for adoption into family-based care were encouraged, but there were not enough adoptive families for all of the children to be taken in. In light of this reality, the BEIP team worked with government officials to randomize the assignment of children out of institutional care. In this rare instance, an experiment was possible that would compare the impact of family care to care in an orphanage. A range of outcomes were studied, from standard measures of growth and anthropometrics to neurological development and early indicators of social and emotional health.

Not surprisingly, the BEIP team's research indicated that children cared for by families fared far better than those who remained in the orphanages. However, the research also underscored that there are certain periods in a child's life that are particularly crucial to their healthy development. The BEIP team found that children placed in families before the age of eighteen months showed greater "catch up growth" and development than those who were randomized to families later.[2] It was clear that all children removed from orphanages and placed in families showed improvements in development, but these benefits were most accelerated in the youngest children.

As Sierra Leone's civil conflict drew to a close, debates arose about the capacity of the broader society to absorb the thousands of highly traumatized children taken from their families. Some argued that formerly abducted children were a "lost generation"—that given the intensity of their trauma and deprivation, a return to their families and communities would be impossible. However, with support from local advocacy groups and international organizations like UNICEF, researchers around the world argued that, similar to the lessons learned from the BEIP research, placement in families would provide the best environment for children to heal and recover.

There is a long literature on how attachment relationships are critical both to helping children weather trauma and also to mending its damage. John Bowlby coined the term "attachment behavior" during his research on mother-child relationships in the 1950s, work that was foundational to the development of modern-day attachment theory.[3] This attachment behavior describes situations where a child looks to their primary caregiver as a haven of safety and a source of comfort.[4] Early research on attachment relationships between caregivers and children was not limited to the West. Mary Ainsworth, a student of Bowlby and later a close collaborator, conducted important work on attachment in six villages outside of Kampala, Uganda.

Ainsworth was originally drawn to fieldwork in Uganda to understand weaning practices that she had heard entailed sending children away to "forget the breast." Ainsworth's research followed twenty-eight infant-mother pairs.[5] Using some of the same coding schemes she had developed in her work with Bowlby, Ainsworth distinguished between children whose attachment to their mother seemed secure compared to those who manifested anxious attachment behaviors.

Ainsworth followed the mothers and young children in Uganda a little beyond the first year of life, all the while coding her observations of key attachment behaviors. She concluded that "the mothers of securely attached infants had been more accessible and more positively responsive" compared to the mothers of "anxiously or insecurely attached infants."[6] Were these manifestations of attachment specific to Uganda, or something more universal? To explore this comparison, Ainsworth repeated her study ten years later using similar methods. This time, her sample included twenty-six mother-infant dyads in the Baltimore area. She concluded that "attachment behaviors previously identified were essentially identical in the Baltimore sample, and so were the phases of development." She saw these two studies as providing support for Bowlby's claim of an "evolutionary and genetic bias for human infants to become attached to their principal caregivers."[7]

However, Ainsworth also observed that in the collectivist culture of Uganda, "there were some differences attributable to cultural differences in mothers' infant-care practices." Ainsworth described these cultural and contextual differences—such as caregiving by multiple family members, including siblings—as shaping how infants responded to strangers, as well as "the circumstances under which an infant could use his mother as a secure base from which to explore." Based on these findings, Ainsworth stressed her conviction that "cultural context must be taken into account" when understanding attachment.[8]

Just as attachment sets the foundation for early development, it also plays a key role in healing from trauma. Judith Herman writes in *Trauma and Recovery* that "destruction of attachments" is part and parcel of the experience of trauma. The pathway to healing from trauma is a journey of restoring trusting relationships. This process is not linear but instead moves in oscillating stages, from re-establishing safety, to mourning and remembrance, and eventually to reconnection with ordinary life. Herman notes that the return to everyday life involves the gradual development of trust in others: "The social alienation of the disorder must be addressed through social strategies. These include mobilizing the survivor's natural support systems, such as her family, lovers, and friends; introducing her to voluntary self-help organizations; and often, as a last resort, calling upon the formal institutions of mental health, social welfare, and justice."[9]

Trauma, especially trauma resulting from violence, has a strong bodily element. As we know from developmental psychopathology, childhood trauma can shape the architecture of the developing brain. Bessel van der Kolk has written in depth about these relationships in his book *The Body Keeps the Score*. He reminds us that

Research . . . has revealed that trauma produces actual physiological changes, including a recalibration of the brain's alarm system, an increase in stress hormone activity, and alterations in the system that filters relevant information from irrelevant. We now know that trauma compromises the brain area that communicates the physical, embodied feeling of being alive. These changes explain why traumatized individuals become hypervigilant to threat at the expense of spontaneously engaging in their day-to-day lives. They also help us to understand why traumatized people so often keep repeating the same problems and have such trouble learning from experiences. We now know that their behaviors are not the result of moral failings or signs of lack of willpower or bad character—they are caused by actual changes in the brain.[10]

Judith Herman too recognized the embodied elements of the trauma response and need for healing, focusing on the mind-body connection. She notes that "establishing safety begins by focusing on control of the body and gradually moves outward toward control of the environment. Issues of bodily integrity include attention to basic health needs, regulation of bodily functions such as sleep, eating, and exercise, management of post-traumatic symptoms, and control of self-destructive behaviors."[11]

Reasserting control over one's body also requires a secure environment around the individual in which to heal. In writing about the women she had worked with, many of them survivors of sexual assault and incest, Herman describes these necessary environments as including "the establishment of a safe living situation, financial security, mobility, and a plan for self-protection that encompasses the full range of the patient's daily life. Because no one can establish a safe environment alone, the task of developing an adequate safety plan always includes a component of social support."[12]

Recalling the stories from Isatu, the dedicated student who survived years of family separation to thrive in a foster family, we see many examples of how her attachment relationships pulled her through her years of terror. Isatu's deep and abiding connection to her sister Amina was a lifeline for survival, both during the abduction and after. Both girls looked out for each other at every turn during their years with the RUF and then again in their years with a foster family. Many of our study participants described how kinship ties or tight friendships in captivity could guarantee help with back-breaking chores or a means of securing extra scraps of food when rations were thin. During their years with the RUF, Amina and Isatu's sibling relationship helped them avoid sexual abuse, a remarkable fact given the prevalence of such abuse among the RUF. Both girls described looking out for each other and taking steps to protect and care for each other despite the brutal actions and desires of their captors.

Isatu and Amina may represent a subtype that researcher Thomas Boyce terms "dandelion" children.[13] Place Isatu into just about any context, and she will take root, thrive, and flourish. She is a hearty soul. Nothing will stop her. Isatu's determination provides an arsenal of resources which in turn galvanize further support and encouragement, propelling her hard-fought journey.

On the other hand, Sahr—the boy who was kidnapped as a toddler by captors who carved "AFRC" onto his chest—might be taken to represent what Boyce calls "orchid" children. When given the correct conditions, such children flourish, demonstrating particular interpersonal and creative sensitivity. However, when subject to trauma and life stressors, they may be particularly vulnerable. Sahr's story captures a toxic mix of trauma, interrupted attachments, and a social support system that could not provide him with the nurturance and care he needed to reconnect with ordinary life after his release from the rebel forces.

Moses recalls the day that he arranged to interview Sahr, when the boy was in his later teen years. He arrived at Sahr's home only to learn that the teen was still out in the fields: he worked farming rice and potatoes in exchange for room and board. The owner of the farm maintained a small rooming quarters for several young men working for him. Sahr was very well known in this area. Moses asked about his whereabouts, as he had missed the appointment they made. A group of elderly men gathered and began to share their opinion of the boy. "I remember it well," Moses noted. "They did not hold back with their opinions."

It turned out that Sahr was well known, even if it was for a wrong reason. "He was not anonymous at all," Moses told me. It became clear that he would need to come back another day to meet with Sahr, but the man and his friends wanted to tell Moses what they could about Sahr. They sat around joking and telling stories.

Waiting for Sahr: A Story Told by Moses Zombo

"This town is the headquarter town of the Tankoro Chiefdom," the eldest of the three men said to me in a matter-of-fact tone. "It was quite a bustling town before the war," he added.

This came as a bit of a surprise. Baiama Town, or what was still left of it, did not look like the headquarters of the chiefdom that had once hosted Kono's largest town. We had just arrived from Koidu Town, which was the center of commerce in Tankoro Chiefdom. The sixteen districts of Sierra Leone are further split into 190 chiefdoms, whose elected officials provide local leadership. Though Baiama may have once been the epicenter of Kono, the contrast following the war was stark. Koidu Town was already teeming with people just a few years after the conflict ended; people meant jobs and trade. Baiama Town, by contrast, did not have a single shop in view. Its residents depended on farming to support themselves. And their farming, like that in most of the country, was only for subsistence.

"We need people to come back," said a second man, who wore a sweatshirt and a woolen cap. "We need especially the young folk to come back. Without them there is not much hope for the town's recovery."

(Continued)

"The trouble with the youth nowadays is that they want development ready-made," said the eldest man, rolling up the sleeves of his gray tunic. "They want to live and work in a place already conducive for good living. That's why they are all in the cities. It is the reason some have made Freetown their home."

It was obvious that this town was struggling to attract people. The dirt road snaked between patches of tall elephant grass and rubble. A few houses, wrested from the debris of previous buildings, stood out. The salvaged cement blocks still bore paint from the original building. These walls were held together by unpainted layers of plain cement, like a mosaic. Even the roofing was a mixture of old and new corrugated iron sheets, with the new sheets covering the interior sections. It was a pragmatic approach, bold and unpretentious.

"We are not a mining town," said the youngest of the three. He must have been in his late fifties. "As long as there are no mining fields or companies around here . . ."

"Yes, but ours has never been a mining community," said the man with the woolen cap. "Yet we used to have very fine people here, both young and old."

"That is why we are open to people like your friend," said the eldest man. He was referring to Sahr, the young fellow that we had come to visit. "He is a difficult character. But he is young. Maybe he will learn."

"Learn?" said the youngest. "What? When?"

They all burst out laughing. Hearty laughter too. "Tell that to his roommate," said one of them between laughs.

"The guy must be allergic to water," said another. "How much does it take to get a bath and a change of clothes?"

"You must have seen his roommate's face that night. 'You will kill me with your body odor!' he yelled at Sahr. 'Sleep on the floor or better still go, find someplace else to sleep, *dorti kolombo.*'" It was the youngest man talking between peals of laughter, referring to Sahr as a "dirty lizard."

"But you have to agree with him. We used to say a person who does not regularly take a bath or change clothes could attract snakes to their bed," they said to more laughter.

"But seriously," said the eldest, "we need people. Even crazy folks like him. That is why I have always advised patience with the lad. This is not his home, yet he is here with us. Many who hail from here don't even come to visit."

Their mood suddenly was reflective. For a moment, the only sound we heard was the endless chatter of thousands of weaver birds in the trees around us. They were quite a lively lot, weaving in and out of the branches as they built their nests and discarded unwanted ones. The yard was littered with discarded nests, and more continued to fall. Up in the trees, new ones were being woven with great urgency.

"They are the sign that life is coming back to our village," the eldest man said, referring to the weaver birds. "Just about the time that we were displaced from here, they left. They were the first to leave. Now that we are back, the weaver birds are back. Hopefully, with a little prayer and perseverance we can be what we used to be once more."

Eventually, Moses did meet with Sahr and with his family, and he pieced together a heartbreaking story. Because Sahr was so young when he was abducted, his family had known him only as a toddler. He spent critical years of his early development being raised by the RUF. His formative years were spent in camps with other abducted children. To survive, he developed a very disinhibited style of interacting with others, seeking soothing and relationships anywhere that he could. He would engage in attention-seeking and indiscriminately friendly behavior, which made him a darling of the NGO workers at the different ICCs where he was housed. Upon his release, his family had a very difficult time identifying him, given that he had grown and changed tremendously over the years.

The extended time that Sahr spent bouncing from ICC to ICC posed additional challenges to developing solid attachment relationships with dedicated caregivers. At one point, Sahr spent two years with a foster mother who claimed that he was her own son. In Sahr's interview with Moses, he told us that he had "pretended" to be her son because he "wished to be free" from endless stays in ICCs. Years passed before he finally ended up in the care of his true family. Sahr's extended time in captivity, breached foster placements, and protracted time in institutions also undermined his chances of developing secure attachment relationships.

In his years between different ICCs, Sahr quickly developed strong attachments to the female expat NGO staff who cared for him. He flourished under their encouragement and the fun he discovered when they taught him to ride a bike. He grew to love riding bicycles. The sense of independence and agency it offered was both soothing and a source of joy.

Unfortunately, exactly the aspects of what helped Sahr to cope and manage his disrupted attachment relationships caused him difficulty later. In his time at the ICCs, Sahr could ride a bicycle as much as he wanted. He would spend countless hours on any bike he could find. Nothing held him back. However, when he was back with his family in their village, the only way to ride a bike was to rent one. Sahr had no means to pay for that. Even when he did pay, with help from his mother, he frequently failed to return his bike on time. He would lose himself in the joy of biking and sometimes returned the rental bike very late, with no ability to cover the extra cost.

The young men who rented out bikes in the village became angry. They felt that Sahr was intentionally showing them disrespect. Sometimes their hostility became physical and fights broke out. Sahr's uncle, the most powerful man in his family, wanted nothing to do with the situation. Even though he could easily afford to buy the boy a bike, he was frustrated with Sahr's inability to focus on his schooling.

Sahr had a loving mother and grandmother who were both deeply committed to him. But with no control over the household finances, they had no means to address the situation. On one occasion, community members surrounded Sahr, beating him for not paying enough for his time on a rented bike. Sahr held out a knife to scare off his attackers. Alarmed, Sahr's mother stepped in to try to stop the violence. She told us, "I saw no reason in beating the boy to correct his behavior."

Sahr's mother commented on his emotional difficulties in an interview with Moses: "At times he is very sad," she said. "He sometimes sits quietly by himself. I think it was because of the problems he had with people in the community." Sahr eventually stopped attending school completely, fueling further arguments with his uncle. His mother noted: "Well, I think he likes school, and he is intelligent. . . . You know the burden of being called a rebel and other challenges made him leave school. As a child he couldn't cope with all the stress."

Sahr's uncle felt that keeping Sahr engaged in school was an endless chore. "It was a struggle to make him attend regularly. The complaints would always come back from the school that he did not go there but went to ride bicycles instead. I used to deal with that and give him advice to take his schooling seriously.

But because I spent much of the day at work and away from the house, I would only get to know about it when I returned from work, instead of being around when the incident would be taking place. He was a difficult kid."

Nonetheless, Sahr's mother and grandmother loved the boy dearly. His mother explained that "he came back because he loved us . . . when a child loves you, you should in return show him that you love him." However, Sahr's uncle remarked that Sahr's time with the rebels had changed the boy. Some family members said that Sahr "would be best left alone where he was." Sahr's uncle said, "There is an elder brother of mine . . . who said we should not take the boy back. . . . He said the boy had joined the rebels and become one himself. He said that the boy had carried arms and that because of that lifestyle he would not be suitable for living in a family like ours anymore. But I explained that there were many people who had given up arms and were living with average people like us and being good. I said if he said we should not take him back we should remember that he carried our family name and he was the son of our sister. I said if he did not want the boy back at least I would take him."

Yet Sahr's uncle felt the grandmother and his sister were spoiling the boy. "My mother doted on him and would not even eat her food in his absence. Even if you urged her to eat she would still reserve some for the boy. As soon as the boy arrived at the house she would tell him where she had kept the food for him. . . . It was only when I would be around that the boy would be on the defensive, as I would press him about his responsibilities to schooling. He would give feeble excuses."

Attachment disruptions and their consequences for mental health and daily functioning in former child soldiers have been studied by various scholars. Interesting work from Tim Allen and his team, for example, has investigated the relationship between a sense of attachment to the armed group and reintegration experiences using interviews among youth involved with the Lord's Resistance Army in northern Uganda. They found that young people who had a strong sense of attachment to the armed group struggled much more within the reintegration process.[14]

Without question, early attachment relationships and the nature, availability, and quality of attachment figures over the course of child development have a huge role to play in shaping later emotional and behavioral health. It is clear that for children involved with armed forces and armed groups, attachment relationships must be understood in terms of the developmental period, nature, and length of disrupted attachment. Beyond biological caregivers, others in the life of a child can make a difference as a stabilizing force for healthy development. However, when such reliable forces are not available to the child, the consequences can cascade across each level of the social ecology. Again, the social ecology surrounding the child, at every layer from the family, to peers, to the broader community of caregivers, has the power to unlock potential and nourish it toward flourishing—or, as in the case of Sahr, to undermine it.

For Sahr, the range of disrupted attachments and breached family placements in his life likely contributed to challenging interpersonal behaviors like those observed by the men poking fun at him in the small village where he had ended up. We see similar behavioral problems, rooted in attachment disruptions, in children who experience multiple foster placements. Research by Rose Marie Penzerro and Laura Lein followed a cohort of 415 youth in foster care in San Diego, California, for over a year. Using standard assessments such as the Child Behavior Checklist, they observed that behavior problems were both a cause of and a consequence of placement disruptions; however, they also identified that children who did not originally evidence behavior problems may be a subgroup at particular risk, as they may respond to multiple disruptions with increasingly self-defeating behaviors.[15]

However, even children beset by challenging behaviors can thrive when met by strong and committed attachment relationships. In contrast to Sahr, the story of another boy in our study, nicknamed "Big Money," demonstrates how attachment relationships can be a touchstone for healing.

In interviewing that boy's father, we learned that the nickname came about from an experience in his infancy. The boy was born with a medical condition that required early treatment for the boy and his mother—at great cost for his father, living in a small rural village. His father, a retired civil servant, was happy to pay for this medical procedure. He was relieved to see his baby boy healthy and thriving as he recovered. But from that day forward, he recounted with a chuckle, "this boy was destined to consume money," and so "Big Money" became the name that everyone called him.

Unlike Sahr, Big Money was enveloped in the unswerving love and dedication of the head of his household. In an interview the boy said, "My father is the one I love most of everyone because he does everything for me. Although things are hard, yet he goes all out to help me and provide for me. So he is the first."

As a boy, Big Money had shown promise in school. His father stated that the boy was "top of the class in exams." It was during the holiday season, when Big Money was only about seven or eight, that his school was raided and he was taken by the RUF. Much like Sahr, who spent four years with the rebels, Big Money spent a long time with the RUF, surviving an estimated five years of captivity. Those many years and the physical changes inherent in the transition from childhood to adolescence made it hard for his father to identify the boy. Big Money recounted how his father had searched for him: "By then my father too had heard announcements on the radio that there were children whose families were being traced after the rebels had previously captured them and they were in places such as Daru. So, my father went to Daru to check."

However, the father was searching for his son using his family name, instead of his famous nickname. "When he went he was using my original name, which was not what I was carrying at the time," the boy explained. "So that is why he found it difficult." Big Money's father recalls searching photo boards and visiting soccer fields of displaced children in search of him. It was in one of those very fields that a lucky break occurred. A group of boys was playing soccer in a faraway field and shouting energetically. He heard one boy shout directions to the others, calling out Big Money's nickname. "So my father said, 'That is my child!' So he came back, and he eventually found me." As Big Money told Moses: "You see, it is good to have nicknames."

All human beings face adversity in their lives, especially when they grow up with limited resources. Early bonds, the loving nurturance and connection between children and attachment figures, beginning in infancy with maternal interactions, serve as a touchstone—a foundation and anchoring base from which to navigate hardships. A compelling truth about the situation of child soldiers is that for most of these children, their involvement in an armed group was a traumatic disruption to what was otherwise a normal developmental course. This is very different from children raised in situations of abuse and neglect—where a long history of family dysfunction and disorganized or interrupted attachments have been the norm.

For many children involved with armed forces and armed groups, the pathway back to healing also meant overcoming attachment difficulties. Being subjected to forced abduction and socialization by an armed group during very tender developmental periods, especially for children taken at younger ages like Sahr, made interpersonal relationships particularly challenging.

In our study, we found that children abducted at a young age and held for longer periods of time were particularly vulnerable to increased internalizing problems (difficulties such as social withdrawal and sadness) as well as externalizing problems (difficulties such as fighting and aggression) over time.[16] When separated from attachment figures at a young age, there is an additional risk to very young children because the key developmental foundations of secure attachment are not yet fully formed.[17]

By nature of the conflict itself, each unique journey through the trauma of war brings with it distinct experiences of attachment and loss. Returning home to a family environment also involves navigating critical attachment challenges. Big Money had the love and support of his father to steer his ship through these challenging rapids. Sahr, alas, was left rudderless.

PART II

Journeys Home

————

9

Finding the Way Home

When the war ended, coming home took courage and required trust on both sides. The fear of rejection could be paralyzing. Families ached to let the children taken from them know that they were wanted and loved. Communication, whether phone calls or word of mouth, slowly melted away the doubt and fear of separated children and families. Some families sent notes, others videotaped tearful pleas begging lost children to return home. News about the children who had been located spread rapidly via whispered messages and stories of a glimpsed loved one, still alive after years of doubt. Rumors would drift from village to village, signs of hope and sightings passed along by market women and young men returning from temporary work deep in the bush.

A study participant abducted by the RUF at the age of five described the measures that organizations took to "trace" missing children and connect them to loved ones: "The NGO was looking for our relatives. They used to put us in a vehicle and roam about the streets of Kenema . . . and maybe our relatives or somebody would recognize us and take us to our parents."

This is precisely what happened to a young woman we will call Fanta. "One day," she explained, "we were taken to a camp where I saw my grandma's sister . . . so I ran to her." Fanta's extended family had lost touch with her parents. They had fled to crowded refugee camps in Guinea. She lived with them for a few years, until her luck changed on a day that a relative came to visit. She recalled:

> My mother's younger brother went to the village and to our house and begged for water. By then he had not seen my father yet. I went and brought the water. When he saw me, he asked if I am my brother's younger sister. . . . Then I said yes and ran to him and embraced him. He then called my parents and they came for me.

Even for those who had dreamed of such reunions for years, the reality of coming home was fraught with mixed emotions. Each great hope was tainted with sharp memories of trauma, loss, and the struggle for survival. When child-tracing efforts led to a potential match, both sides pondered the pros and cons of reunification. Abducted children were now grown teens or even young adults. Mothers yearned to hold and caress their lost little girls and boys but now had to contend with fully grown young men and women, often unrecognizable. Some girls taken as children returned with children of their own.

Fathers fussed about how to pay for school fees and feed additional hungry bellies. Tensions were high, but the stakes even higher. From the perspective of the returning youth, they feared that the brutal years of life with the rebels had hardened them into unrecognizable adolescent pariahs, impossible to love. Indeed, many of the formerly abducted children exhibited behaviors that were difficult for their families to understand and to manage.

In 2008–2009, we conducted repeat in-depth interviews with twenty-one youth and thirteen of their caregivers or guardians.

We also traveled around the country conducting seventeen focus groups with war-affected youth. In a series of lively discussions with young people, the resounding message was that the effects of war were unrelenting, even many years later. In Kenema, youth described war experiences as linked to present-day drug and alcohol problems: "Some are still on drugs and their attitudes are different . . . their actions and the way they interact are aggressive . . . a majority of drug addicts now were with the fighters" during the war.

In Makeni, a focus group of young women expressed concern for girls caught in a cycle of using transactional sex to survive: "It is the women who are affected the most. . . . There are some of our peers who go into the streets and sleep with men just so they can survive." Indeed, even in the hotels where our research team stayed, it was not uncommon to see a beautiful young girl, in clothing far too extravagant for the rural area, hanging out in the corridors late at night in hopes of sleeping with a soldier or militiaman for money.

Our interviews with caregivers and adults reflected many of the topics that arose in the focus groups with youth. One mother explained, "Those that were with those people in the bush were obedient, but the problem they had was that they were highly temperamental." Another mother emphasized school as the true testing ground: "I always got complaints from the school. At one time the teacher even threatened to expel him from the school if he didn't change his attitude."

Returning children were directly tested. Upon their return home, former abducted children spoke of being taunted or provoked, of being teased to the point of anger or humiliation. One mother said, "With the return of those children, people were disgruntled about them because according to the popular opinion, these children have destroyed our lives, houses, and property. Therefore, these ex-child combatants were teased and called different names." In some cases, the community response was so strong that families would even turn their back on a child. The same caregiver continued, "there was total rejection of them; some people even disowned their own children."

As our interviews revealed, how returning children managed the provoking really mattered. To take the bait and lose one's temper—or worse, to fight back, like Sahr, whose story we told in Chapter 8—was a trap. Taking that bait could slap a label on a young person that would be hard to ever remove. One of the study's female participants said,

> Throughout this country in the aftermath of the war, as long as you have been with the rebels, there are those who would never have a clean heart for you. Some would think that you probably killed their father or mother or that you might have been the one who burnt their house down. So, there will always be this lingering suspicion of you. And you have to be very careful in anything you do.

The children who could conduct themselves appropriately were very careful. They would go out of their way to demonstrate how demure and well-behaved they were. This effort would often pay off. A young man in our study noted,

> I am happy because I can now move around the community freely. Nobody points fingers at me as one who was with the rebels. I now attend school, play with my friends, and do the right things. In the mornings, I dress properly and go to school. After school I will go to the market, come home to cook and eat, and later on study. People know I am good now.

In Sierra Leone, like many other low-income countries, it is customary to take in the children of relatives or friends when needs arise. Those with adequate work and income carry a weighty obligation to help others. Even nonrelatives, if trustworthy, may have several children from remote villages staying with them to attend local schools. In Sierra Leone, this is a practice sometimes referred to as *men pikin,* or "minding children." After the war, children without mothers and fathers were often taken in by aunts, uncles, and grandparents. Children whose biological families could not be found were placed into foster families.

Not all reunions were happy ones. In some cases, children cared for by others might be subject to years of household servitude and abuse. A young woman in our study explained,

> I lost my mother at a very young age. My stepmother treated us very badly. . . . That younger brother and I are the ones who survived from the war. The rest died during the war. So, she used to serve garri [from the less nutritious cassava root] for my brother and me while she served rice to her own children.

In contrast, we found that in many cases, nonbiological caregivers showed tremendous dedication and love for the children in their care. The story of Mahmoud and Uncle tells such a tale.

As Uncle described in his interview, he had cared for Mahmoud since he was a young boy. But on a visit home with his biological father, the boy "was captured. . . . The father escaped after some time. He came over and told us about it. All of us felt so bad, especially me, who had brought him up since he was a baby."

Mahmoud had always wanted to be a doctor and had been very serious about his studies. Once it became clear that he had been captured by the RUF, "everybody was worried. His mother would cry all day long. His father died of this thought." Years of separation followed. In the end, it was Uncle who found Mahmoud and eventually brought him home from captivity.

Uncle shared the story of their reunion:

After some time, somebody came here and told me he saw
Mahmoud was in one of the rescue centers where some
children here camped to be disarmed. I went there and was
able to identify him as my own child . . . I talked to the as-
sociate in charge until he was finally handed over to me.
They asked me if I would be able to take care of him; I
replied in the affirmative.

Immediately, Uncle noticed that the war had changed Mahmoud. Like many formerly abducted children when they first
came home, he was easily angered and emotional. Mahmoud also
demonstrated traumatic stress reactions, sometimes blacking out
or reenacting war memories.

Emotional and behavioral changes, such as re-experiencing
traumatic memories as well as hypervigilance and emotional
numbing, are all considered among the classic symptoms of
PTSD, according to the American Psychiatric Association's *Diagnostic and Statistical Manual of Mental Disorders.*[1] As Uncle described, "I found out that all his attitudes had changed. He was
so violent and was behaving abnormally. At times he would take
up sticks and start to imitate an attack saying, 'I'll shoot you!
Where are you going?'"

Despite Mahmoud's acting out, Uncle remained calm. He
tried his best to speak soothingly to the boy: "I'll call him and
tell him that this is not a jungle and we don't want to see those
actions." Uncle said, "I was taking him to the hospital, where
he was being treated with some injections to help him cool
down." It is unclear what injections the boy was given in hospital, but one might guess that he was given tranquilizers, since
both antidepressants and antianxiety medications were barely
available on the standard list of psychopharmacologies available

in Sierra Leone at the time. After the care they were given at the hospital, Uncle reflected, "he is gradually coping, only he is so hot-tempered." The symptom of being "hot-tempered" is noteworthy. It is a theme that will appear later in our intervention work, which focuses on the emotional dysregulation that is typical among the responses of trauma-exposed youth.

Recognizing the boy's extreme mental distress, Uncle became a sounding board for Mahmoud. Although he was not a trained therapist, he provided a safe place for Mahmoud to share his experiences. Uncle was not frightened off by Mahmoud's behaviors; he remained committed. He began to see that this support alone had an impact. "If I talked to him . . . he'll explain to me that most of the time he is not conscious of what he does. But I continued talking to him, and he is gradually changing."

Slowly, Mahmoud opened up to Uncle, gingerly unfolding his painful story and the memories that haunted him. Our interviews with Uncle clearly showcased his active listening skills and a patience that many a therapist would envy. Uncle notes: "I had to talk with him in confidence and ask him what his role in the war was. He said they were the ones who went to conduct reconnaissance on a town or village that they wanted to attack. They'd go, observe, and come back to tell the fighting forces about the situation on the ground before an attack was launched."

Mahmoud explained to Uncle that since he was young when he was taken, his role was like that of many small boys. "He did not carry a gun; after the attack their role was to take the properties and belongings of the village people who would have run away . . . they gave information before an attack was launched, and they would stay with the civilians for a week or two, observing, before they went to give detailed feedback to the rebels. That was his role."

Listening was not always easy because Uncle, too, had suffered and lost loved ones during the war. Listening to Mahmoud's stories could trigger difficult memories. Like the homes of villagers in Mahmoud's story, Uncle's home had been attacked. He too had experienced the terror and had to flee with his loved ones. They had lost everything. "When the attack was launched on our village," he said, "we ran to seek refuge in the bush. I was there with all my family. We lived on wild fruits; we had nothing. All our rice and other foodstuffs were taken away from us . . . all that was in my possession they took. But as long as I had life, I had hope."

Despite knowing that Mahmoud had inflicted some of the same searing pain on others that he and his family had suffered during the war, Uncle remained committed to helping Mahmoud. Faith fueled Uncle's love, patience, and dedication to the boy. Uncle's commitment was firmly rooted in this faith. "Since I am a fervent Muslim, I thought it was the prayer that helped my child. I prayed all day to see him . . . and indeed, my prayers . . . were answered."

Mahmoud's return to Uncle was like an answered prayer. For both of them, the simple fact that the boy had survived was a source of hope. Like many of the youth in our study, the early days of return were a sort of honeymoon. Uncle explained, "That was a red letter day. When they announced that the war had ended . . . we had our peace . . . all of us prayed and danced for a lasting peace. We were so happy to see Mahmoud. Some members of the family shed tears of joy. I wept bitterly for the manner and condition in which I saw him."

The family went out of their way to signal their joy at having Mahmoud back home. "I asked my wife to prepare a big chicken in stew for him," he said, "after which we went for some shopping; I bought some secondhand clothes for him." Even the broader community was stunned and overjoyed to have Mahmoud home. "He was being admired and looked upon constantly like a paramount chief. . . . His mother celebrated throughout that week." (In the government of Sierra Leone, *paramount chiefs* are nonpartisan members of parliament.)

Mahmoud had seen such brutality in his years with the rebels that he seemed stunned that the family had survived and that they remained so dedicated to him. As Uncle reflected, "We provided all that he needed. He expressed that he was so happy to reunite with us. He said he thought all of us would have been dead by then. We kept him at home and gave him all he wanted."

But the celebrations generally hid a set of more complex feelings about the return of the children formerly associated with the RUF. A great deal of trepidation remained. Uncle reflected, "Some people feared them because they thought they still had their former rebellious ways. As a result of that, some community people didn't want to welcome them." At the time of return, both the government and local organizations were engaged in what were called "sensitization campaigns."[2] Uncle was involved in organizing these sensitization discussions: "We called a meeting and pleaded that they are our brothers and sisters and that we should not leave them all on their own. We educated them about peace and reconciliation." In the end, the children were able to remain in the village; it took time, but eventually "everybody accepted them."

In addition to the community's efforts to self-organize and advocate for acceptance, care for the returning children fell on the shoulders of locals with little outside support. "No help was rendered. No educational facilities. We as parents took the onus to take care of and educate our children because we know they are future leaders of society."

As Uncle saw it, the formerly abducted children were in good physical health when they returned, which was a blessing in that it gave his village a fair platform from which to build. "One good thing that happened in this village," he said, "was that all the children who were captured returned in good health and strength. Uncle also noted that the former CAAFAG were getting along well with other youth in the village who had not been involved with armed groups.

Uncle helped to lead a community effort to promote inclusion. "We formed a committee for farming activities. They were so obedient. They would go to the farm with us." Uncle and his community members made an intentional effort to support and provide guidance to the returning youth. Individual leaders like this are the "active ingredient" that can kick off a virtuous cycle of healing and reconciliation.

When asked to compare those who were with the rebels compared to those not involved, Uncle explained:

> I see it in their academic work very seriously. For those who were involved, some don't even attend school now. They ride around the streets unless we strictly supervise them, and we advise them to take academic work seriously. If I had the opportunity to design a project for ex-combatants, the first thing that I would do is to pick up all the children in the street, gather them somewhere, talk to them, counsel them. . . . At the same time, they'd be going to school. Doctors would give them treatments to get the drugs out of their systems so that they behave normally. For the girl children I'd enroll them in a vocational institute. Those who have children would also be encouraged to do something better for a brighter future.

Despite the challenges, Uncle felt hopeful. "I have nothing to say except to express my joy and happiness for seeing my child . . . he behaves well and I'm so happy . . . that he is doing well on his academic work and has realized that he needs to change." With the right development investments and political leadership, individuals like Uncle might have the chance to impact even more lives. "I want him to become a doctor or some other reputable citizen in the society. That is why I'm doing my level best . . . I don't want my child to be a dropout, but a respectable person in society . . . I'm sure if I encourage him, I believe he can make it up . . . but without that I don't think he'll become the doctor he intends to be."

In post-conflict settings, we must do more to encourage more people like Uncle. The need for brave and committed natural helpers is immense. Oftentimes in interviews, youth spoke about this as a desire for "guidance." To lose family members was to lose a pipeline to a naturally occurring protective process—a link to parents, aunts, uncles, and siblings who could run interference with frustrated teachers, provide a shoulder to cry on, or offer simple words of advice and perspective.

To lose loved ones also meant losing guidance in navigating the fragile and impoverished post-conflict environment, where jobs were few, housing and food were insecure, and access to school fees was often impossible beyond the primary school years. This loss was often a raw, real, and enduring source of pain.

Uncle's gift was to see the opportunity within the deep hunger for advice and support that many of the returning youth craved. Uncle never ceased to see Mahmoud's return as anything short of a gift. This abiding hope, fueled by faith, allowed him to stand by Mahmoud, even when things got difficult—essentially *loving him through it.* When asked by our interviewing team if any of the youth who returned from their time with the rebels continued to act out, Uncle responded, "Actually, my own son, Mahmoud, causes some problems at times, but I see these problems as a result of his long stay with the rebels." Uncle's insight into Mahmoud's troubles proved a true balm through the hard times, especially when other village members "come over to me with complaints."

For others, like Sahr's uncle, being responsible for a young man with emotional and behavioral problems in a close-knit village might be seen as detrimental to their good reputation. But Uncle's commitment to Mahmoud was fueled by a deep reserve of love and compassion. With patience, even in the most trying times, a moment would emerge when "some of these community members showed some understanding somehow."

Uncle manifested the spark necessary to ignite a virtuous cycle of positive outcomes, even under challenging circumstances. Among the most resilient young people in our sample, usually there is a synergy of this type: a spark of inner perseverance or desire to achieve social, economic, or academic success that propels the young person—and then is met by others around them, who pick up that spark and help fan the flames of desire for something better. Although there are bumps along the way, these virtuous cycles can become a formidable force, propelling the child forward, despite all odds.

10

Post-traumatic Growth

In the field of trauma research, there has been growing attention paid not just to understanding what factors shape riskier versus more resilient life outcomes, such as those we explore in this book, but also to the hotly debated question of whether good things might be born out of such immense pain and suffering. Among the most controversial topics in trauma studies is the concept of post-traumatic growth.

According to Richard Tedeschi and Lawrence Calhoun, post-traumatic growth refers to processes of positive change that result from "highly difficult life crises."[1] They argue that some individuals emerge from experiences of trauma with even stronger levels of functioning and elements of improved emotional and behavioral health than had existed pre-trauma. Examples of such change might include having a greater appreciation of life or a changed sense of priorities, or in some cases, deeper and more connected intimate relationships. Their research revealed that some survivors of extreme trauma were able to recognize a greater sense of their own personal strength as well as a recognition of new possibilities or paths for life. Some individuals exposed to extreme trauma even reported a deeper sense of spiritual development.

Critics of post-traumatic growth as conceptualized by Tede-schi and Calhoun have pointed out the risk of the "superhero trope." Eranda Jayawickreme, a professor of psychology at Wake Forest University, argues that Western culture is imbued with ideas that suffering brings achievement—no pain, no gain.[2] From military drills to valiant responses expected from veterans to the death and destruction witnessed in combat, Americans often like to claim that "what doesn't kill you makes you stronger."

However, such thinking can also reveal the sharp reality of a double-edged sword. As he describes in a podcast interview, Jay-awickreme himself witnessed a tremendous amount of trauma as a child growing up in Sri Lanka during its civil conflict in the 1990s, seeing the consequences of civil conflict between the Tamil Tiger rebels and the government forces. "My everyday experience as a nine- and ten-year-old going around Colombo . . . was seeing the bodies of people who had been abducted, tortured, killed and left on the side of the street. Looking back on that . . . one thing that I'm struck by is just the extent to which I thought that was normal. I had no comparison." He reflects, in retrospect, "I think that set the stage for a pretty high degree of normalization of extreme violence."

He was fascinated as a teen with the plotline common in many American movies, from Clark Kent to John Wayne—a young man encounters horrible trauma or loss, but with time, his past trauma becomes his superpower. After surviving trauma, he can do extraordinary things. As Jayawickreme points out, the great risk of the superhero trope is the suggestion to trauma survivors that they should find some growth or strength from their experience. This is simply not always true. Trauma and adverse events are experiences of horror and pain; we don't wish them on anyone. For some people, changes may arise that are positive, but there may also be changes that are negative and long-lasting. The diversity of outcomes—not always growth—is a reality that must be respected, not minimized. Jayawickreme notes that making claims about whether someone's life is better overall because of the trauma they lived through is not a realistic or respectful stance toward the survivor.

Reflecting on how trauma had affected his own reaction to subsequent experiences, Jayawickreme describes how, having just arrived in New York City, he had responded to the terrorist attacks of September 11, 2001. He recalls: "My first thought was 'Well, this is bad, but it also weirdly feels like home'. . . I don't think it struck me just how bad it would've felt to other people around me." Looking back, he realized that he had been responding with a sense of detachment. "What seemed relatively normal to me, as someone who grew up in Sri Lanka was something that I was realizing was not normal to many other people, at least for people who lived in this part of the world."

He deepened his inquiry into the methodological and conceptual challenges pertaining to how post-traumatic growth had been considered in literature in psychology. He quickly observed that much of the research had been conducted cross-sectionally—meaning studies that analyze data from a population at a single point in time, yet the research findings were presented in terms of personality *change* over time. What most questionnaires on post-traumatic growth were really investigating was the effectiveness of active reframing of expectations by looking for good coming from difficult events as a coping strategy. In fact, as several studies would underscore, such an approach could have the converse effect, leading individuals to feel even more distress because this way of reframing, in reality, just didn't fit.

Rather than an expectation of good things from past trauma, Jayawickreme began to consider how the framing of adversity in binary "bad" and "good" outcomes really obscures the very complex reactions that characterize most experiences. "I don't doubt that the sense of detachment, the sense of normalizing trauma and adversity can be useful when you are in that context. But it also comes with costs, especially when you don't live in that context anymore." When Jayawickreme thought about his boyhood experience of growing up during Sri Lanka's civil conflict, he reflected, "As I've gained more distance from my life in Sri Lanka, I have become more aware of just how ubiquitous this normalization was. I understand the benefits of it from a mental health perspective, but I also see the cost."

In recent years, his research has dug even deeper to unearth the unique and complex sense of self and others that such experiences may engender. He explains that "any type of unusual or unexpected event that pushes people to experience the world from a nonnormal perspective, that enables these people to think about the world from the margins. And to the extent to which you experience unusual events, unexpected events, that enables you to be open to different ways of thinking about the world and understanding human experience." He adds: "it's a different kind of superhero trope. It's not developing some new skill, but really doubling down on what it is that you have inside of you."

In recent work on the topic of responding to traumatic experiences, Jayawickreme has been exploring approaches such as Acceptance and Commitment Therapy to unearth core values: "the idea that one of the challenges when we are faced by adversity or struggle or suffering, is that . . . the impact of that event prevents us from living our lives the way we want to. Or living our lives in light of the values that we care about." In speaking of this therapy, he explains, "one thing that we are trying to do in these interventions . . . is to highlight for people . . . the importance of their own values. Despite the fact they're going through challenges, despite the fact that there might be events outside their control that they're experiencing, [the emphasis is on] what's important to them, what matters to them, and then how can they commit to behaviors that are consistent with those values."

Therapeutic processes that own and hold true both the complexity and the mixed reality of trauma and its consequences, he tells listeners, help to "separate out that struggle from who you are as a person, and understand that you are not purely defined by your struggles. That you're also someone who has values and that you can still commit to that life."

The assumptions baked into the classic portrayal of post-traumatic growth are ultimately limiting. New perspectives approach the issue from a different lens, explains Jayawickreme:

I think one problem with current research on post-traumatic growth is the term itself. There are two assumptions baked into the phrase, post-traumatic growth. One is that trauma is needed for you to grow, but also that you are going to become a better person. That is a much more simplistic understanding of what happens to you when you experience a major life event that I think is the case for most people.

I think it's quite likely that . . . people can become more compassionate. They can gain great insight into their own lives. They can commit to their values again. But we should be sensitive enough not to say that that means that the trauma or the adversity was worth it. Someone could become compassionate, . . . someone could commit to living their values and still experience significant challenges in their mental health or in other domains of their life.

The dynamics of trauma and response in Sierra Leone are not that far from those described by Jayawickreme in Sri Lanka. While we saw tremendous instances of individual resilience, we also witnessed young people for whom the effects of trauma were undeniably destructive, leading to social isolation, bad relationships, and in some cases early death. A high rate of mortality is evident in our sample—the children we studied in Sierra Leone were much more likely to die young than we would expect. And the rate of early death for male participants was twice that for the female participants in our sample.

Mortality is a blunt example of lost human potential, but there are many other ways in which the experiences of trauma and loss in post-conflict Sierra Leone have deprived youth. The lost potential of human lives appears in our study in a multitude of ways, including among young people who struggle with persistent mental health difficulties. In the pursuit of education, livelihoods, and other means of self-advancement, the vestiges of conflict can have serious consequences. Common mental health symptoms such as feeling despondent, withdrawn, and hopeless about the future can mean that even when opportunities arise, it's much harder to actualize them. In a school or work environment, having difficulty managing strong emotional situations, such as the criticism of a work supervisor or corrective actions from a teacher, can lead to failures, both in grades and promotions.

Circling back to several of the stories of young people profiled in our study, we can see many of these same dynamics at play. Sahr, the often isolated boy who loved to ride bicycles to soothe his emotions, is a tragic case of lost potential. Sahr was deeply loved by his mother and grandmother, but he lacked support from the powerful uncle in his family. When community rejection took hold, without support from a key family figure who had sway in the community, he was left to struggle in isolation. In contrast, Isatu, the diligent student who was kidnapped alongside her sister Amina, suffered her own traumatic separation from her family, but her perseverance in the wake of adversity compelled others around her to help her reach her goals. After the conflict, Isatu decided to become a doctor—a commitment to serving her country that exemplifies the deepened sense of self and compassion that can emerge when individual talent and drive is nurtured in the context of a loving, enabling environment, despite the trauma of war.

In reflecting on her life, Isatu credits what she learned from surviving in the bush and the many people who aided her with helping her become a better medical professional. "Looking at my own life [I ask] what positive impact I will make in society afterwards? So that all these positive contributions that have been made in my own life can be of benefit to others. And I mean not only my patients, as my patients are very dear to me, but just the rest of the people in society."

To this day, Isatu maintains an enduring compassion for others and a strong sense of faith. Isatu remains deeply involved in her church and sees her faith as a major source of her motivation to contribute to bettering the lives of others. And in our sample of former child soldiers, the good news is that Isatu is not alone. Our study has documented a sizable group of former child soldiers who want to transform their experience in ways that help others. Several, like Isatu, have developed an interest in health careers. Joseph, a young man from Kono, was inspired by the experience of surviving RUF captivity to become a nurse. He explained that even though he was never forced to fight directly, the memories of what he saw affected him greatly: "I was not involved in combat, but seeing people, seeing dead bodies, wounded people. . . . It affected me so much as a kid . . . seeing people die is very traumatizing for a kid at that age." He described struggling with intrusive memories of the past, especially when reminded of past trauma: "All of a sudden, I start to see dead bodies, wounded people, blood, people with guns, people fighting, and the sound of gunshots. I think that is very traumatizing."

Despite struggling with the real consequences of the violence he witnessed, Joseph remains driven to make a better life, become a nurse, and pursue a career. Joseph and Isatu are examples of fulfilled human potential and even flourishing, despite—but perhaps not because of—horrific trauma. In both cases, Isatu and Joseph are able to put their best selves forward and exert their sense of agency toward their life goal of helping others who experience difficulty. We cannot draw a causal link from their trauma to their goals today, as it may be the case that both Isatu and Joseph would have been similarly motivated even without the horrors that they experienced. Nonetheless, they demonstrate that it is quite possible that young people experiencing such trauma and loss can go on to achieve great things and draw from their experiences to benefit others. In both cases, the agency and effort demonstrated by these young people is recognized by others, and may help unlock additional support and resources to get ahead.

11

Boots on Muddy Ground

Our study sought to document the process of coming home. To understand the return journey of these young survivors and their families, we had to assemble a team of local staff up to the task. Moses and I set out to interview candidates. Our team would need to balance stamina, grit, and compassion. We set out some clear criteria: members had to be well-respected in the community, have some history of work in human services, and above all, show concern and compassion for working with very vulnerable young people.

Mr. Stephen was one of the first people we hired. He was an older gentleman, dressed head to toe in light brown khaki. He moved and spoke with a stiff formality. His presence brought seriousness and respect to the situation. The set of his jaw and the deep wrinkles in his face spoke volumes about a life that had seen it all.

Miriam Yorpoi was a soft counterpart to Mr. Stephen. She was plump and exuberant. A former schoolteacher, Madame Yorpoi had a wardrobe of eye-popping African print dresses in bright colors. Her calm and wise manner and her big heart made her a trusted confidante to many in Koidu Town. Christianity was central to her life. She was deeply involved in her church, often helping to organize prayer groups and activities. When the war came to Kono, Madame Yorpoi fled to Guinea. She eventually made her way to Freetown a few years later, after the rebel incursion had reached Guinea territory. In Freetown, she found a job teaching children in makeshift schools in a camp for internally displaced people that was supported by the IRC. There she met Moses and found a shared passion for helping others.

In order to work in the capital during the war, Madame Yorpoi was staying with family members who had a home in Freetown. The day the rebels attacked, she had hidden along with her girls in a small chamber of the home as the rebels moved methodically from room to room, smashing doors open with their guns. They found her huddled with her two daughters. Despite her desperate negotiations, the rebels took her twelve-year-old girl. She recounted the story for Moses: "I lifted my face to the heavens and spoke directly to God, saying: 'Will you allow this?'" She continued her fervent prayers. Within moments, her young daughter, frightened and speechless, returned. The rebels had let her go.

In Koidu, Madame Yorpoi's personal experience with the war, as well as her knowledge of the local grapevine, made her a popular community confidante. She was a tremendous asset to the study. We knew if there was ever a problem, Madame Yorpoi would handle it with compassion and wisdom. A critical advisor to our team, she helped us navigate the cultural context of how we asked questions, from ensuring true informed consent to handling sensitive risk of harm cases.

Tracing and finding the youth on our roster became all the more possible when we hired Billy. Billy was possessed by an unstoppable energy, like a man fueled by a bucket of double espressos. He was relentless in tracing down a clue and making connections. His mind whirred almost audibly. We would provide him with a name from our potential participant list and he was off to find them in a swirl of dust, like a cartoon character. He would report back at the end of a workday, sweating and gleeful to share what he had found out that day, speaking quickly and excitedly about his efforts to locate youth on the list. Sometimes it was hard to follow Billy, but we would write our notes frantically as he chatted on. Over time, he developed an elaborate plan for tracking the youth and families we were inviting to participate in the study. He hatched networking schemes that extended like a thick web from village aunties to the big men who employed half the town.

In addition, a handful of younger former NGO workers were also hired. It was a team of bright, young, energetic people who had worked for large NGOs in the months following the war, but whose job opportunities had dried up as the world chased after the next hot global crisis, leaving Sierra Leone behind. Unfortunately for them, underemployed talent was in abundance.

Hopeful applicants came for interviews with us. They would knock expectantly at the red steel door. A small, rusty panel at the top allowed us to make eye contact on tippy-toes and welcome the visitor into the building. On breaks, we could step into the dust of the courtyard and see towering spires, minarets painted green, white, and blue—the colors of Sierra Leone. Early in the morning, the call to prayer would drift through bullet-sprayed buildings as the pink dawn broke. Roosters would join the hubbub, crowing, making for an exquisite sound. Small versions of the ubiquitous African dog—red in color, demure, and mangy—roamed the streets.

We wrote field reports about our hiring process for Marie de la Soudière, the director of the Child Protection Unit at the IRC. Elegant and poised, with her black hair piled in a ballerina's bun fitting for her past as a dancer, Marie insisted that the children shouldn't languish in centers. These former child soldiers (her French accent hanging on the word *sol-diers*) needed to be back home wherever possible. What would help smooth the journey? We didn't really have any evidence one way or another.

Who would do well and who wouldn't? Why? What support was needed to help children and families thrive? The IRC had raised funds to ensure at least six months of financing to help families pay for school fees—for those who agreed to send the children back to school. After that, it would be up to the families to make ends meet.

When I looked over our eclectic team of data collectors, ready for that sweltering first day of training, I felt a bit intimidated. My first experiences with training local staff in research methods had been in more developed settings, where we could offer tea breaks and training room tables lined with matching folding chairs. I was used to providing bright *HELLO, MY NAME IS:* tags on round tables crisply set with spiral-bound notepads for jotting down the critical dos and don'ts of interviewing. *Do* sit at the child's level. *Do* offer materials to draw and scribble. *Don't* push. *Don't* do anything without permission of both the parents and the child—collected independently. *Do* allow the young person to tell their story in their own words. *Don't* use leading questions.

We spent long afternoon sessions roleplaying the freshly learned techniques of good research interviewing. Koidu Town was much different from the training sessions we had led back in Cambridge. We were working in an enclosed, sweltering hallway between two concrete buildings. Tea breaks and flush toilets were nowhere to be found. Birds flitted between the high crawling vines above our heads that crowded out the hot sun peeking into this narrow space. The walls of the corridor were painted a cheery yellow.

We roleplayed while sitting sideways on long, handmade wooden benches. The thick layer of varnish on the wood gave off a strong smell of resin as the material baked in the afternoon heat.

"Okay, Miriam, now you play the part of a young girl being interviewed, okay?" I would request, followed by, "Mr. Stephen, you play the part of the interviewer, alright?"

They nodded in solemn agreement.

I'd continue: "Let's start from the beginning. Pretend that you are knocking on the door of a house that we have sampled. What is the first thing you are going to say?"

The staff were a bit stiff and shy at first, but soon formalities gave way to energetic roleplay. They gestured as they played their parts.

"Good day oh!"

"Ow dis monin? Ow di bodi?"

"Di bodi fine! Ow yusef?"

We learned from each other during these training sessions; I taught the team research skills, and they taught me how to speak Krio. Sierra Leone's lingua franca has a wonderful and joyous rhythm; it is a very fun language to speak. Pregnancy is referred to as *di belleh bizness;* a woman *got belleh* (belly) from making *mami an dadi bizness* (sex). Children were *pikin*. When it came to talking about the war and its effects on children, a famous phrase was *bush no dae for trow bad pikin,* which roughly translates to "you can't just throw a bad child to the jungle."

In fact, the degree to which "bad children" (as some thought of the returning former child soldiers) had been able to return to their homes and villages after a brutal eleven-year civil war was remarkable. The overwhelming pattern was that of increasing acceptance over time. We wanted our research to help us understand what worked and what didn't to help influence successful life outcomes. At the time, there were not strong standards for how reintegration should be done.

Some NGOs have developed very innovative ways to bridge the divide and help children and families reconnect. The IRC, for example, used handheld video cameras to film powerful video testimonies from family members, pleading for their child to return: "*Hawa, come home, our girl. We know the rebels stole you from us. Don't be afraid. Don't be ashamed. We love you. Come home.*" When shown these videos, hearts steeled by years of survival would melt. The messages from home of love, acceptance, and a sense of commitment paved a pathway home for those who took the leap of faith to return to their villages.

Some young people had been held by the rebels so long that they had come to identify with nicknames given them by rebel abductors. As one young man explained, the nickname he identified with, Rebel Boy, was given to him by an RUF commander. He told us what the end of the war looked like for him:

> I was in Kailahun when the UN started to visit the place. We used to hear them make announcements that anyone who had been captured and was separated from your family members, whether they were alive or dead, you should assemble in a particular place so that they would be able to transport you. So, I was happy. The man I was with [the rebel commander] was not happy about that. . . . He was actually an important man among the rebels . . . when I told him I wanted to come to my people, he did not welcome the idea. . . . He even told me to stay with him and promised to be responsible for my schooling. But I looked at the way of living there and decided I should come back. . . . They had made a law that as long as a child had come to the heliport, no one could stop the child from being there.

Rebel Boy explained that many of the RUF commanders tried to hold back children who wanted to leave, but those lucky enough to get to an interim care center would get case management and support to find their families. His story was similar to that of the boy nicknamed Big Money:

They used to ask us, "Which street in Kenema were you?" So when you told them they would take you on a motor- bike and carry you to the house. They would go and ask for your people. . . . We went to the place and the house but we did not find anyone there. By then my father too had heard announcements on the radio that there were children whose families were being traced after the rebels had previously captured them. . . . So my father went to check. However, when he went he was using my original name—which was not what I was carrying at the time—so that is why he found it difficult. . . . Some of my friends said, "Oh, there was one of our friends here who told us his nickname was [Rebel Boy]. They said he has been taken to Kenema as he said his family are there." So my father said, "That is my child!" So he came back and he eventually found me.

Such tales of family reunion were not uncommon. Even with the RUF indoctrinating children, carving deep scars into their juvenile flesh to mark them as their own, as soon as abducted children had a chance to reclaim their families, they almost always took it.

With training and practice, our team of data collectors were ready to gather these stories. We had very few refusals. Young people were hungry to share their experiences. They were also touched that anyone cared to check up on them since they had returned home. The stories they had to tell were astonishing.

12

A Mother's Courage

As we embarked on our research, tales of great courage and loss began to emerge. Moses relayed the following story about a brave mother whose love and perseverance brought her girls home.

Mariama was a happily married mother of four who lived in Sierra Leone's diamond-rich Kono District. Prior to the outbreak of the country's civil conflict she had hardly ever been out of the district. Mariama spent her days caring for her two boys and two girls. One fateful day, Mariama's town of Koidu came under violent and ruthless attack by the RUF rebels. Many of the town's residents were killed, and numerous civilian survivors were taken captive. Mariama and her husband escaped the carnage. However, not one of their four children was able to escape with them.

"We lost all our senses during the attack," she said, describing the mayhem during which she was separated from all four of her children. "It was like the end of the world." As for the pain of being separated from children left to a terrible fate, Mariama just could not find the words. The other mothers who shared their experiences in the focus group discussion offered her comfort as she sobbed with emotion. "We mothers still carry the pain like fire in our hearts," she said through her tears.

Mariama and her husband crossed the border into Guinea, where they resided in a refugee camp. For years she looked forward to finding her children as wave after wave of refugees arrived in Guinea from Kono. For years she turned up nothing. By then, virtually all of Kono District had come under the control of the RUF. People fleeing from the district brought harrowing stories of what was going on there. Then Mariama finally got information that her two girls were alive and in a village under the control of a rebel commander.

Once she heard the news about her girls, Mariama could not rest or sleep. Her daughters had been about six and nine at the time of their separation. They were the youngest of her four children. She had hoped to hear that they were with their older siblings, but this news confirmed the worst of her fears. They were alone, with the rebels. Mariama soon reached a decision. She was going back into Sierra Leone to get her children.

When she told her husband of her plans, he was appalled. "He told me that if he lost me in addition to the children, he would die shortly. But I responded that I would equally die if I did not reunite with my children."

Mariama set out on foot into rebel-controlled Kono District all on her own. She carried on her head some dried meat and palm oil, which was all that someone in her position could scrape together and save. When she set out, she knew that when she entered rebel-held territory she would have to walk through several villages past armed men who could kill on a whim. Yet she did not hesitate. As she pushed onward, she told the armed people she encountered that she was going to see one of their commanders.

She arrived at her planned destination by nightfall but had to wait another day for the commander to arrive from some business in a nearby location. Meanwhile she was able to walk to the rebel compound, and there she saw both of her daughters. They were alive! They were thin and looked tired and frightened. She was not allowed to speak with them. Only the commander could authorize her meeting with her children.

Once the commander arrived, Mariama presented her gifts and expressed her thanks to the man for having taken good care of her daughters, adding that she had yet to find her two sons. She said their separation had been slowly killing her and their father. She concluded by asking to take her daughters back with her so they could reunite with their ailing father in Guinea. The commander responded that he appreciated her taking the initiative to approach him and that he would reward her efforts by letting her take a child—but only one, the younger girl.

Mariama would not settle. She looked the commander directly in the eyes. She explained calmly that she needed to take *both* of the girls to meet their ailing father and that her purpose of coming could not be served by leaving either of them behind. Now the commander reminded her of the disposition of the people she was dealing with. "He said to me, 'Woman, you should count yourself very lucky. When we took these children, we killed off those who were not good looking. Your children are still alive because of their very good looks. By letting you take one of them I am making you an exceptional offer. So, you will do well to accept it before I change my mind.'" Mariama began to realize the danger of the situation and promptly voiced her agreement.

She set out the next day along with Finda, the younger girl. What she did not know was that her other daughter, Sia, had made the very daring move of going after them. Dreading the prospect of living in isolation from all of her loved ones, Sia escaped by herself. She had listened to her mother's account of her journey to the rebels, and hoped that she and Finda would take the same route home. Unsuspecting rebels on the way confirmed to Sia that a woman and girl were headed in that direction. Sia half-walked and half-ran all the way to the border.

After Sia escaped, a small group of the commander's men were sent to bring her back. Unaware of the danger, she crossed a small river along the Guinea border just before the RUF rebels appeared. They had arrived at the border a quarter of an hour too late.

13

The Helpers

It is in the nature of humans to help one another. While extreme events can be incapacitating for some, they can also galvanize astonishing acts of selflessness in others. When we help children make sense of frightening events or mass casualties, it can be comforting to point out all of the people who come to the aid of others. They are always there. Helping has healing powers both for those helped and for those who do the helping. In fact, there is a long literature underscoring the healing power of altruism, which has great relevance for our work on trauma today.

Helpers of all sorts rose to absorb the pain in Sierra Leone's war. Moses told me a stunning tale of a middle-aged woman named Mary, a wheelchair user, who was a volunteer at the camp for internally displaced people where he first worked. Mary's home was near the camp. Given her personal experience, she was concerned that children with disabilities were at risk of being overlooked in the programming implemented in the camp.

As a remedy, each day she would trundle her rusty wheelchair into the dilapidated entrance of the camp, twisting through rutted red dust and tangled scrap metal, to hold sessions for children with disabilities and their parents. Without pay or materials, her dedication became nearly a daily affair. And what a difference she made.

The average number of children per household in that camp was between five and seven. Household heads were already at the limit of their abilities as they strove to provide food, care, and protection for their children in this unpredictable place. A child with special needs could easily get lost in the shuffle. In addition, most children with disabilities were in households headed by a single female. The needs were greatest where the abilities and resources were most constrained.

Many of the children with disabilities were at risk of abandonment. Moses recalled one boy of about two years of age:

He was struggling to learn toilet habits. His mum, a single woman, scraped a living from making and selling local soap. Each day she was faced with a tough choice. She could, on the one hand, carry this two-year-old on her back all day as she hawked her wares on the rugged streets of Freetown. She could, on the other hand, leave her child behind in the care of her neighbors, who could only afford to pay the kid partial attention. She would return home after a tough day to find irate neighbors yelling at her because her boy had defecated on their front porch. Having children to provide and care for made it much harder for poor women like her to find marriage, in spite of her best efforts. Having a special-needs child among the number made it near impossible.

Another case he described was that of a household with a bedridden girl of about eight, who likely had cerebral palsy—in Sierra Leone, adequate assessment and diagnosis of childhood disabilities is rare. Though she could not talk, Moses explained, "she recognized faces within a range of about five or six yards. [She] would shriek with delight each time she saw a friend she recognized. She was such a sweetheart. But it did not help that she could not control the flow of spittle from the corner of her lips." The girl was often ignored, kept indoors or within the seclusion of the backyard, the family seemingly embarrassed by her condition.

For children with disabilities, Mary's work broke the shackles of a reclusive existence. She would gather them together in one place, in full view of camp residents, and demonstrate the proper treatment they deserved by her show of care and attention. Mary herself had in her childhood spent some time in a missionary-run facility. She had internalized strong values regarding the rights and treatment of persons with disabilities. But, as Moses explained, "her biggest asset was her generosity of spirit." Evidence of this was abundant in almost all that she did, but especially in the way she touched and cared for the children.

For example, she would very regularly use her *lappa* or wrapper, a traditional article of clothing, to wipe a kid's runny nose, Moses observed, "in a manner that only a child's parent does. She was quite resourceful too. A cup of water was all she needed to bathe and soothe a crying infant in the noontime heat." Crucially, "she did not hold back on discipline either. Before the close of each day the group would hold a session to review the day and reflect on matters such as each child's conduct and relationships. In these sessions her demeanor would be quite stern, even when she used improvised sign language."

Moses saw that Mary's example inspired others. "It was Mary's show of genuine interest and warmth to the diverse cases of disability that sparked similar emotions in the hearts of the displaced population." Over time, as people in the camp took notice, the NGOs pulled together to help set up a small area for Mary to host her gatherings for children living with disabilities. It was transformative not only for the children, but for their parents too, held back by fears of being singled out or rejected for their child's condition. Soon, celebrating children of all abilities became a family affair. Their siblings began to come along to the little tarpaulin booth where Mary held her sessions to help with the chores and share in the play. As Moses noted, "before long, respectability developed in place of stigma for families with disabled members. One woman's inspired example was what made all the difference."

Mary's courage helped the camp leaders recognize that the number of children affected by disabilities was substantial. When exchange visits were organized, which brought children with disabilities from the main camp for internally displaced people in Freetown to meet others at a specialized camp designated for those with amputations, Moses explained, "there would be initial tears and hugs from parents who were total strangers, and then mutual words of courage and support. This was quite important for a nation that was going to carry a significant caseload of disability, from physical wounds of war, but also from the horrific amputations that plagued many of the parents and could potentially be a source of stigma and shame." Mary wanted nothing but the satisfaction of witnessing some measure of well-being for children who, like her, were living with a disability.

Like Mary, Miriam Yorpoi soon became a local hero upon her return to the war-torn Kono District. Kono was among the country's worst-affected districts as the very diamonds that had made it so prosperous became a much sought-after resource by the parties to the conflict. By the time the savagery of the war was over, the devastation was immeasurable. Both property and family ties had been torn asunder. Moses explained, "returning home was far from a smooth process, as the divisive events of the war added another layer to the complexities of extended families, polygamous unions, and outmoded customs." In particular,

Moses was speaking of customary patriarchal practices, which excluded women from decision making and, in many cases, land ownership.

It was in these post-conflict disputes that Madame Yorpoi's skills shone brightest. Reclaiming and repossessing what was left of family property was a particularly contentious issue when various members of one common family returned home to rebuild their lives. These disputes threatened to bring further conflict to families that were yet to heal from the scourges of war. It was often the case that the prewar head of household would be dead. This created a problem, Moses explained, "leaving no obvious leader or unifier of a broken bunch of survivors. Various households would have developed separately over the war period with each carrying perceptions and sometimes misconceptions of betrayal and abandonment by other family members."

In Kono, Madame Yorpoi became a peacemaker. Moses witnessed her magic firsthand. He recalled, "it took a great deal of protracted negotiations and counseling to re-establish peaceful coexistence among such members. Few possessed the needed attributes of trustworthiness, patience, negotiation skills, and power of sacrifice to accomplish the task." Madame Yorpoi was just such a person. Able to serve as both mediator and counselor, on occasion she would offer up a room in her house while negotiations were being made with the rest of the family.

She told Moses about many cases of young pregnant girls or nursing mothers who had been let down by partners or guardians:

> They would revert for support to what was left of their families as a matter of right. But securing such rights was never a certainty, and the poor girl or woman would need someone to stand by her in the pursuit of it. Many of the children had not only suffered the traumatic loss of loved ones and

the sting of community stigma, but also the loss of access to financial, emotional, and even informational resources. Many young people lamented that there was no place for them to find guidance or advice from a trusted source.

Moses recalled Madame Yorpoi often saying that in some cases, words are just not enough. He explained that

> Even while in exile in Guinea her house had served as a kind of safe house for women and girls facing the threats of domestic violence. Miriam Yorpoi eventually caught the attention of Médecins Sans Frontières, who listed her among their team of recognized volunteers among the refugee population. Now back in her hometown after years in exile, she became a burning force of compassion. Her heart broke for the children forced into armed groups or the children exposed to the threat of exploitation and abuse in their homes. Madame Yorpoi said her experience taught her that counseling community members and engaging in dialogue with them was effective in preventing exploitation and abuse of children and women. She deployed her skills exhaustively, and when asked what drove her passion to help others, she would reply that it was probably the struggles she had experienced herself.

Miriam Yorpoi grew up with her mother, who was a traditional birth attendant. She then married a kind man who later in life suffered a terrible stroke that left him bedridden for four years before he died. Madame Yorpoi relocated her family to her husband's ancestral village during that time. She cared for her children and her ill husband while also working as a teacher and farmer. Drawing on this experience, Madame Yorpoi firmly believed that adversity could build character and empathy. She would often teach her students and the young people she mentored that helping others could serve as a powerful tool for dealing with one's personal challenges.

For families who had been even less fortunate than her own, Madame Yorpoi stepped in to help wherever she could. In Kono, she became a wise counselor and a source of guidance for many. She helped innumerable returning young people advocate for patience and a chance to start over when meeting with local leaders and teachers. To those without a mother or a father, she served as a touchstone, a shoulder to cry on, a loving aunty whose advice they could cherish in matters of the heart or the pocketbook. Sometimes it was both.

As Madame Yorpoi had seen, for too many young women during the conflict and after, their only resource was their own body. Transactional sex simply became a way of survival for women and girls in the post-conflict environment. In some families, those who had taken in a girl might even encourage it. Madame Yorpoi helped young girls recast their choices with a look at the long game. She talked through the long-term consequences of dropping out of school, the lasting and life-changing reality of an unwanted pregnancy, or the pain and stigma of a sexually transmitted infection. After some reflection, young women were able to use this information to make safer choices in their own best interest. When girls came to her desperate for school fees, clothes, or a means to get ahead, Madame Yorpoi helped them to slow down, to break the problem down into small, manageable steps. After this exercise, they often found they had many more options than they had originally conceived. Years later, we would integrate this exercise into our mental health groups for war-affected youth: sequential problem solving.

Just as Madame Yorpoi had done for years, we began to observe in our research the reality that when individuals have experienced extreme trauma, the part of their brain involved in executive functioning can easily become overwhelmed. Sometimes bad choices are made in the context of cognitive and emotional overload. We have seen similar dynamics in higher-income countries too, especially among refugee families who struggle to adjust to a new language and culture, and often struggle to secure jobs and housing. In such situations, the simple act of breaking the challenges into "baby steps" can help to make problems seem more manageable.

In our research in post-conflict Sierra Leone, school-fee payment was exactly the sort of target problem some girls struggled with. A young woman who has lost family in the war, without a father or a protective uncle, might despair of getting those fees paid. However, when problems such as these were brought to the group and possible actions broken down step by step, girls often saw that each of the smaller steps along the way might lead them to their goal. Even the simple act of speaking with a neighbor or another relative could help. There might be ways to make money that don't require taking on a male romantic partner. They might help a neighbor in a small business, or plant a small crop and sell the fruits of their labor. Other, formal options existed too, like microfinance, or taking out a small loan to help a self-run business to thrive.

For young men, losing a father, brother, or uncle might mean lost opportunities to learn a trade or work on family land. However, for some of the young men in our study who had no family to lean on, dangerous trades became attractive, such as selling drugs and resorting to petty theft, known as being a *tiff man*. To become aimless was a very undesirable thing indeed, as it increased risks of falling in with a bad crowd, including local gangs in urban areas. Such aimless roaming is referred to as *waka waka* in Sierra Leone. It is a far too frequent habit for many young men in post-conflict settings.

According to the United Nations Development Programme, in the immediate years after the end of the conflict, it was estimated that about 70 percent of the country's youth were underemployed or unemployed, with large numbers actively searching for employment.[1] In a landscape of bereft of fathers and uncles, slain in the conflict, some men took on these roles, sometimes taking several young men at once into their household to mentor them and teach them a skill.

In Koidu Town, a focus group revealed the experiences of a cluster of young men who had exercised their own sense of agency to attract a mentor. They had spent months roaming without purpose after school each day. However, one of their favorite hangouts had brought them into contact with a hardworking local business owner, Mr. Tucker. Mr. Tucker was a stout and strong man. He spent most of his days wearing a grease-stained jumper and peering with tremendous concentration under the hood of any one of the many Jeeps and trucks in his care. He had started out fixing vehicles with a mentor of his own. He now owned his own garage. The boys approached him, pleading their case: "Uncle, we want more to do than being idle all day."

Mr. Tucker had seen the boys around the village and knew that in their hearts they were good kids. He decided to give them a chance. He and his wife prepared sleeping quarters for the boys and a hot meal each day. In return, he expected the boys to get up at sunrise and report for duty at the garage. They worked each morning and each evening, shadowing him to learn the ins and outs of carburetors and tire repair. They would finish the day with clothes smeared with grease and a wide smile of accomplishment lighting up their faces.

For young people set adrift, helpers emerged in Sierra Leone in the absence of formal social or mental health services. History has provided us with examples of the critical role of helpers in mitigating the effects of trauma. Even under situations of extreme duress, the critical buffering role of attachment relationships to help children make it through difficult times has been underscored repeatedly. In a seminal study published in 1944 by Anna Freud—daughter of Sigmund Freud—and Dorothy Burlingham, the pair documented the behavior of children cared for in English nurseries during World War II. In observing children who had not suffered physical injury but who had been repeatedly exposed to wartime bombings, Freud and Burlingham noted, "so far as we can notice, there were no signs of traumatic shock to be observed in these children. If these bombing incidents occur when small children are in the care of either their own mother, or a familiar mother substitute, they do not seem to be particularly affected by them. Their experience remains an accident, in line with other accidents of childhood."[2]

If a caregiver's dedication, love, and patience could be bottled, it would be an elixir that would fortify any child. If we are to successfully reintegrate former child soldiers or any child who needs to recover from extreme adversity, we need to better understand the thinking of these mentors and everyday heroes and find ways to support them. There is still a long way to go.

14

The Sting of Rejection

Humans are tribal creatures. Just as collectivity and social embrace can heal, nothing is deadlier than being cast out of the clan. The sting of rejection can be toxic. In our research, one enduring factor associated with poor outcomes appears time and again: stigma. In a collectivist culture like Sierra Leone, to experience community rejection, especially rejection from one's family and community, is a pain beyond imagination.

When abducted children returned to their communities or families, it was common for those who had been with the rebels to be subject to community provocation. There were daily insults and jeers shouted from dusty street corners and bustling markets: "*look at that little killer,*" or "*you have rebel blood in your veins.*" These words were painful for children who were forced into association with rebel groups and had no choice in the matter. Patricia, who was abducted at age eight, explained: "People used to call us rebels, so we always have that stigma. We were not fighters, but hostages."

As the children and parents whom we interviewed pointed out, it was distressing and disorienting to be publicly shamed for a situation that was already laced with personal trauma and horror.

To return only to be rejected by the community—and in cases like Sahr's, by his family as well—rubbed salt in their wounds.

These community provocations were a test. Those who weathered the taunts and persevered were seen as somehow strong of spirit, but for those who didn't pass the test, the consequences were poisonous. Children who could not control their behavior and emotions well in the face of community provocation were on a dangerous path. Such taunting often deepened and persisted, creating a cycle of community rejection that soon made it impossible to carry out a simple errand or go to school.

Considering the personal trauma that already weighed on them, the provocation faced by the children in our sample was heartbreaking to hear of. One young man told us:

> At first, when we had just returned, people pointed accusing fingers at us, saying that we were with the rebels—there was no respect for us. People were pointing fingers at us saying "this one killed my father; this one killed my mother; that other one burnt down our house. Some were even pointing fingers at those who had looted their property."

It made a powerful difference when adults advocated for the children. One young girl recounted, "my mother would tell people that they should not blame me for being with the RUF; they were to blame God because I was so small when I was captured. Since my mother welcomed me, it was easier for people [in the village] to accept me." To have a parent or caregiver—or even an older brother or teacher—accept you could make all the difference. This protective outer ring could hold a child at its center and give them just time enough to heal.

A mother in Moyamba explained how frustrating it was to deal with people who blamed the children who were abducted:

People referred to them as rebels and pointed fingers at them. Sometimes the child combatants cried as a result of the provocation and complained to us. It annoyed me at times and I would go to the parents of those kids who had provoked them. We would usually tell them that the children did not join the rebels by their own will, but rather, they were abducted. They would not have joined had they not been captured.

A parent who advocated with such courage and dedication could play a definitive role in their child's future.

As we and other teams of researchers have studied the effects of exclusion on children, we have come to see stigma as one of the most powerful predictors of a child's future well-being. My team's study in Sierra Leone built upon a well-established body of research that helped us to describe the ways in which stigma contributes to poor mental health.[1] *Social stress theory* demonstrates that groups of people who are disadvantaged, marginalized, or isolated suffer from poorer physical and mental health because members of these groups are both exposed to additional stressors and also have reduced access to coping resources.

Certainly, discrimination had an inverse relationship with family and community acceptance in our data. The more rejection young people faced, the less support and acceptance they perceived from their families and community. This inverse relationship also affected mental health. For example, higher levels of family acceptance were linked to fewer feelings of anger and hostility. Improving community acceptance over time was associated with higher levels of adaptive attitudes and behaviors among the young people in our sample.

We also observed that post-conflict factors such as discrimination played an important role in shaping psychosocial adjustment in former child soldiers over time. For example, in statistical models adjusted for demographic covariates and other war-related experiences, a past history of injuring or killing others was a significant predictor of increases in hostility over time. However, once perceived discrimination was included in our statistical models, the strength of the relationship between wounding / killing and hostility was reduced by almost half and was no longer statistically significant, indicating that it was the effect of community stigma that continued to perpetuate poor mental health over time.

Similarly, stigma was also a main driver of persistent depression in rape survivors: discrimination largely explained the relationship between being a rape survivor and depression later in life.[2] For rape survivors who did not experience community rejection, depression outcomes, in general, improved over time. On the other hand, rape survivors who experienced higher levels of stigma had higher levels of depression over time. Simply put, much of the relationship between past trauma and poor mental health over time was explained by persistent community rejection rather than the experienced sexual violence itself.

Other research on child soldiers has revealed similar findings. In northern Uganda, Jeannie Annan and Chris Blattman observed that abductees and nonabductees experienced similar levels of family and community rejection.[3] However, Verena Ertl reported that stigmatization in former child soldiers was significantly higher compared to other war-affected children.[4] Dr. Kennedy Amone-P'Olak, also working in northern Uganda, had similar findings, reporting that stigmatization was the only "social and relational challenge" that former child soldiers self-reported at a significantly higher rate than adolescents who were not former child soldiers.[5] Several studies also noted that fear of stigmatization by society was a barrier to former child soldiers accessing mental health services. Such a finding indicates that mental health programs that rely on eligibility labels, like being only "for former child soldiers," may create barriers to access for those they are intended to reach as they may propagate stigma via unwanted labels.

Beyond lack of control in the face of provocation, there were other outward signs former child soldiers expressed that could elicit stigma. For Sahr, his hot temper became a tool that resentful community members used against him. They would prod at him and tease him until he snapped. His inability to control his strong emotions could be manipulated in ways that reinforced people's fears about those who had been with the rebels. Every time Sahr fought back, he confirmed the community's suspicions that he was irreparably damaged by his past. When he pulled a knife, intending to defend himself, he became a pariah, unable to live in his home village any longer.

In truth, although individual and even group mental health interventions will likely remain far from the reach of many children formerly involved with armed forces and armed groups, thoughtfully constructed and inclusive interventions can go a long way in helping young people build their interpersonal skills and ability to regulate their emotions. In later years, when we drew from our study findings to develop mental health interventions for youth, we specifically avoided any labels that would indicate that programs were directed to any one stigmatized group. Our Youth Readiness Intervention (YRI) was designed to work both for children associated with armed forces and armed groups as well as for those who had experienced the trauma and disruption of war without involvement as a child soldier.

To address the interpersonal deficits that can accompany trauma exposure, we placed a great deal of emphasis on building prosocial attitudes and behaviors. The ability to put one's best self forward might become an important catalyst, setting off a virtuous cycle of additional social support and relationships to counteract the risk caravan that could occur in light of community rejection.

There is a saying in Sierra Leone that we use in the YRI manual: *good wod pul good kola.* Loosely translated, this phrase means that "good words will bring good things." Kola nuts are extremely valued in Sierra Leone and used as a token in everything from a wedding exchange between families to an important meeting between leaders. By being able to put one's best self forward, youth who may otherwise raise suspicion can navigate troubled waters. Some war-affected youth never get the chance to develop such skills. Their difficulties with relating to others and strong emotional reactions, likely due to past trauma, set them up for community conflict and eventual rejection without support.

Evidence suggests that the effects of stigma can travel intergenerationally, with rejection and hatred extending beyond former child soldiers toward their own children. Such dynamics are particularly devastating for the children born of rape to girls abused by rebel groups. These forced "child mothers" suffer from discrimination, stigma, and an array of psychosocial problems upon their return.[6] In Myriam Denov and Atim Angela Lakor's qualitative study of sixty children born in captivity in northern Uganda, the children of former child soldiers were marginalized based on both their parents' former affiliation with the Lord's Resistance Army as well as by their label as children born in captivity.[7] These mothers and their so-called "rebel babies" faced painful stigma and community rejection along with verbal and physical abuse and violence upon return.

Girls could also develop very complex and fraught attachments to the young men who had held them in captivity and forced them into sexual relationships. Over time, some of these relationships evolved to include a tremendous sense of attachment. The story of Patricia, a young girl captured in Kono, exemplifies these realities. Patricia was abducted by the RUF at age eight and spent two years with the fighting forces. "My fears were that I must be forced to fight, to be raped, and to smoke marijuana. Because I used to see my friends being forced to do such things—friends that were older than me." When Patricia was with the rebel forces, an older rebel fighter took interest in her. "The only man who proposed to me," Patricia said, "was the fighter that took me away, but I was very small, and he told me that when I reached the age of marriage, he would marry me."

The older man's interest in the girl upset his wife. "I remember the person who captured me . . . he came with me to his wife and told her that he liked and wanted to marry me when I had grown up and that she should take care of me." As Moses explained, having more than one wife was culturally acceptable at the time, but jealousy could make such situations toxic. Patricia noted, "At that time, his wife started maltreating me. That was some of the reason that made me escape."

In fact, Patricia was in great danger during her two years in captivity. On several occasions, the rebel commander's wife attempted to kill her. One time, when the commander was away, his wife took Patricia to the bush and attempted to stab her to death. Patricia recounted the story: "Even up until now, I have the mark—the woman nearly ended my life with the knife they were using during the war." The attack on Patricia was only interrupted by the return of the commander. "As she was about to stab me the second time, her husband came and asked us what we were doing, and I told him that his wife asked me to escort her into the bush and stabbed me."

The commander was able to get Patricia care for her injuries. "The man took me to town," she explained. In time Patricia's injuries healed, but she remained in captivity. Eventually her friendship with the sister of the commander's wife—the wife who had tried to kill her—led to her escape. The sister witnessed a second attempt on her life. "The commander's wife beat me and threw me in a fire; all my [vagina] got burnt and I was not even wearing pants. The sister told me that she saw some people escaping, and she told me to escape with them. I then agreed to go with the people."

Patricia reflected on how her ability to make friends had saved her. "My good attitude toward the woman and the woman's sister saved my life and helped me to escape," she explained.

Patricia survived several attempts on her life and suffered severe physical injuries. After her escape, she was able to make her way back to her village. Her family tried their best to take care of her. Her mother said: "We do our best to help her with her basic needs, for example we help her with her medical bills and we give her money for her cosmetics. You know, for a young girl these are necessities. There is no problem with that." Nonetheless, Patricia did struggle with stigma in the community when she returned home. Patricia says that her family treated her well "and used to encourage me with the saying that I am their daughter in spite of anything." The family support helped, and the NGO's efforts at changing community behavior was also important for countering community provocations. Patricia recalled the messaging that had been used: "That they should stop calling us rebels, that they should love us and accept us in society. With that, they were treating us very well; we are all one now."

Patricia's mother was well aware of the community and peer challenges that her daughter encountered. "Initially she had problems," she acknowledged, "like her peers mocking her in school." Patricia's mother had been a fierce advocate. She faced up to the school leaders and demanded a more compassionate response: "I had to go and tell the school authorities about her situation—that she didn't willingly join the rebel forces but that she was abducted when she was eight years old. Now that she has come back alive, I told them not to provoke her. So, the school authorities discouraged the stigma, and the provocation stopped."

The trauma that Patricia had endured was staggering, and her mental health suffered. At times, it was a lot for her family to handle. "When she came back, she had bad characteristics in her—like she was stubborn and rebellious—but now she is totally different," her mother recalled. Patricia also spoke about having frequent headaches upon returning. Despite a loving family, poverty and her early initiation into relationships led to a reliance on male partners to pay for her school fees. "The war affected my future because before the war—when I was captured during the war—at that time I was a child; it was during that time that I started sexual intercourse," Patricia explained. "That never gave me a reason to finish my education."

When she first returned home, her family struggled to keep her in school. "I started attending primary school here and took the national primary school examination and passed for a junior secondary school . . . I attended one year there and left due to poverty." By the third time the study team interviewed Patricia, she had dropped out of school.

"I came back home because of financial constraints," she explained. "During the time I was attending, it was my boyfriend who used to sponsor me in my schooling, and due to that my uncle and the rest of the family said that I have got someone to take care of me and that I should be with him, meaning that I should go along with him."

For Patricia, like many war-affected young girls, a male romantic partner was not a reliable way to pay school fees. He was "out of funds and I had to drop out of school," Patricia said. "He came to his parents and asked them to help him with some amount of money so that I can go back to school, but no one helped. So, I finally stopped going to school."

Patricia's mother explained that Patricia was living with her boyfriend: "Well, she is not yet married but she has someone she is courting. But what caused that was because I had no money to pay her fees that year." Her mother seemed frustrated with the situation: "He promised that this coming year, God willing, he will enroll her back in school," further elaborating, "even if I have the chance today, she will go back to school."

When the team reunited with her in 2016, Patricia was no longer with her boyfriend and had returned to live with her mother. She now had a young child. She explained: "We are not together now because he left me." Patricia remained resourceful nonetheless; she was selling fried cakes at the roadside to make money. She spoke of wanting to start a business so that she could help her younger brothers and family. "I'm doing a lot of things; presently I'm the one taking care of myself," she said. In reflecting on how poverty could drive women into unreliable partnerships, she spoke proudly of what she had accomplished. "Some men always expect women to be in a bad condition, but if he sees me now, he would know that he made a mistake by leaving me."

15

Social Ties

Can communities become more accepting? If so, what does that take? Getting back to that image of social ecology as the rings of potential protection surrounding a child, the vision of a cohesive society is a utopia of support. Of course, the vision is often more an ambition than reality.

Typically, people who work with children affected by war focus on individuals. Helping to change one person's behavior is a much more straightforward act. For example, recall the bike-loving Sahr, who struggled in his relationships with others during his reintegration. There are a number of actions that the evidence shows can help people in this type of situation. We have programs to help people build interpersonal skills. We can also teach practices of self-regulation and mindfulness, such as deep belly breathing or attending to the present moment. Such skills might have helped Sahr improve his emotion regulation, his ability to make friends and manage tensions with others in his community and family.

We also have a toolkit of social and emotional interventions that work on the household level to improve family functioning by reducing conflict and promoting healthy communication. For Sahr, such interventions might have greatly enriched his relationship to his rejecting uncle and helped him to be better supported by his loving mother and grandmother.

But even beyond those two layers of influence, Sahr suffered greatly from a community that lacked social cohesion. He was easily marginalized. In order to combat social stigma, we need to develop programs that can improve acceptance in the entire community. But trying to influence the dynamics of a whole village or town is much more difficult. Communities are ecosystems, infinitely more complex than individual behaviors. There's a Krio term that always reminds me of this: *al men tek em,* or "we need everyone." Can we promote this type of change on such a large scale? And if so, how?

Pushing forward community-wide change is difficult. Some community-level interventions have been tried and evaluated in Sierra Leone, but unfortunately, the results are mixed. For instance, we observed a number of what are called "community sensitization" campaigns—efforts to encourage communities to welcome and support children who returned from their war—and their initial impact. These efforts usually involved "town hall" meetings, held in a local gathering place, to discuss the involvement of children in rebel forces and the potential for them to return home. Facilitated by the government and partner NGOs, these discussions reminded villagers that the abducted children were forced into their involvement.

These meetings served two purposes. First, they kicked off a dialogue about healing that was clearly quite important. Secondly, they provided a chance to "take the temperature" of a community—to see whether the placement of children there was possible. Facilitators might suggest that abducted children who wished to return home should be seen with forgiveness. But in some cases, expressions of resentment and anger were too strong. When such negative dynamics persisted, the National Committee for DDR might may deem a village not yet ready for formerly abducted children to be returned to the area. But more often than not, community discussions did lead to formerly abducted children being returned to their homes and communities—a tangible sign of the power of forgiveness.

While initial sensitization efforts did have some positive impact, a more formalized approach of continuing these facilitated community discussions might have better sustained efforts over the long haul. From what we observed in our study, family and community dynamics were left to take their natural course, which meant that when things started to go wrong, there was no means to monitor the situation and take action.

Reviews of other community initiatives in post-conflict Sierra Leone indicate similar dynamics. In 2009, Mike Wessells, an expert on community-based efforts to support healing and the reintegration of children involved with armed forces and armed groups, prepared a report for Save the Children International.[1] It reviewed evaluations from unpublished literature on community-based groups focused on child protection and well-being, with an emphasis on groups that had been externally initiated or supported. He reviewed hundreds of evaluation reports, including those on local child welfare committees and disarmament, demobilization, and reintegration (DDR) programs serving children. He observed that externally initiated programs faced real challenges of sustainment. In fact, large infusions of donor funding early on, before meaningful local leadership and buy-in were established, were dangerous to a program's longer-term survival.

Community investment and ownership appeared to be a crucially important limiting factor. For those programs that had survived over the long term, their community ownership was strong. Sierra Leone certainly provided a perfect example of this dynamic in action. Immediately after the end of the war, humanitarian organizations had helped to organize several community-based child protection committees. However, a few years later, most of the child protection committees were inactive or no longer existed. Nothing had translated into a more sustainable system to address child protection issues.

Other research demonstrated the complexity of community-level change. One of the most compelling examples was the rigorous evaluation conducted on the Fambul Tok community reconciliation initiative. Fambul Tok, meaning "family talk" in Krio, was rolled out in 200 Sierra Leonean villages, with 2,383 individuals involved.[2] The Fambul Tok intervention involved meetings where perpetrators could share their stories and request forgiveness, and victims could express the anguish and loss they had experienced. The idea behind Fambul Tok was to process truths and difficulties of the past with the intention of turning toward a more harmonious future together.

Elders and local leaders were brought in. Entire villages came together for these events. A rigorous randomized controlled trial was conducted using state-of-the-art methods. The results, published in *Science,* were a bit cautionary. While the Fambul Tok intervention did increase forgiveness of perpetrators and strengthen social capital, it came at a substantial cost for the victims, whose rates of depression, anxiety, and PTSD increased.[3]

The mixed experiences of the Fambul Tok intervention were reminiscent of the community sensitization campaigns. They did a good thing; they got people talking. They brought elders and youth into conversation. However, our research and that of Mike Wessells also revealed that with time and without cultivation, their effects faded. Without institutional support and intentional effort to nurture positive community relationships carefully, with all sides considered, even the most well-intentioned efforts can sour. True reconciliation, true reintegration, takes time and commitment.

The good news for Sierra Leone and many other war-affected settings as studied by Wessells is that there are naturally strong networks, passion, and commitment—forms of rich social capital— to be channeled if the correct pathways can be discovered. Social ties run deep in Sierra Leone; they remain an enduring natural resource. The sense of connectedness that ties people to one another is hard to fathom in the United States, in any generation. I often explain this sense of collectivity to people outside Sierra Leone by sharing the following story.

In 2004, Moses and I were preparing to share our research at a meeting of the International Society for Traumatic Stress Studies held in Atlanta, Georgia. Moses had been awarded a prestigious scholarship meant to support researchers from places where financial and educational resources were scarce. He had spoken directly to the event organizers to arrange the logistics of his travel, and he was confident he wouldn't need any other help.

The terms of the scholarship required Moses to purchase his flight and then, upon submission of his receipts, he would be reimbursed. Moses didn't tell me that he didn't have enough cash on hand to buy a round-trip ticket to Atlanta. He quietly pursued his own strategy to overcome the situation. He could afford a one-way ticket, so he planned to purchase that and then buy the return ticket once he could gather enough money from incoming paychecks. Proud of his resourcefulness, he never considered asking me for assistance.

On the day of his flight to the United States, however, his plan quickly crumbled. When he arrived at the airport, he was informed by the immigration officer that he would not be allowed to leave the country without a return ticket. The clock was now ticking. Moses had ninety minutes to purchase a ticket for the flight back or risk losing the money he had spent on the outbound flight.

Realizing his predicament, Moses calmly began to cast his eyes around the airport. Missing this flight was not an option. He was possessed by a steely confidence that he could assemble the money. He knew people. Quickly, Moses found a family friend and explained the situation. The gentleman emptied out his pockets to help. Over the shoulder of the family friend, Moses spotted a former neighbor; he called out and explained his predicament again. Soon he had even more cash.

As the minutes ticked by, Moses shared his story with a former teaching colleague and the cousin of a friend. Everyone contributed, digging into the limited cash that they had on hand. His friend's cousin worked at the airport and arranged with him to have the remaining portion of his ticket paid out of her salary. In under an hour, Moses was able to pull together the thousand dollars he needed to buy the ticket. He finalized his purchase and boarded his flight with just minutes to spare.

Most people from North America or Europe find this story astonishing—it is hard to imagine something like this happening in an airport in London or Boston. In many other settings and cultures, we cannot fathom having such a deep sense of connectedness to the others around us. The ties and obligations of family, friends, and neighbors to one another is a rich natural resource that cannot be ignored.

When formal systems are weak, social cohesion and social support, in many forms, may play an outsized role. In our research, we have encountered headaches when trying to measure these concepts. There is a range of standard social support measures in common use in research, but they mainly draw on a Western orientation, with questionnaires addressing such issues as "do you have people who care about you?" or "do you feel loved?"

Certainly, these questions do measure something meaningful in every environment. However, when we employed these methods in Sierra Leone, we immediately noticed what we could call a "ceiling effect" among responses. Nearly everyone indicated that they had relatively high levels of emotional support. In fact, this response was so common that we could not really find ready distinctions between one group of interviewees and another. Everyone felt deeply connected and tied to those around them.

It was only when we added a scale that got into other elements of social support too, such as instrumental support—the willingness of others to help you get things done in your day-to-day life, such as watching your property, lending you money, or giving you a ride if you needed it—that we finally began to see some variation. We began to measure informational support, such as the willingness of others to advise you on dealing with challenges in life or to help you make connections to get a new job or a way to advance yourself. Then we really started to see differences. So many of the children we interviewed lamented not only the intense grief of losing loved ones, but also the lack of immediate help as well as long-term mentorship that accompanied the loss of those relationships. It was common for the children to register a deep sense of loss over not having anyone to provide guidance to them. Everyone benefits from having people who acknowledge and listen to us and help us navigate the tough decisions that we face in life. For youth affected by war, this was one of the hardest needs to fill.

Social support in many forms abounds in Sierra Leone. As many of the stories in this book underscore, connectedness in Sierra Leone is a way of life. It is an indelible reality that many of us from urban environments may find hard to understand. Along with that deep sense of connection to one another comes a sense of mutual duty. The formidable sense of connection and obligation that allowed Moses to pay for an international flight in less than an hour was the harnessing of a force more powerful than most can comprehend. This quality is not uniquely Sierra Leonean, but it is a way of life in many low-resource settings. The good news is that it is a natural resource that, for once, is not in short supply.

PART III

Reintegration

16

The Puzzle of Girls' Resilience

Upon return from captivity, girls were more likely to struggle with high rates of depression, anxiety, and hopelessness. They were also more likely to experience family and community rejection. Yet, when we recontacted our sample fifteen years later, the pattern had reversed: boys had notably higher rates of mental health problems and were more likely to experience family and community rejection. Males in our study also had higher rates of involvement with police and of considering suicide.[1] It wasn't immediately clear why girls would fare better over time. We set off to find the answer to this puzzle.

Going back to the early years of the study, we knew a lot about the losses and trauma these young people had experienced in childhood. However, we wanted to know more about their interactions over time with their peers, families, and other loved ones. We asked about how they had fared in finishing school, or how, if at all, they had secured a means to support themselves and their family. Since young men made up a majority of the sample, we went to extra lengths to track and understand the lives of the women and girls as well as the boys in the sample.

We were slowly peeling back the layers of both risk and protection around the young person to understand what patterns emerged. After consulting with local leaders, we constructed questions for scales that would capture both community and family acceptance or rejection. Similarly, we recorded measures of post-conflict stigma, family support, community support, and other social interactions. Fifteen years later, in young adulthood, we were also able to ask about highest grades completed as well as about employment, involvement in crime or being in trouble with the police, current use of alcohol and drugs, whether or not they had intimate partners or children, and the different features of these relationships.

Given our interest in mental health, we continued to ask about struggles with anxiety, depression, and post-traumatic stress symptoms, as well as suicidal ideation and attempts. Using a statistical technique called latent class growth modeling, our analyses suggested that the sample fell into three groups based on patterns of change in community and family relationships over time. The first group, relatively large in size (66 percent), fell into a pattern that we labeled "socially protected," meaning that over the fifteen years of follow-up, they had relatively low problems with family acceptance and low levels of stigma. Our young doctor Isatu embodied many characteristics of members in this group. She had always been adored and buoyed by both her foster family, her sister, and the extended network of community supporters who came to her aid.

The second group was labeled "improving social integration," indicating that they had experienced challenges in both family acceptance and community stigma upon return, but over time, these dynamics had improved. The third group was labeled "socially vulnerable," as they had persistent low levels of family and community acceptance and troubles with high stigma. Almost every participant in this group was a young man (97 percent), all much like Sahr, who really never overcame his challenges both with his family and broader community.

The shift in the vulnerability of girls compared to boys over time was surprising. As we had documented, in the early years after reintegration, girls had much higher levels of community rejection, less family acceptance, and higher rates of mental distress, including anxiety and depression. Fifteen years later, when everyone in our sample had entered young adulthood (their average age was now twenty-eight years), the dynamics had entirely changed, with boys more vulnerable overall in their mental health and in their family and community relationships.

Despite the shortage of mental health interventions available in Sierra Leone, the truth remains that time heals. A majority of both male and female former child soldiers in our sample demonstrated a pattern of improvement over time in their symptoms of anxiety and depression. However, for female participants in our sample, the level of improvement was far greater, according to several indicators. For instance, classification of individuals falling into the "likely clinical" threshold for problems like depression and anxiety was no longer much higher for the female participants. In fact, they showed levels of depression and anxiety that were comparable to male participants (though still at rates that would be considered much higher than populations not affected by war, with 47 percent exceeding the typical clinical threshold on our assessment tools for symptoms and impairments related to anxiety and depression). When it came to clearly trauma-related conditions such as PTSD, we saw steady improvement for female subjects, but the pattern for male subjects was less clear. In fact, the rates of likely PTSD in the male sample after fifteen years of follow-up were comparable to the rates observed in the sample soon after the war.

What explains the differences we observed by gender? Some theories hold that, in general, women are socialized to be more oriented toward maintaining strong relationships and positive interactions with others. Thus they may be more equipped with skills and motivation to navigate interpersonal dynamics, even those as painful as community rejection and familial shame. Resourced in this manner by their connections to others and their interpersonal ties, women may thus be positioned to both contribute to their community and more likely to be able to find their place within it after such horrible traumas. In contrast, it may be that for young men, more gendered expectations for stoicism and physical strength may be prized. Such a need to be "strong" or "tough" despite the pain may have not allowed young men the space needed to heal over the long haul. Furthermore, the war has undermined the fabric of day-to-day life and the economy into which young men and women are expected to find their way. It may be the case that the pressures on young men to secure a livelihood and provide for their families may be extreme.

In her ethnography of fatherhood in Sierra Leone, Kristen McLean wrote about the pressures on young men to secure a means of providing for their families.[2] Across the board, there were very limited opportunities in the post-conflict environment. Although men yearned to be good fathers, they had few ways to make enough money to provide food and shelter and send their children to school.

Indeed, when many child soldiers came home, the boys tended to congregate in collectives related to employment. This collective approach could build both a sense of identity and assistance in securing work opportunities. Even today, people in Freetown will argue that all of the moto drivers are former child soldiers—implying that their background explains their erratic and aggressive style. Nonetheless, this act of banding together and wearing one's past externally was considered acceptable, and even desirable, as a means of projecting a "toughness" and maintaining street credentials among these work collectives.

The personal stories revealed over the course of our study upheld some of these patterns. In Sahr's case, for example, his interpersonal difficulties made it impossible for him to fit in. As a result, Sahr struggled to access the potential protective factors inherent in peer relationships. Upon leaving his home village, Sahr reconfigured a family for himself, settling into a new role while working on a farm with a group of boys.

In contrast, for the young women in our sample, to be associated with the armed groups, to be singled out as a former child soldier, was a mark of shame. This indelible label could be seen as a cross to bear, signaling that a young woman was "unmarriageable." To be cut off from the potential of marriage was a very perilous situation. To be unmarriageable as a young woman was a blistering scarlet letter of community rejection. Accordingly, many young women went undercover, seeking to conceal their past and create a new identity. By fleeing their past, they hoped to shed the labels pinned to girls involved with armed groups. They wished to trade the image of being somehow "defiled," or seen as promiscuous, for new monikers of "student," "mother," and "wife." With a new identity now installed, these young women were positioned to weave a fresh narrative of meaning and reconstruction.

In Sierra Leone, efforts at DDR were very experimental just after the conflict. Policies and interventions that at the time were untested were put in place and are now standard practice in DDR. These included important innovations such as child tracing for family reunification, spearheaded by leaders like the IRC's Marie de la Soudière. In addition, NGOs and the Sierra Leone government worked very closely together to establish interim care centers with attention to psychosocial programming to support reintegration and emotional well-being, including art and recreation programs.

Despite its many innovations, Sierra Leone's DDR process also became a case study on overlooking the unique needs of women and girls. The way initial DDR programs were constructed, labels mattered. To be on a list of former child soldiers could bring with it certain services and benefits. Eligibility criteria were established in order to better allocate the limited resources available, and initial decisions were made to focus on those directly associated with the fighting forces.[3] To establish this link, admission to some ICCs required that former child soldiers turn in a weapon. In the words of one caregiver,

> The DDR asked us to hand over all the children that were involved in the war to them. There was a problem later when they announced that they'd only give some privileges to those who carried weapons. We asked about those who escaped. They said only those who took up weapons.

Girls and young women were overlooked by such policies. Girls had experienced abduction and forced bondage. They had been forced to cook, clean, carry supplies and equipment, and tend to the wounded. Many young women and girls had hauled weapons for their commanders, but rarely would they have their own. When turning in a gun became the ticket to services, the girls were often empty-handed.

It also took quite some time for the government and NGOs to recognize an additional burden that weighed heavily on young women and girls: rape. Sexual violence of all kinds was ubiquitous in the war. For some girls, especially those treated as "wives" of rebel commanders, the level of repeat rape and assault is hard to imagine. In our survey interviews of former child soldiers served by ICCs, 5 percent of boys reported experiencing sexual violence. For girls, 45 percent reported experiences of rape. The true numbers for both groups are likely even higher given that some respondents, due to the pervasive stigma around sexual assault and abuse, would have felt too ashamed to report their experiences.

In addition, many young women and girls had unwanted children born of rape. For these young mothers, the child represented a painful memory. They found motherhood forced upon them as they navigated their own trauma, poverty, insecurity, and eventually, community stigma. Returning fatherless with young children also placed an inordinate financial burden on young women. Thus many women faced a double burden, and reintegration programs overlooked their additional needs as mothers and victims of war.

Upon return, formerly abducted mothers had neither moral nor economic standing, which constrained their capacity to reintegrate successfully. Research on war-affected women in post-conflict Sierra Leone found that women who could not provide for their families were often marginalized, while women with means were more likely to be successful in reintegrating and rebuilding their livelihoods.[4] Thus, the exclusion of women and girls from DDR efforts had major implications for their re-entry and reintegration into society. Failure to account for the particular needs of women and girls undermined what might have been a stronger foundation for their educational, economic, and social potential.

Returning with a child born of rape was no minor issue in post-conflict Sierra Leone. For many girls, their children served as a living, breathing reminder of a traumatic past. However, the realities of survival also blurred the lines. After years of sexual violence and abuse, to be "married" to one of the upper-level commanders was a way for a girl to evade sexual violence from others. A girl might tolerate a relationship that she may not typically have chosen as a means of protection.

As years passed in captivity, these relationships would naturally become more complicated. Even if their origin was one forged of necessity and self-preservation, human connections and mutual obligation also grew. The literature on Stockholm syndrome advances the concept that an abductee might come to empathize with their captor.[5] When children are born into the equation, it becomes all the more complicated.

The complexities of leaving captivity and complicated relationships that had produced children were revealed most clearly upon the return home. Haja, a young woman in our sample, returned home with a small child. The NGO community worked hard to anticipate the particular challenges that she would face and to ensure a fostering situation with extended family who could help to care for her little boy. Then she began to disappear for long periods of time, ostensibly to work. Through her friends, the full picture began to emerge: Haja was maintaining a relationship with her rebel commander, and was acutely aware that to have this relationship revealed could mean the end of the support she so desperately needed. It was in her interest to keep this secret concealed in a programmatic and policy environment that failed to see the unique needs of women and girls.

So what explains the positive outcomes that we observed, whereby girls overall were more likely than boys to show improvement over time in both social reintegration and mental well-being? There may be some clues in the ties that bind women and girls to one another, like braids woven tightly.

I witnessed these powerful connections firsthand when I brought my own children to Sierra Leone for the first time in 2018. Because I had meetings and a conference to run during my trip, I arranged for Moses to take Anna, then sixteen, and Joey, fourteen, to visit an ICC run by Caritas, the in-country partner for our research. A bit evolved from the old ICC days just after the war, this care center was home to a small group of young girls and boys who had lost family due to illness or the 2017 mudslide, which killed an estimated 1,141 people.[6] Deforestation around the country has made it particularly vulnerable to heavy rains, augmented by climate change. A moratorium on housing construction was in place, but not enforced. For years, a small, informal settlement had lived contentedly in an outcropping of makeshift homes lodged in the loose red earthen side of Sugar Loaf Mountain. The view was stunning. However, three solid days of heavy rain from August 11 to August 14, 2017, had caused flooding around Freetown and the Western Area. No organized effort was in place to warn residents of the risks. Early in the morning of August 14, the lower part of Sugar Loaf Mountain, just below the settlements, collapsed, followed by a raging wall of mud, water, and debris that tore through houses and tumbled tree trunks in a matter of seconds. The mudslide flooded homes, trapping many still asleep. When it was over, more than 3,000 residents were without homes, over a thousand were dead, and a rain-soaked red scar slashed the bright green hillside.

Compared to the rescued child soldiers of the war-era ICCs I had seen in 2002, the children we met in the Caritas ICC were notably better provided for. They wore clean clothes and had more than one pair of shoes. They had three square meals a day and the undying love of Sister Agatha and Sister Bernie. Sister Bernie wore a pale blue T-shirt over her long skirt and light gray habit. Sister Agatha beamed and welcomed us into the courtyard that rainy afternoon. At first the children were sheepish, but as soon as they saw my two kids, their stance softened.

I had asked Anna and Joey to come prepared. Not only had they crafted lesson plans for story time and a science experiment, we had toted loads of books, toiletries, and clothes to give away. When every last item that could possibly be given had been distributed (including the comfort bags of eye masks and small toothpaste tubes from the Delta flight), Sister Bernie began to clap energetically. She burst into a rousing rendition of the tune from the PBS children's program *Barney:* "I love you, you love me, we're the perfect fa-mi-ly!"

It was impossible not to chime in. Soon our voices were a wall of sound as we followed Bernie's nods to move in a circle. The song now had a call and response element to it. By the end, Sister Agatha and Sister Bernie had convinced all the children to sing. Anna and Joey knew the tune from their preschool years and sang along, sending me knowing glances as they recognized how the words had been creatively adapted.

After the singing and a few warm-up games, the children peeled off into small groups. A jubilant and talkative group of teenage girls surrounded Anna, smoothing their hands along her long brown hair. She looked at me with surprise and elation. Anna was transported into a sacred space of West African girl-hood as they began to braid her hair.

Now the tone became more serious. Two taller girls, clearly pushing their teen years, stepped to the front of the pack. Their fingers moved swiftly through her copper-brown locks. I remember the look on her face as she was surrounded by the girls, an outsider now inside a sacred fold. The girls stood together tightly, apart from the adults and apart also from the boys. The joy of braiding and tending to this new stranger absorbed them entirely. The whole experience lasted at least half an hour as they chatted softly and exchanged jokes and giggles.

In Sierra Leone, braids are important. Women and girls alike spend hours in close conversation as they comb, separate, tug, and pile high works of magnificence. During this time, they share the contents of their hearts, revealing their hopes and also sharing stories of hardship and abject violence in a country where rates of sexual violence still persist at very high levels. Perhaps as a natural response to real risks, in Sierra Leone, sisterhood, love, and friendship are woven thick. These female connections also serve as a lifeline to hoist many drifting young women out of tough situations. Tragedy can forge bonds as strong as ropes. It may be these ties that have helped many of the young women in our study put their lives on the long road to recovery, finding ready company in their sister fellow travelers.

17

Reverberations of Violence against Girls and Women

In February 2019, Julius Maada Bio, Sierra Leone's new president, declared rape a national emergency after a series of high-profile sexual assaults. In one case, a five-year-old girl had been raped and died as her family attempted to seek care. The streets of Freetown filled with protestors. For many women and girls in Sierra Leone, stories of sexual- and gender-based violence are not new. As our own statistics attest, wartime sexual violence in Sierra Leone was staggeringly high.[1] And such violence and child maltreatment in the country have been widespread for many years since the end of the war as well.[2]

The pervasiveness and impact of sexual violence during the war and in the decades after the conflict have been the focus of important work by a number of scholars; however, for local women and girls, very little of the research has resulted in concrete action. International interest in the topic has waned after the International Criminal Court concluded its trials of those who bore the greatest responsibility for atrocities brought upon civilians during the civil war. Since that time, women and children in Sierra Leone have largely suffered in silence. Based on Sierra Leone's 2019 Demographic and Health Survey, around 60 percent of all women in Sierra Leone report having experienced physical or sexual violence. The prevalence of forms of physical, sexual, or emotional intimate partner violence are just as high.[3] In 2021, the Rainbo Initiative, the only organization in Sierra Leone providing free medical and psychosocial treatment for survivors of gender-based violence, reported an increase in reported sexual violence cases during the COVID-19 pandemic—86 percent of those cases were children.[4]

In Sierra Leone nearly 30 percent of girls are married before the age of eighteen, and 70 percent of survivors of reported sexual assaults are under the age of fifteen.[5] It is a common practice of families in some regions to demand that a rapist marry a young girl who has been "defiled" by sexual assault. Among women and girls in both urban and rural areas, female genital mutilation also remains a common practice, with 83 percent of women and girls aged between fifteen and forty-nine years having undergone the procedure.[6] Altogether, more recent data on sexual violence and child maltreatment is distressing. The COVID-19 pandemic has exacerbated these dynamics while creating gaps in the available data. In fact, a nationwide demographic and health survey has not been conducted since 2019.

Although our data indicate that the male participants in our sample didn't fare as well over the course of time as their female counterparts, Sierra Leone remains a male-dominated society. Scholars conducting research in the country have argued that the civil war led to a certain level of normalization of violence against women. Certainly, unequal, gender-based power dynamics are reflected in attitudes and beliefs of both men and women. Research in Sierra Leone has demonstrated high levels of belief among both men and women that wife-beating is justified.[7] Beating and other forms of physical discipline of children are widely accepted and common in Sierra Leone. In fact, some research by our team and others has demonstrated that parents navigating the precarious high-poverty environment of postwar

Sierra Leone view intense discipline as a central component of child-rearing and a means of ensuring safe and proper development.[8] Physical discipline in schools was in fact legal until 2021.[9]

Negative responses of parents to NGO efforts to reduce physical punishment and other forms of child abuse suggest that grassroots approaches are needed to address this pervasive problem.[10] However, the ban on beating in schools, as led by Minister David Sengeh, suggests an important step has been taken to shift the culture away from corporal punishment.[11]

Given the longstanding disadvantages facing women and girls in Sierra Leone, attempts to change these dynamics must be approached with care and consideration for the society as a whole. For example, it has been proposed that women's social and economic advancement in society may have a counterintuitive effect, increasing rates of intimate partner violence as gender roles and concepts of masculinity are threatened. In such cases, male partners may attempt to regain control through violence.[12] Thus particular attention must be paid to include and uplift all members of society, including men who may be threatened by shifting power dynamics.

In addition, not all the factors affecting the prevalence of violence against women and children and the maltreatment of young people in Sierra Leone are in the hands of the people. The Ebola virus disease (EVD) epidemic, for example, diverted attention and resources from addressing teen pregnancy. During the EVD outbreak, an extended stay-at-home period lasting nine months, there were 14,000 more teenage pregnancies than usual.[13] Such a steep rise in teenage pregnancy is a true indicator of how easy it is for progress on the rights of women and girls in Sierra Leone to backslide. Many onlookers feared the COVID-19 pandemic would have similar effects on girls education, but those fears were largely unfounded. Although Sierra Leone still struggles to prevent and attend to the consequences of teen pregnancy, it has built on its experiences from EVD and created dedicated classes in more than 300 community learning centers that have helped reintegrate more than 800 adolescent girls affected by teen pregnancy into more formal schooling.[14] In these progressive policies led by David Sengeh, Minister of Basic and Senior Secondary Education at the time, we see another sign of potential for change that must not go unacknowledged. However, as reported by Dr. Sengeh's office, the government's ability to reach more girls was hampered by the dwindling number of international donors investing in Sierra Leone.

The Sierra Leonean government has made noteworthy legal commitments to prevention of and protection from sexual violence and child maltreatment. The Constitution of Sierra Leone contains language to ensure equal rights of women and children, such as prohibiting forced labor, barring inhuman punishments, and providing equal educational opportunities. Sierra Leone has also enacted several statutes focusing on protection against violence and trauma, especially in the home environment.

In addition, the Sierra Leonean government has ratified international and regional treaties that commit to protect women and children against domestic violation and exploitation in the form of sexual abuse, child labor, child marriage, and military service. The current administration has made broad public commitments to protecting women and children from harm and ensuring their security and well-being, and these commitments have, in fact, been centerpieces of the political agenda. For instance, in President Maada Bio's first presidential address to parliament, he committed to combating issues such as sexual violence and teenage pregnancy, child marriage, and others. In 2018, First Lady Fatima Maada Bio launched a "Hands Off Our Girls" campaign to end child marriage. President Maada Bio's proclamation of a state of public emergency over rape and sexual violence in Sierra Leone the following year was short lived, but the measure was followed by parliament finally passing the Sexual Offences Amendment Act of 2019. In 2020, the president launched the first-ever National Male Involvement Strategy for the Prevention of Sexual and Gender-Based Violence in Sierra Leone, and the country also overturned a ban on pregnant girls and teenage mothers attending school. In 2022, Sierra Leone began taking steps toward decriminalizing abortion.[15] Most recently, in January 2023, the country enacted a groundbreaking new law, the Gender Equality and Women's Empowerment Act, to increase the number of women in decision-making roles across the private and public sectors.[16]

Sierra Leone still has room to grow in establishing more robust protections for women and girls. Although the Child Rights Act establishes eighteen years as the minimum legal age of marriage, the Customary Marriages and Divorce Act permits child marriage if there is parental consent, and the rate of child marriage remains high in Sierra Leone: 30 percent are married before the age of eighteen, and 9 percent are married before the age of fifteen.[17] However, these laws are not the primary barriers to protection against sexual violence and child maltreatment in Sierra Leone.

Notwithstanding the robust legal commitments that the Sierra Leonean government has made regarding the rights of women and girls, on-the-ground realities reflect a pronounced gap between legal commitments and implementation of them. The country faces significant barriers to progress, such as lack of government resources; insufficient donor support; and a shortage of skilled health, social services, and mental health professionals.[18] As a result, lack of budget allocations and technical staff among government employees limit Sierra Leone's ability to implement much of its ambitious policy agenda. The Ministry of Gender and Children's Affairs, a relatively new governmental body, has yet to acquire enough skilled staff to effect change in this area.[19]

Even though this ministry has a mandate to protect the rights of women, most international and domestic NGOs assert that it does not have the infrastructure or support it needs from government to handle its assigned projects successfully.[20] In the education sector, at least one-quarter of all positions at the district level are vacant.[21]

In regard to external support, donor commitments have been insufficient to address the pressing need for meaningful change and support for women and girls in Sierra Leone. Thus little has been done to pilot new programs or new approaches. The donor pool has been historically small, but it has shrunk further in recent years as Sierra Leone moves away from the "post-conflict" label and as conditions on the ground make it more difficult for donors to see returns on their investments.

Many organizations have curtailed their work in Sierra Leone because of the EVD outbreak and the COVID-19 pandemic. In 2011, foreign aid made up 32.3 percent of Sierra Leone's GDP, but in 2020, it made up only 3.3 percent.[22] This dramatic decrease in aid has left Sierra Leone with a dearth of funding, whether for rebuilding in the wake of both EVD and COVID-19, for coping with current economic struggles with inflation and food insecurity, or for dealing with the impact of climate change.[23] In addition to concerns about the obstacles to delivering aid, donors to local ministries and NGOs may be growing increasingly hesitant to fund organizations without adequate human resources and capacity building, those suspected of corruption, or those failing to provide accountability. Increasing donor trust is paramount to raising aid levels to meet Sierra Leone's needs. To do so, the government must address its past problems with accurately and transparently tracing donor aid.

Beyond resource shortages, there are barriers for those who attempt to act on the country's legal commitments. For example, the issue of violence against women and girls has become highly politicized, with women's rights activists reporting that new rape penalties are being used to improperly target political opponents. There are enduring issues of trust in certain institutions. For instance, Sierra Leonean women have indicated that they do not feel protected by the existing domestic laws, partly due to mistrust of the court system.[24]

Sierra Leone has taken commendable initial steps toward ensuring legal protections for women and children. However, the next step in actualizing such protections will require increased government spending on employee hiring and training, and capacity building from the grassroots to the government level. The government must also work to regain donor trust and support through transparency and accountability in the management of funds. In turn, donors should prioritize funding in areas that complement Sierra Leone's enabling legal environment and that take a culturally sensitive and whole-society inclusive approach. Any further deprioritizing of donor funding to fight sexual violence and child maltreatment in Sierra Leone could have a regressive impact.

Conflict-affected countries like Sierra Leone suffer from compounding failing systems that increase the risk of political backsliding and a resurgence of violence. However, such contexts also have the potential to see the greatest change. Against all odds, the Sierra Leone government and people have shown a willingness and desire to reshape their social fabric to empower women and children as members of society. Sierra Leone is therefore in a moment of opportunity for women and girls, one not to be squandered.

18

Good Deeds Always Come Back

BY MOSES ZOMBO

Aunty Jestina was a very popular figure in the National Workshop Camp, a once-thriving rehabilitation program for those learning trades located on the western edge of Cline Town along the Freetown-Waterloo Road. The camp, which became a postwar home for the internally displaced, was a congested and squalid place. People fleeing the fighting in the east end of Freetown had taken shelter in this scrapyard with its abandoned warehouses and discarded machinery. The West African peacekeeping forces had established something of a safe zone that was the only hope of thousands of Freetown residents fleeing the carnage of January 1999.

There was no pre-planned hosting facility for internally displaced people, and it was quite a challenge to bring order to a place that was suddenly home to so many. In the midst of it all, though, some people still stood out from the rest. Aunty Jestina was one such person. A portly single mother in her mid-fifties, she was soon well-known as one who would not compromise on her principles irrespective of the situation in which she found herself. In her world, boys hung out with boys and girls hung out with girls. With teen pregnancy on the rise, she had reason for concern.

Aunty Jestina was soon known for her stern lectures to any boy who tried to cross the line and mess with her girls. She openly voiced criticism of parents who were surrendering to the pressures of the time and letting their kids roam free. "How do you call yourself a parent," she would say, "when all you do is give birth? True parenthood is not in the birthing but in the raising." She would bring the same uncompromising standards to housekeeping, even in this place of chaos. Everyone in her household had to follow the housekeeping rulebook to the letter.

It made no difference that what served as the home in the camp was a makeshift structure of plastic and bush sticks. It did not matter that your backyard was an extension of someone's front yard and your front yard an extension of someone's backyard. It was virtually impossible to observe boundaries and maintain one's own space in this tumultuous environment. Yet Aunty Jestina's small compound still stood out from all the rest for its high standards of cleanliness. Only dogged determination and an unyielding combative spirit could have achieved such a feat. No one doubted Aunty Jestina was one tough woman. But beneath the veneer of toughness was a truly warm soul. When she was in the mood, she would share a lesson or two on life's experiences. One such was her lesson on the all-powerful topic of "goodness."

"It always comes back to you," she said, a chewing stick in her mouth. "Goodness is always repaid when you need it the most, and expect it the least." She went on to explain how the two youngest of her daughters were not really her blood relations. She had never met their father. She met their mother on her deathbed. That day, she had been visiting a good friend in hospital when the woman lying on the bed next to her patient asked to speak to her. "She asked me to be a mother to her," she said. "She was not much younger than myself but I got the message. Her situation was desperate."

Aunty Jestina explained that the woman had asked her to stand in as her family member at the request of the doctors. She was dying of cancer and the doctors wanted to speak to a family member. But she had no such person available. She had come from Liberia with her two daughters of about nine and eleven years; she had no other family in Sierra Leone. Her husband had returned to Liberia, promising to come back and join them, but two years had passed and he had not returned. During that time, she had taken ill and had been hospitalized. Now the doctors had terrible news. They explained that the family should prepare for her death, which could happen in just weeks. Once the doctors made the pronouncement, the critically ill woman turned her attention to the care of her two daughters and voiced a dying wish to Aunty Jestina.

"She asked me to take care of her two daughters till their father returned. She had no doubt that he was coming back for them. 'Just maintain contact with the place we have been staying,' she told me. 'That is the place he knows.'" At this point, it was obvious that Aunty Jestina was fighting back tears as she recalled the exchange. "Oh, women. The things we have had to endure," she went on. "To know you only have a week to live. You cannot so much as rise up from your bed. And to have to carry the weight of your broken family." The tears were flowing freely at this stage. She would use her *lappa* to wipe them as she looked around to make sure none of the children were close enough to see.

"How do you refuse a dying woman's request for the care of her poor children?" Aunty Jestina asked between sobs. "Being a mother yourself, how could you possibly refuse? My children were aghast when I brought the two girls to our single-room home. But not only was it the right thing to do, it was rewarded in ways I could never have thought."

Aunty Jestina went on to explain that it was less than a year afterwards that the city had been attacked by the RUF and the

AFRC, the splinter group of the Sierra Leone Army who aligned with the fighters. Aunty Jestina was no stranger to displacement—she had earlier fled the war in the provinces to come to the city. But this time there was no place to hide. The only exit from the city was already taken by the fighters, who were raping and murdering the civilian population. The Kissy area, where Aunty Jestina lived, was at their mercy for days on end. Civilians would relocate to neighbors' houses and huddle in basements and latrines to avoid detection by the fighters. She explained that during that horrible time she was separated from her son, her daughter, and the elder of the two girls she had fostered.

"It came to a stage when we either had to get out or stay and die," she said. "We had no more food, and there was deathly silence all around us. The people in our group decided that at dawn we should leave for Cline Town. Word had reached us that the place by the seaport, a whole mile away, was being secured by the West African forces."

Aunty Jestina told the story of their walk to Cline Town. They took a circuitous route, using footpaths and traversing backyards in order to avoid detection as much as possible. To make matters even harder, the group of over a dozen people sometimes had to crouch, clamber over debris, and occasionally make a dash for cover. This was quite an ordeal for a heavy woman such as Aunty Jestina. As she explained: "It was the second day of my fast and I had vowed to God to take neither food nor water until I found my missing children. I was already very low on energy. But the sight of corpses and burnt-out houses would by itself have made me feel faint. I was so often lagging behind that the others could not wait for me to catch up. All, that is, except my little girl."

She recalled how the girl, the younger child of the woman she met on her deathbed, followed her with an undying dedication. No matter how far Aunty Jestina fell behind as she struggled after the group, panting in the heat, the girl would always retrace her steps to lead her back to the rest of the group. Because of the discreet manner of the group's movement, they would have been impossible to find without this help.

As everyone else swiftly fled in terror, the girl kept going back and forth:

> She not only made sure that I found them, but also, she kept me going. Sometimes she would stand and wait and call out to me from where I could see her, and other times she would actually come up and take my hand. It was her encouragement and act of sacrifice that kept me going. I was beyond exhausted. I was shifting between hope and despair. At some point, I was starting to resign myself to the idea of not being able to reach safety.

It was at such a moment, she said, when she was feeling faint from fatigue and hunger, that the girl's angry voice split the silence: "Aunty, we don't want you dying on this road!" Aunty Jestina remarked, "She must have been very frustrated with me to talk like that. But it woke me up somewhat. I kept putting one foot in front of the other, knowing I would pass out any moment. Then she was walking beside me. I didn't quite hear what she was whispering and I thought she was pointing me the way the others had gone. But suddenly, I realized she was pointing to the military checkpoint. And in the distance, about a hundred yards beyond them was a crowd of civilians moving about freely."

Jestina shook her head in disbelief at the memory. "I collapsed at the checkpoint, crying in relief. Somebody offered me water in a polythene bag but I just held it to my chest without drinking. Shortly after, my little girl came back with word that some people had seen my children among the crowd. I immediately put the water to my lips, knowing that my prayers had been answered. But I have never been more thankful for having cared for a child that was not mine."

19

Meaning Making and Transformation

People can reinvent themselves. Being able to look beyond a painful past and craft a new narrative is also a powerful act of healing. In the life stories we have come to know in our study, some of the most remarkable outcomes are examples of scrappy reinvention.

Saidu's story is one of these. During his first interview as a young teen, fresh scars were still visible, marring the skin of Saidu's babylike face. Saidu peered at Moses hesitantly through handmade sunglasses. Moses recalled: "In a place like Kono, you'd hardly find any place to buy dark shades [but] he had them on; they were metal. I still remember what they looked like; they were rectangular-shaped and fairly ill-fitting." The sunglasses did little to conceal the ragged injury and the disfigured eye, milky white and unseeing. "You could see that this wasn't some minor childhood injury that he'd suffered."

Moses later learned that an explosion had hit Saidu with shrapnel. "He got shot in the eye. He had lost his eyesight . . . the damaged eye wasn't in good shape at all," he explained. The boy had been lucky to survive the blast, which had also peppered his face, chest, and arms with scars from shrapnel. Without medical care, he had been left for dead, but he had managed to survive.

Saidu was in an apprenticeship program, as Moses recalled: "some trade apprenticeship—I think it was metals." He had likely made those improvised sunglasses himself. His mood from that day of the interview had stayed with Moses. "He was somber—I think he was the kind of guy who was rather serious, not light-hearted and happy." Moses also recalled another striking detail: his clothing. It was a blazing hot day, but Saidu had worn a jean jacket over his T-shirt and matching jeans. "That was one of the things that was interesting about him—that his clothes weren't only very clean, but they'd also been neatly pressed. They'd been ironed in a time when there wasn't much ironing of anyone's clothes."

Their interview had covered a lot of territory. Saidu was subdued but also insightful. As Moses recalled: "I thought how hard it must be on this guy, for somebody who really likes and takes care of his grooming, to have to lose an eye and suffer from a facial injury." Over the course of an hour-long interview, never once did the boy discuss his disfigured eye. It was as if he couldn't mention it, couldn't yet integrate it into his self-definition. Moses also had the good sense and compassion not to push him. It hadn't come up, and Moses hadn't asked. He followed Saidu's lead.

When Moses returned to interview him many years later, we were all intrigued. We always relished the chance to see what was happening in the lives of the children in our study. To protect the identities of those within the study, as research study ethics often requires, we typically don't give Moses and Musu—who conduct the interviews in Krio—much more than basic contact information. Given the hundreds of young people in the study, they don't always immediately remember the person until they have begun the interviews. Although we retained over 67 percent of the sample over the waves of data collection in 2002, 2004, 2008, and 2016, sometimes there would be a case that we could not locate in one wave who would be found again in a later one.

This was the case with Saidu. Moses recalled with a smile: "It had been around eight to ten years since I last saw him . . . so a lot of time had passed. I didn't know this was the guy I was looking for."

Moses had forgotten about the eye, and our research notes didn't describe the details of the case. He was simply a name and address on our list of sampled interviews. Moses said, "I had a name. I had some contacts I was trying to reach. After a long search—you know, some really thorough work!—I came to this house, and there was this guy."

Moses approached a group of men where the participant was said to work: "He was the lead guy for a group of young boys. He was older than they were, but he had these ten-year-old boys who were hauling firewood. He was organizing these guys to get it off the truck, pile it up, and chop it into smaller pieces. So, he was the big guy around them."

As Moses drew closer, he noticed that the man in charge was very well dressed. While the other boys were in T-shirts, he wore a pressed dress shirt, tucked into clean trousers with a leather belt. His shoes were well made and polished. Immediately, he realized that it was Saidu. A lot had changed. Saidu was beaming, and there was a buzzing, positive energy in the air. Moses laughed at the memory:

It was so striking how this fellow who I'd seen the first time was morose, cross, and sad. Then, the next time I saw him, he ran the show with a group of, like, twelve or so boys, and they were all a very delightful group. It was a real beauty to behold!

I saw that he was missing one eye. The damaged eye had improved somewhat; it wasn't as bad to look at as when I first met him. Somehow, I think natural healing has helped with that. He wasn't wearing glasses or anything. You could clearly see that there was now indeed a scar on the side of the eye socket.

Moses noted the multiple levels of transformation. "Between our first and second meetings, even his community had evolved quite significantly. When we first went, there were burnt-down houses and a very small population. People were coming back from exile and camps." By the second interview, the village had changed. He recalled, "people were more settled in. The community itself had really evolved positively."

Saidu had evolved too, as Moses reflected: "It was really good to see somebody who hadn't only moved forward from those days but was even aware of how different he was now." Moses could not resist pointing out the comparison; he asked Saidu, "Do you remember we had an interview about eight to ten years ago, and you were an apprentice?"

Saidu replied, "Yes, I remember."

Moses continued: "Back then, you were wearing dark glasses." He let the observation hang in the air.

Quickly Saidu responded, "Oh, that? Back then, I used to be embarrassed about the eye."

Moses then realized how far Saidu had come: "I saw when he said that, that it had been so hard for him then. But he was just reinforcing that he was past that kind of thing. He was a different person now and fine with his scars . . . he was an example of a guy who's aware that he's come a long way—that he has bounced back from what used to be his shame and embarrassment."

Over time, this quiet and shy young man had woven a new narrative. With some innovation and know-how, he parlayed his skills into innovative problem solving—a kid who can fashion his own sunglasses from scrap metal must have those skills in droves! The forces of protection around him had been activated by loving caregivers, providing opportunities to work and apply his intelligence. Soon, his entrepreneurial spirit led him to become well-regarded among his peers. They didn't see him for his injury, they saw him as a leader.

Moses learned how Saidu had moved from his apprenticeship in metalwork to his present-day work: "He believed that chopping up firewood and selling it was way more rewarding than metal work. Secondly, he was pursuing this work in partnership with his family members, so he was happy to be surrounded by his siblings and make money together." In reflecting on the shift from the dour mood of the past, Moses attributed this to Saidu's social ties: "He was a very popular guy in the neighborhood; he was well-liked, even though he'd previously been with the rebels."

One truth of our study is that narratives can change. A somber young man embarrassed by his scars, who covered them with handmade glasses and fastidiously ironed clothes, could one day become a leader and entrepreneur, not ashamed at all of his injury. Instead, he could wear it like a badge of courage along with his freshly pressed shirt and fine leather shoes.

For many war-affected youth, starting a business or finding a livelihood provided a powerful sense of purpose and identity and an opportunity to weave a new narrative. Some scholars on the experiences of child soldiers have pointed out that past skills in leadership honed from years of surviving brutal captivity might actually serve as a resource that young people can channel into leadership and management skills later in life.[1] As we see in Saidu's situation, the result can be transformative.

20

Adversity upon Adversity

Just as violence begets violence, one tragedy can set the scene for another. Nothing captures this dynamic more powerfully than the way that failure to rebuild Sierra Leone after the war set the stage for the horrors of the outbreak of EVD.

Things started with a jolt. In the spring of 2014, I received a frantic message from our colleagues at Caritas Freetown. In the remote regions of Sierra Leone's border with Guinea, a variant of hemorrhagic fever had been identified, and it was spreading. EVD is often accompanied by a terrifying array of symptoms—including bleeding from the eyes and ears—and it has a fatality rate of 50 percent.[1]

It was crushing to consider what might happen should the virus reach the large population centers in Freetown, Makeni, and Bo. The war had left the country's health-care system in shambles. Not only were large hospital systems lacking staff and supplies, the systems for training and bringing up new medical professionals in Sierra Leone were also far under capacity, and now many people were dying. The country had only a few hundred doctors for the population of nearly 8 million people.

During that time, our understanding of resilience and collectivity was tested in a most horrific manner. As feared, new

infections began to spread like wildfire. The first case in Freetown was identified in July 2014.[2] A period of abject terror unfolded, a period that did not end until March 2016, when Sierra
Leone was declared Ebola-free.[3] The years in between were a
blur of terror. In the early days, my team resisted leaving, yet
university policy came down hard. They insisted that we evacuate
all faculty, staff, and students immediately. Back in Boston, it was
painful to feel so far away and to watch this horrific epidemic
unfold in the newspapers and on television.

It was also devastating to watch how containment and security measures reigned while humane care was sadly lacking. Given
general distrust of local authorities and the militant disease control measures put in place, such as curfews, checkpoints, and stay-
at-home orders, those who fell ill were terrified to interact with
the Ebola treatment units. Nonetheless, in the name of disease
control, thousands of people were sent away for "care," which
often amounted to separation from loved ones by health professionals clad in full-body isolation suits who meted out the basics
of food and water. Though the measures being taken were of
course necessary to curb disease and protect health professionals
at risk, this approach of prioritizing containment over care only
increased fear among the community. Ebola treatment units
lacked staff, IV fluids, and other basic supplies. Foreign workers
infected with EVD received supportive care, such as IV fluids,
and were evacuated to Western destinations. Those suffering from
EVD in Sierra Leone were left mainly in isolation to battle the
disease alone.[4]

We would receive emails and phone calls updating us on the
situation in the field. The news was heartbreaking. The capital
was under lockdown. Stores were shuttered, and work began to
dry up. Basic supplies were hard to find. We soon learned that
Musu, a dear colleague who had worked on our research project
since 2008, had lost her husband. The circumstances of his death

are an example of the many ways in which the focus on containment over care for EVD was deadly, in ways extending far beyond those directly infected with the virus. Musu's husband had diabetes and had fallen ill. She had raced her husband to the hospital when he began exhibiting symptoms consistent with diabetic shock. But no action could be taken until a test for EVD came back clear. The test took three days—until then, he could not receive care. Musu's husband died waiting.

The rich collectivity of Sierra Leone's culture soon became a major risk factor for spreading infections. In Sierra Leone, it is a traditional practice to touch and bathe the bodies of those who have died.[5] Without these practices, it may be said that someone was not buried well, and their soul may not then rest in peace. In the early days of the EVD outbreak, the distrust in authorities led many families and communities to perform traditional burials undercover, which only spread the virus further. A series of deaths resulted from hotspots among funeral attendees and those who prepared and cared for the bodies of infected individuals who had died.[6]

Soon, the virus was raging beyond control. At the same time, rumors spread that EVD was a fiction. In Guinea, aid workers were attacked, and several were slaughtered. Distrust was rampant. Because containment was receiving much more attention than compassionate care, people hid signs of infection. Family members tried to care for one another. EVD became an inferno.

Watching from afar, we were in anguish. Travel to Sierra Leone was barred, yet we felt obligated to act. Since starting work in Sierra Leone in 2002, we had built a staff of over thirty local research assistants and collaborators. The team had worked hard. They were experts in everything from how to conduct in-depth qualitative interviews to how to carry out repeat surveys and ask about sensitive topics such as mental health and traumatic events.

As Ebola began to spread rapidly and make its way toward Freetown, the phone calls and emails took on a new tone of urgency. "Don't forget us," they pleaded. We wanted to show our solidarity, and this was a time to rise up rather than shrink away.

It rapidly became clear that we couldn't press ahead with our usual program of research. A lot of other projects were suspending operations, but we were concerned about our staff, as well as their families and loved ones. Working for our project has been a critical source of professional employment for so many. The staff felt that with some adjustments, appropriate personal protective equipment, and the ability to conduct data collection without physical contact, the research could continue. However, in an attempt to control the rapidly spreading infections, the government of Sierra Leone implemented several days of stay-at-home orders. Schools were closed and curfews established. Eventually all work—and means of income—came to a halt.

When we spoke to the staff, they wanted to contribute; they wanted to make a difference in the fight as well. Our partners at Caritas were already on the front lines, starting feeding programs for impoverished children and distributing cleaning supplies and personal protective equipment to stop the spread of infection. They were also helping with sensitization campaigns to impart accurate messages about EVD and how to stop its deadly spread, including new approaches to helping families bury loved ones without the risk of contagion.

We all felt that we could contribute our research skills to the response. There was little information at the time on beliefs and attitudes that shaped risk behaviors for the spread of EVD. There had been very little attention to how prior trauma and war experiences might also have a role to play. Might there be associations with past trauma as well as current mental health difficulties and how people interpreted health messaging and health promotion behaviors? In this gap, we saw an opportunity. We could deploy our staff and their tremendous skills and also make sure that no one lost work. We could in our own small way use our research skills to contribute to the fight against the virus.

With help from private donors and colleagues from the Harvard Humanitarian Initiative, we developed a new study to investigate knowledge and attitudes related to both risky and health-promoting behaviors in the context of EVD.[7] Using technology that the team had set up for our other research projects, we programmed a survey in Boston and used Android tablets already in the field to turn our attention to research on fighting the EVD epidemic.

Our team prepared carefully to launch data among over a thousand residents in the communities of Freetown. They would use field epidemiology methods to sample at least one adult in households randomly selected from census enumeration areas.

We had long research discussions about whether random digit dialing and phone interviews might be possible. It was decided that these were a nonstarter. The team conducted their interviews outside, in courtyards and under trees, with one staff member on watch to ensure privacy and the other leading the interview. Our medical colleagues agreed that if participants and staff were free of EVD symptoms and no physical contact was involved, these interviews could be done safely.

The findings of this study demonstrated critical connections between mental health problems and the ability of people to make good decisions to keep themselves safe. People whose trauma and loss manifested in anxiety were also more likely to avoid crowds and other practices where EVD risk was raised. However, for individuals with PTSD, we observed lower levels of EVD prevention behaviors. We were able to share these findings with partners working on the Ebola response to bring greater attention to the psychosocial elements of the outbreak. We eventually published our findings in the journal *PLOS Medicine.*[6]

It was Louis Pasteur who observed that "chance favors the prepared mind." We had no idea that we might be able to contribute to the Ebola response—it was not at all our topic of expertise. However, when faced with an urgent call to action, we had an obligation, and we had prepared ourselves in ways that we hadn't realized.

Many years later, I would help colleagues put together the idea for a longitudinal study of children affected by the Ebola outbreak.[7] The idea for this study, led by my fellow Boston College global practice professor Thomas Crea, was to use the methods from our study of child soldiers—including the surveys, the methodology for field work, and the basic concepts of risk and protective factors arrayed throughout the social ecology—to understand factors shaping risk and resilience among children: those directly infected with the virus, those indirectly affected by disease among family members, and those who were not affected. By following them over time, as we had done in the child soldiers study, we would be able to understand how these processes interacted and shaped one another. Findings published by Crea and the team in 2022 showed that social distancing and EVD-related stigma were both sources of distress among study participants, particularly among children. The results suggested that isolation due to infection and enduring stigmatization demanded "coordinated responses to prevent and mitigate additional psychosocial harm" of infected individuals and their families.[8]

Our research study in post-conflict Sierra Leone provided the trained staff on site and existing methodology for responding in a timely way to the EVD crisis. The lessons learned in structuring these two studies assisted a longitudinal study of children after the Ebola outbreak, furthering research in risk and resilience. It is important that the work we do feeds and launches new projects. Such commitment to ongoing partnerships and building of new ones as the opportunities arise is key to creating the multiplier effects needed to advance the field, as well as protections for children and families.

21

Write on the World

In truth, the stories of all young people captured in these pages are the stories of survivors. Children and adolescents living through war must draw on their own courage and resourcefulness to navigate the realities they face. The concept of children's agency is part and parcel of any discussion regarding youth living in conflict-affected regions. In developmental science, it is a well-documented reality that, as children mature, they are able to exert more choice and influence over their lives. In different cultures, the concepts of *child* and *childhood* have a range of definitions and expectations. These realities are further shaped by gender and other dynamics, such as social class and tribal affiliation. As the case of children associated with armed forces and armed groups underscores powerfully, young people exposed to such extreme circumstances cannot be seen simply as members of "vulnerable" groups deserving of protection or humanitarian intervention. They must be considered as individuals with needs, rights, and the agency to act and make decisions in accordance with their evolving capacities.

The United Nations Convention on the Rights of the Child (UNCRC) defines children as "every human being below the age of 18 years unless, under the law applicable to the child, majority is obtained earlier."[1] Like the developmental concept of maturation and agency, the concept of the evolving capacities of the child is a fundamental principle of the UNCRC, articulated in Articles 12–15 and central to the interpretation of the rights of children as they mature from infancy through adolescence to adulthood.[2] Capacities of individual children to act on their own behalf and to participate in decisions that affect them are seen to be constantly evolving as the child matures in their social and cultural context.

The importance of considering children's views and their right to participate in decisions that affect them is a core theme of the UNCRC.[3] In particular, children's experiences concerning safety and development must taken into account to better understand how to advance children's security. Under UNCRC principles, such consideration must also allow for their evolving capacities and reflect their best interests.

When taking up the issue of children associated with armed forces and armed groups and how programs and policies can best promote their longer-term health and well-being, children's views and their abilities to make decisions for themselves play a critical role. To survive years of captivity and being socialized into an armed group requires tremendous personal agency. Critics of current humanitarian programming have cautioned that programs and policies that paint children as innocent victims minimize the tremendous resourcefulness that young people have exhibited in such circumstances. In Sierra Leone, we saw that a young person's sense of personal agency and their ability to persevere in the face of challenges were key factors in determining future outcomes.

An analysis by researcher Helen Berents observed the critical role of personal agency in contributing to young people who successfully navigate post-conflict environments. She conducted interviews in Colombia, Sierra Leone, and Uganda, noting, "children in peace-building processes raise unique problems because, having lived through these experiences, their actions frequently do not conform to dominant understandings of the 'child.'"[4] As Berents argues, young people may leave their experiences with an armed group equipped with perseverance, as well as a significant sense of personal agency and leadership skills. To simply expect former child soldiers to then return to the role of the innocent "child" is incomprehensible. This agency is a skill that can and should be tapped. When harnessed, this sort of perseverance and drive can be potent.

The interplay between potent individual agency and protective elements in the social ecology can be powerful. The case of Joseph, the young man in our cohort who became a nurse, captures this dynamic well. Joseph was a young teen when he was captured by the rebels as his family attempted to escape to safety in Guinea. From his description, he was tasked with fetching water, gathering wood, and finding food sources such as potato leaves to feed the rebel troops. Joseph described to Moses his sense of despair at being taken from his family, but also how he maintained a sense of agency in captivity.

For Joseph, books became a lifeline and also a characteristic pastime that made him stand out. Joseph told Moses, "I carried my books during my leisure time . . . I would pull out my books and start to read." Joseph's actions, which quickly caught the attention of rebel commanders, "even made some of the commanders love me." Rather than sending the thirteen-year-old to the front lines, the commanders began to appreciate his talents: "They even asked me to write letters for them."

As rebel commanders took note of Joseph's intelligence and interest in books, what unfolded was a virtuous cycle of agency, mutual care, and protection that supported Joseph through his two years with the RUF. Joseph described his relationship to his rebel commander as one of affection. "Even though I was a kid. . . . This guy showed me so much love. . . . This guy protected me. . . . He did not allow me to even touch a gun."

With time, Joseph came to live with the rebel commander and his wife. "I was living in his house. I was not there as house help, but I was doing domestic work for him . . . iron his clothes, polish his shoes." The rebel commander was protecting Joseph because he needed the boy's skills in reading and writing. The commander treated him "like his secretary," Joseph explained, "because he was not educated."

Joseph's abilities also protected him from being taken by another commander. There were times when other members of the rebel leadership would come to see his commander, and those were moments of terror. "The house was not secure," said Joseph, and other rebel leaders "would come . . . with guns."

Joseph knew well that if his commander were killed or if he gave up Joseph to another commander, his life could change in an instant. He would do all that he could to avoid others developing an interest. "When sometimes they met me doing something they would say, 'your boy is clever!'" In those moments, Joseph kept his head down and immersed himself in his writing, which grew by leaps and bounds. Joseph remembers surviving those days in the bush by writing. "I will write, write on the world," he remarked.

Eventually, the commander died. Joseph told us, "when he died, I felt so insecure." For a child to lose such a powerful protector could have been tragic, but instead Joseph's ability to build and maintain relationships led to his escape. The commander's wife still cared for the boy and took pity on him. "When he died, I told his wife that I wanted to see my parents," Joseph told us. "She graciously accepted." She eventually arranged for his return home.

Wartime relationships are complex; they never confine themselves to simple words like *good* and *evil*. Many of the commanders and their wives were themselves children and youth who were abducted, involved in the conflict against their will. Even in the darkest of places, a sense of humanity and care could still be found. In reflecting back on the two years that he spent in captivity, Joseph remarked, "you know, I was loved." After the commander's wife returned Joseph to his family, they too viewed his captors with compassion: "I went to my parents and explained this sad story to them. They also felt it . . . the guy was nice . . . not everybody during those days was bad."

When Joseph looks back at the steps he took to change his fate, he credits the commander who shielded him. Joseph feels the commander saw in him "potential" and "would not expose me to any danger." In fact, "he tried to protect me," Joseph explained. He also credits God. "God just made everything possible," he said.

At first, people in the community were anxious and feared Joseph. But his behavior and drive to meet others' expectations helped to calm people. After coaxing and sensitization, his mother explained that the townspeople became "relaxed." In the end, Joseph's return home was joyous. His mother recalls, "People danced and rushed to church."

Joseph had a burning drive to study and to advance himself through education. When asked if the war had changed her son, Joseph's mother replied, "He has not changed his lifestyle. He is quite studious." But she also reckoned with the reality that "the war affected their education as they made no progress."

Nonetheless, Joseph's desire to advance himself was undeniable. "I want to be in the office," he explained. "I want to be somebody with a tie and with a coat, you know; I admire people like that."

As might be expected, Joseph did very well in school in Freetown. After the war, he attended a respected high school. He eventually became the school prefect there and taught for a while. Joseph was inspired to study nursing because his mother used to be a nurse, and his uncle was also in the medical field. "I have an uncle who is a senior medical practitioner, and he encouraged me to enroll for nursing." At first Joseph had been surprised: "I did not even know that a man could be a nurse. . . . He encouraged me to start at a very low level . . . then after my state-enrolled community health nurse examination, I decided to go for the West African Senior School Certificate Examination again and was successful . . . the second time."

Real experiences with death and dying during his time with the rebels inspired Joseph to join the medical field. "I will say I was destined to be educated. Most of my colleagues that . . . went through the war, most of them are motorbike riders, some are drop-outs—they are not doing anything." However, like Isatu, Joseph had a drive, a sense of agency that distinguished him. He explained, "I think all that inspired me . . . during the war, seeing people" who were sick or injured. He recalled the story of a young girl he had known during his time in captivity: "We were all together. She got sick. I think it was malaria . . . I can still recall the symptoms she was having during those days."

Even as a young boy, Joseph had tried to step in to help the girl, who was also held by the rebels: "I cared for her. I would go near her, I would encourage her to eat." Without a proper diagnosis, medicines, and training for how to intervene, he hadn't been able to save her life; the girl, just a "small kid," died. He was heartbroken.

Her death inspired him to take action: "Now that I am in the medical field I recall her condition, her symptoms, and can say, 'that girl died of malaria.'" For Joseph, this knowledge has been accompanied by a sense of empowerment and motivation to be an effective leader. "All of these things are inspiring to me."

22

The Education Gap

Being educated is not just a mark of pride for many children in Sierra Leone, it is a foundational step for advancement. For war-affected children and parents around the world, from Sudan to Ukraine, the chance for children to pursue an education remains a beacon of hope amid a sea of discord and suffering.[1] In humanitarian emergencies, parents and young children interviewed about their hopes and dreams speak time and time again of education as their utmost priority. While access to quality education can catapult them to a better life, such opportunities remain out of reach for most.

Soon after the end of Sierra Leone's war, researcher Myriam Denov interviewed a group of boys and girls living in the settlement of Beledu, Sierra Leone. She noted, "all participants emphasized their desire to continue their education and described education as a pathway to economic and social advancement. It became evident that education constituted a collective value that all participants shared, but that was largely inaccessible."[2]

At the end of the war, schools were destroyed. Policies on access to accelerated education for children who had missed years of schooling were lacking. In fact, for many years after the war, girls who became pregnant (often from sexual exploitation) were excluded from school. Lack of sensitivity to trauma and its consequences and weak policies to support vulnerable children were not unique to Sierra Leone; these are unfortunate patterns repeated globally.

In a study of former child soldiers in northern Uganda, Jeannie Annan and Chris Blattman found that compared to children not associated with fighting forces, the longer children spent in the captivity of a rebel group, the larger the gap in educational outcomes.[3] Further, those who were abducted at younger ages were less likely to return to school after their release.

Even before the civil war, Sierra Leone's education system was struggling. The country was unable to accommodate the millions of children seeking public education. In 1990, only 55 percent of children eligible for primary school were enrolled.[4] Schools at all levels demanded fees from parents, slamming the door in the face of impoverished children. While little detailed data is available for the immediate prewar period, it is clear from indicators of educational outcomes in the country, such as very low literacy in rural areas, that the system was not meeting its goals. The United Nations Educational, Scientific, and Cultural Organization (UNESCO) estimated in 2022 that in Sierra Leone 51.6 percent of males and 34.9 percent of females over age fifteen were illiterate.[5]

As we embarked on our data collection in 2002, our qualitative and quantitative data from Sierra Leone confirmed the findings of Myriam Denov and her colleagues.[6] When we asked Sierra Leoneans what helped young people to reintegrate after the war, they repeatedly spoke of the critical role that education played. As one young woman in Kono District put it: "The most important aspect that should be given priority is education, because lots of children have not attended school since their return but have gone back to the street." Over 75 percent of the caregivers we interviewed saw education as a centerpiece of healthy reintegration.[7] In reflecting on educational options, care-givers cited both formal schooling and skills training as equalizing forces. One caregiver said: "I know if a former child soldier learns a trade, their future will be just as bright as any other child who was not captured."

In community interviews, increasing access to educational opportunities for children formerly involved with armed forces and armed groups was seen as a means for improving social cohesion and mitigating the effects of prolonged family separation and years of living in captivity. In Kono, a young man described the link between productive activity and successful reintegration: "the community becomes happy when they see us engage in productive activities such as schooling, trading, mining, or farming." Thus, a successful and productive return to school could serve as a signal to those in the community who feared that there was "rebel blood" coursing in the veins of the former child soldiers. To be successful in school, to perform well and be able to get along with others, helped smooth the pathway to community acceptance. Another young man stated this reality quite plainly: "we were accepted because we were sent to school."

Not every young person could fully benefit from educational opportunities, however. If conflicts with teachers or other students erupted—as we know is common among young people suffering trauma-related distress—it could raise concerns and worsen community relations. Any incident involving one adolescent with a bad temper or poorly controlled emotions could be taken by teachers and community members as "proof" that formerly abducted children were damaged goods.[8] One boy in our study explained, "if you are stubborn and unsettled, they get worried."

Beyond signaling acceptance and a return to routine, schools also serve as a place where teacher and peer relationships are formed and social support structures are extended. In our social ecology of resilience, both peers and teachers provided protective layers of support that promoted resilient outcomes when reintegrating former child soldiers. For many returning children in Sierra Leone, the war had led to separation from teachers and shattered friendships. Peer networks had been destroyed, communities fragmented, and schools shuttered. When they returned home, school provided essential protective resources. An older adolescent from Kono explained why education was important to her: "through the help from NGOs, we continued school so I could interact with my friends." Attending school, she said, contributed to her mental well-being: "so I would not be depressed and discouraged."

The mental health consequences of the war could also pose a tremendous barrier to productive participation in formal education. "Education came to a standstill," said a young woman in Kono. "The RUF killed people and therefore created so much fear." She explained that the conflict "made me think of my parents all the time. I have suffered from mental stress since then."

A young man from the Bo region talked about how his past trauma caused him interpersonal challenges: "Even among my friends, I become violent and get annoyed over trivial issues." Prior research on war-affected youth has indicated that past trauma exposure may lead to interruptions in attention and learning that make it difficult for youth to fully reap the benefits of getting back into school without additional supports. Trauma exposure has been associated with an increase in school problems, including interpersonal problems, and dropout.[9]

For those in our study whose trauma has interfered with their ability to get along with others, we see a concerning pattern: even when given a chance to succeed, their prospects may be undermined. Sahr, for example, faced conflict with community, interpersonal problems, and challenges with emotion regulation that not only got in the way of his acceptance in the community, it also led him to drop out of school.

Sahr was not able to work in a typical environment, either, due to interpersonal challenges. In the last years of his life, he lived on the margins of society, away from his family, and struggled just to have enough to eat. A boy beloved by his mother and grandmother, Sahr never had the chance to unlock his full potential.

The emotions and behaviors of war-affected children sometimes baffled caregivers. In Kono, one focus group member told of her struggle with her son:

> The war has made a lot of children lose interest in education. Most of them have refused to go back to school, like my child, for example. I have done all I can to encourage him to return to school, but he has refused. Recently he brought a woman whom he introduced to me as his wife. The best that can be done for them now is to establish institutions where they can learn a trade.

In fact, caregivers and community members seemed to have little awareness of how the burden of war experiences on children might influence their ability to thrive in the school environment.

If issues of stigma and community rejection by peers were left unaddressed at school, the environment could quickly turn toxic. Unsupportive teachers could become an active source of stress for returning young people. Compared to other adults interviewed for our study, caregivers of former child soldiers were more likely to cite stigma as a significant obstacle facing returning children.[10] Young people themselves spoke of how disheartening it was to be taunted and teased by peers in the schools and community, both of which were common even in educational settings. "In school, my friends provoked me," explained a young man formerly with the RUF.

But not all schools were alike: efforts to counteract stigma from peers, teachers, and other school leaders had an important role to play. When issues such as taunting and name-calling occurred, teachers could step in to calm tensions. A caregiver from Kono, for example, noted in one case:

> The child now fits well in the community. At first, he was provoked because he had a RUF tattoo on his body, but the teacher intervened, and now he is not provoked. He didn't like to go to school . . . but now he is comfortable in school.

In this case, the teacher was a trusted figure to the boy, and someone he felt comfortable approaching for help. He remarked, "whenever they called me names, I usually explained the matter to our teachers, so they advised them not to do so."

More teachers are needed in conflict-afflicted settings who are invested in making the classroom a safe space and trained in trauma-informed approaches to managing student behaviors and relationships. In recent years, several initiatives have been developed and tested to promote social-emotional needs in schools. Some of these programs, such as the Healing Classrooms initiative of the IRC, equip teachers with skills in classroom management and also facilitate conflict resolution. Such skills enable teachers to hold classroom conversations about challenging topics, from grief and loss to mental health promotion.[11] Innovations on how to scale such interventions are also being explored. In a study in Pakistan, Atif Rahman and colleagues have been testing the use of chatbots and other digital tools to help coach classroom teachers in behavior management and other elements of improving social-emotional learning.[12]

In Sierra Leone, educational opportunities were important to former child soldiers, but so was the availability of schools that fostered tolerance and reconciliation and facilitated positive peer interaction. For young people, returning to school was an important way to bolster and demonstrate prosocial attitudes and behaviors. The mere fact that children so significantly exposed to trauma and socialized by armed groups could return to classrooms, craving peer support and positive interactions, is quite noteworthy. It is a reminder that the current interest in positive youth development, character virtues, and other "soft skills" for life success are just as relevant to war-affected youth as the focus on potential psychopathology resulting from trauma.

However, for those youth whose trauma and loss meant that they struggled with emotional and behavioral consequences, achieving the ideal represented by school success became quickly out of reach. In Sierra Leone, the educational system is slowly waking up to the need for school-based mental health services and access to guidance counselors, at a minimum. To date, there is very limited access to trauma-informed mental health care in school or community settings. But where an organic process has led to teachers and classrooms dedicated to social and emotional healing, such practices had immediate benefits for all.

Clearly, post-conflict Sierra Leone—like all conflict-affected settings—needed trauma-sensitive schools. They needed to prioritize returning war-affected children to normalizing school environments. Yet in spite of the strong desire for education among most returning children, they faced significant structural barriers. After the war, school fees were a major roadblock for youth and their caregivers. We heard concerns over paying for school fees and materials in more than half of our key informant interviews. Emma, a participant in our longitudinal study, was asked how the loss of her father had affected her life. Her mother stated that the death of Emma's father was far worse than anything Emma experienced while with the rebels. Emma's mother explained at the time, "the girl herself says that it is a problem because of the encouragement he used to give."

By the time the team interviewed Emma after the war, she had discontinued her schooling. "My father, who was paying my fees, died. . . . There is no money to pay my fees." Emma, nonetheless, had not given up hope. She continued to dream of getting back into school. School, she indicated, offered a path to achieving her dream of becoming a nurse. "I want the future to be bright and fine. And in five years' time, I believe I will attend and complete my education. I would like to become a nurse." But to do so, she needed to find the money for school fees.

Sampling from the larger group of young men and women involved in our surveys, we selected thirty-one youth for in-depth qualitative interviews. Ten of them reported that they had received school fee support from NGOs; fifteen reported receiving school-related items, including books, uniforms, and school bags, but not school fees; and six said that NGO assistance was trivial (i.e., soap and two packs of biscuits) or that they had never received any help.[13] While those who received school-related assistance from NGOs were generally grateful for it, they still expressed concerns because the amount given was insufficient to cover the various costs of schooling, and assistance was often very short lived.

Another concern of war-affected youth that we interviewed about their school experiences was the reality of being "over age," or far older than their grade level due to missed years of schooling. This concern was mentioned by more than half (55 percent) of our key informants. "I also feel sad when I see my peers in senior secondary school and I am still in junior secondary school," shared a young woman from Kenema. "If it were not for the war, I would also have been in school." Such findings drive home the strong link between educational access, self-image, and well-being.

In reflecting on identity and self-perception, a young man from Kono felt that his experiences during the war had not only stopped the progress of his education but also caused him to struggle with self-image: "The war affected my mind; it put my education backwards, making me feel too big to go back to school." Some of the respondents were so far behind that they were unlikely to catch up.

One former child soldier, who was at least nineteen years old at the time of our interview in 2004, had been with the RUF for six years. He explained that to be back in school and so behind despite his age was really difficult: "I was not happy, because I was taken away from my family to a place I never knew. My education was affected, because I should not be in form one now but in form five or six." Even in form six, he would have been much older than his classmates.

Just as disarmament, demobilization, and reintegration processes were not sensitive to the needs of women and girls after the war in Sierra Leone, schools were especially difficult places for young girls. Some girls who experienced sexual violence and forced relationships returned to their villages with children. As Myriam Denov described in her research on former child soldiers, poverty and a history of sexual violation also left many girls vulnerable to selling sex as a means of survival.[14] Because schools had a policy that expelled pregnant girls, the pitfalls for war-affected young women were particularly dangerous. In Pujehun District, a young woman in our study told a common story: when she returned, the NGOs "gave me books and some other things," but once she was pregnant, their attitude changed. "They do not care for me now," she said. "They said that I am pregnant . . . but the child is no longer with me, and I want to continue my education."

This policy has been changed in recent years, with greater attention paid to how to help pregnant teens finish their educational pursuits. In his celebrated tenure as Minister of Primary and Basic Education in Sierra Leone, David Sengeh advanced a policy of "radical inclusion," which opened doors for children with special needs as well as survivors of sexual violence and pregnant teens.[15] Leadership of this nature was sorely lacking back in 2002; its presence today is a source of hope.

Some caregivers and community members that we interviewed expressed an attitude that it was simply too late for older youth to return to school. Some felt the children—despite their burning desire to make up for years of lost schooling—were just too old. Had such attitudes prevailed in Isatu's case, she would never have made it all the way to medical school.

In some cases, household dynamics presented formidable barriers to former child soldiers pursuing educational goals. After the death of family members, many children were raised by extended family or foster families after the war. Not all caregivers operated with the best interests of their young people in mind. We observed that when a child was taken in under the practice of fostering, *men pikin,* it was much more common for the caregiver to perceive the child as someone who should have other responsibilities before school. In one of our interviews, a young man being cared for by his uncle told the story of a girl being fostered in their home who was given heavy household responsibilities and passed on the same burdens to other children in the house:

> Our father had a brother who died and was survived by his wife, who he left in the uncle's care. . . . He and the woman have had two children. So, one of the children, the girl that I refer to, is a little older than me. Our aunt has put her in charge of everything in the house. So she acts as if everyone were under her authority. . . . Sometimes when our exams

are due, she would give me one large container full of water to sell. I would sell all of it, and once I returned she would ask me to carry another for sale. And this would be the eve of our scheduled date for two examination papers. So, I would hide and go off somewhere to read my notes. She would not take it kindly. When on weekends my uncle returns home from work, she would tell him that I refused to do any work at all in the house.

While many young people like Isatu were burning with a passion to finish their formal schooling, many more caregivers, especially foster caregivers, promoted the idea that former child soldiers were best suited to vocational education. As an adult focus group member explained, having missed so many years of school, youth needed vocational training opportunities as well as accelerated educational programs. She suggested: "The girls should do things like *gara* tie dye and soap-making." However, for the young people whose lives and education had been interrupted, to return to skills training was often perceived as inferior to regular schooling.

The disconnect between the realities, hopes, and dreams of young people and attitudes of their caregivers regarding education, mental health, and their futures remained largely unsettled issues of DDR policy. Policies and programs that could help war-affected youth actualize their desire to finish formal education clearly required investment. Such investments can have the dual goal of promoting educational attainment and also mental well-being, character virtues, and a sense of identity—all critical to successful reintegration. As a young woman from Kenema District summed it up: "I only feel better when I am studying or when my friends and I share ideas together. I usually say that studying is a source of encouragement. I know that if I am educated I will be successful and people will appreciate me."

In a broad sense, education, both traditional and alternative, has been a critical ingredient in the recipe for former child soldiers' reintegration. For instance, the groundbreaking United Nations report on the impact of armed conflict on children, headed up by the former first lady of Mozambique and, later, wife of Nelson Mandela, Graça Machel, emphasizes the important link between school attainment and economic security for returning child soldiers, factors that often determine the successful social reintegration of returning children and prevent re-recruitment.[16]

Data from other settings bear out this argument. For example, in northern Uganda, former abductees were, on average, less than half as likely to be engaged in skilled work because of schooling loss and serious injuries suffered during the war. These constraints, furthermore, reduced by about one-third the average wage earned by these adolescents after reintegration.[17] Research on former child soldiers from El Salvador has documented similar livelihood benefits of education.[18]

At the time of this writing, Sierra Leone has made great strides forward in education, but it still has room to grow. With the appointment of government officials who aim to prioritize these reforms, the prospects are bright, but the task is immense. The dream of war-affected children and their parents and caregivers to access quality education as a pathway back from devastation remains an enduring hope, still salient today.

PART IV

Community and Healing

23

Narrative Healing

Humans make meaning through story much as a craftsperson weaves colorful strands into a tapestry. For war-affected young people who have lost so much, taking control of the loom and weaving their own story can help them see events as part of a cohesive whole, opening a powerful pathway to process strong memories and emotions. To bring this sense of coherence to fractious and difficult events can be a potent act of healing. In their work with the lost boys of Sudan, psychologists Paul Geltman and Wanda Grant-Knight used narrative storytelling to elucidate the life stories of war-affected youth.[1] They observed that the act of narrating and documenting the lost boys' fragmented memories of flight and survival, bringing memories into a structure that had a clear beginning and middle, as well as a vision toward the future, could have healing power.

Relatedly, Narrative Exposure Therapy (NET) has been used with great success among a range of war-affected populations to treat symptoms of PTSD.[2] In a study of NET with former child soldiers in northern Uganda, Frank Neuner and his colleagues observed that they could improve PTSD symptoms in young people by using guided storytelling to recount their experiences in a safe environment with a trained therapist.[3]

In its early iterations, NET was implemented by trained mental health professionals in individual sessions, making it costly and time consuming. More recently, the experts behind NET have been expanding beyond individual sessions to test the impact and safety of doing these interventions in groups. In recent years, there has been a global movement toward task-sharing, or the delivery of certain evidence-based mental health interventions by well-trained and supervised nonspecialists.[4] Early evidence shows that NET likewise can demonstrate good results when delivered in this way by well-trained and supervised lay interventionists.

Research on the Youth Readiness Intervention (YRI) that grew out of our study in Sierra Leone has also demonstrated that well-trained and supervised nonspecialists can serve as effective and compassionate interventionists. In more recent iterations, the intervention is now being taught to teachers within Sierra Leonean schools, thus extending reach to where highly trained mental health professionals are hard to find.

As we see in the early years, where many of the young people in our study struggled, intrusive trauma memories can interfere with mood and wreak havoc on interpersonal relationships. Research indicates that severe trauma experiences can also alter memory processing, contributing to a greater emphasis on generalized memories and less retention of specific memory, which can have implications for learning as well as academic performance. Recently, a group of researchers active in Iraq and Afghanistan have investigated the impact of a memory-processing focused intervention called Memory Training for Recovery.[5] The intervention has been tested in Afghan teenagers, a group often overlooked by most evidence-based interventions, with promising results.

Narrative has been used in many ways to help integrate memories of past difficulties and trauma into a more coherent and forward-looking view of the world. In our work on family-based prevention with war-affected populations both in post-genocide Rwanda and with refugees resettling in the United States, the use of narrative in the work with families has provided a powerful mechanism for honoring the strengths that helped families make it through the horrors of the past. As time and distance from the events of the past allow, in some cases, being able to tell broad elements of the family story both from the perspective of the caregivers and the children can help family members identify areas of shared vision as well as areas of disconnect. Above all, telling the family story from the perspectives of both children and parents can help participants to develop perspective on each family member's experience and enhance communication and connection. We have found this work especially possible and powerful in multi-generational work with refugee families resettled in the United States.

The Family Strengthening Intervention was first adapted from the work of William Beardslee, a professor emeritus of psychiatry at Harvard Medical School and Boston Children's Hospital. Beardslee has had a long and storied career, from working in the civil rights movement to advancing the science of family-based prevention. His particular area of expertise is in the prevention of depression among children in families where a parent is struggling with depression. It is well known that parental depression is a major risk factor for depression in children. For many families, parental depression can be so loaded with stigma that it is treated as a secret. The consequences for children can be devastating. Many children in families affected by depression are left to make sense of their parents' symptoms, such as mood swings, social withdrawal, and even hospitalization, with little information or guidance. The developmental response to adult mental illness can vary, but especially at young ages, children can come to worry that they are to blame. Adolescents can feel all the more rudderless and alone as they navigate life's challenges.

Beardslee's family-based preventive intervention, Family Talk, opened up a vital lifeline of communication for families struggling with the stigma of parental depression. A major goal of the psychoeducation provided in Family Talk is to help children and caregivers understand depression and how it operates. Such open conversations and clear sharing of knowledge can help children to release themselves from blame. When a caregiver lives with depression, children can also harbor fears of developing depression themselves. Beginning to talk about these concerns is critical to building the coping skills and self-care necessary to ward off serious illness.[6] As he documents in his book *Out of the Darkened Room,* the telling of the family narrative is a means of eliciting the family story.[7] The family narrative exercise is an opportunity to talk through both the happy and challenging times. In so doing, each family member can honor their unique strengths.

The use of narrative or storytelling in a therapeutic process can help individuals to move beyond the struggles of the present toward envisioning the sort of future that they wish for one another. In work with families addressing parental depression, Beardslee encourages the telling of the family narrative both from the perspective of the children as well as caregivers. Over the years, we have collaborated to adapt this same intervention, first to the context and culture of families living well despite HIV / AIDS in Rwanda, and eventually to African diaspora refugees resettled in the United States. In our multicultural adaptation of the Family Strengthening Intervention, the family narrative remains a cornerstone of healing.

For individuals who have lived through war, the journey they have experienced—the most difficult moments as well as the moments of survival and resilience—is critical. In the refugee Family Strengthening Intervention, both children and parents have the opportunity to tell the story of the family and how it began, where it is now, and where they hope for it to go. Using words, small drawings, and notations, they collectively reflect on and document their journey along a timeline. To the degree to which individuals are comfortable to share, it's important to honor the great moments of joy but also the moments of pain and loss. The storytelling, the narrative, becomes a way to contain it all.

Among the Somali Bantu refugee families we work with in Lewiston, Maine, and the Bhutanese refugee families in Springfield, Massachusetts, many parents have never shared the story of the events that led them to flee their home country. When their children complain about the challenges they face now, the teasing at school for their accents and different ways of dressing (especially for Somali girls who wear a hijab), the struggles to find decent jobs and housing, the navigation of school systems and bullies, it can be empowering for parents to share with their children why they made the painful choice to leave the country of their birth. For the children we have worked with, it has been a grounding force to understand the culture and context of their origins and to appreciate the difficult choices their parents have made to breathe new opportunity into their lives.

Perhaps one of the most helpful aspects of constructing a family narrative is the history and grounding it provides family members: not only does the narrative look back on difficult events in the past and the strengths that carried the family through, it also tells the story of a family's present struggles and imagined future. This integrated view of a communal future in which family members share their hopes and dreams can provide stability for many families and individuals. It can be the bedrock of hope.

24

Adult Lives

I first met Isatu myself in the foyer of the Hotel Barmoi in Freetown. Moses and I had planned several days to sit together and discuss case studies to be used in this book, but an upcoming site visit by the National Institute of Mental Health (NIMH), who were funding our youth mental health intervention research, cut our time short.

He messaged me: "Theresa, what if I told you that you had the chance to meet with a person of much interest to you while you were in Freetown?"

I was intrigued. I pressed him to reveal his secret, and he couldn't keep his excitement from me. He texted back quickly: "You could meet with the lady who studied medicine abroad and is back in Salone now." Knowing how busy we were, he teased me: "I bet you would like to squeeze a brief meeting into your schedule somehow? I was going to surprise you with the news once you arrived." The site visit by NIMH was vitally important to an approval that we needed in order to move ahead with our services research. This bit of good news was just what I needed to relieve the stress.

Moses went on, "Is it not a sign that we are all going to be in Freetown at the same time as everything begins to come together?" I could not disagree. Before I knew it, he had arranged for Isatu to come to the lobby of the Barmoi.

My heart raced a bit in anticipation. The sky was turning a dim pink as the sun set. I walked down the long tile hallway past the dining area and swimming pool, where local men in business suits were digging into large plates of grilled barracuda and chips. I scanned the people sitting in the reception area for Isatu. The lobby was festooned with large wooden sculptures of figures in traditional dress, holding baskets on their heads. I recognized Isatu at once. She was dressed in a gorgeous African print dress of Dutch Wax cloth in yellow, blue, and green patterns. It was very well made, with pleated flounces at the waist and shoulders. The back was fitted with a bright gold zipper. Isatu sat as if anticipating an important job interview in the waiting area on the leather couches.

I had held countless meetings in that same Barmoi lobby, seated on those same leather couches over the years. I always hated how the leather stuck to my legs in the summer heat. In contrast, Isatu looked cool and regal.

In the course of over twenty-two years of back-and-forth travel to Sierra Leone, I have stayed at the Hotel Barmoi when in Freetown. The founder and owner was a retired physician named Dr. Sheku T. Kamara. He had once gotten particularly involved with our work on youth employment topics. A major innovation of our group mental health intervention for youth was to integrate it into other programs to promote life opportunities through education or job training programs. Most recently, the World Bank and the German development agency Deutsche Gesellschaft für Internationale Zusammenarbeit, or GIZ, had been investing in entrepreneurship programs. However, to start a small business, a young person often needed a loan. To get a loan required someone to co-sign. For many youth after conflict, such social connections were lacking.

Our beloved driver Dikoh was a case in point. Dikoh was in his twenties and had not finished secondary school, but he was desperately trying to make a career for himself. Not owning his own vehicle was his biggest stumbling block. To get a loan to purchase or rent a car, he needed a co-signature. Dr. Kamara and I had had lengthy and heated discussions in that same lobby about limitations in the Sierra Leonean banking and credit system. I said that when it came to loans for entrepreneurial youth from poor families, they often had no one to help them. Dr. Kamara argued that in Sierra Leone there were always "big men" willing to help marginalized youth get ahead. To prove his point, he had offered to co-sign a loan for Dikoh, who was excited but shy and terrified of Dr. Kamara.

I remember Dikoh's spreading grin as I told him the news. Dikoh's smile was distinctive: an open gap in his front teeth had been filled with a bright gold false tooth, paid for by a group contribution from our entire team. Everyone was thrilled for Dikoh. He was off to great things. He had a new smile, a new girlfriend, and big plans to finally purchase his own vehicle and advance his career.

Then Dikoh got sick. I knew of the hospital, the one where Isatu now works, because I had visited Dikoh there when he was hospitalized for liver failure. It was an overcrowded place of rusted bed frames and soiled linens. The hallways were congested and connected by broken cement hallways and outdoor passages. Printed paper signs and name plates were taped to door frames, torn and yellowed, though doors overall were lacking; doorways were often simply hung with tattered sheets.

It was heartbreaking to see Dikoh, once so vibrant, in his hospital bed. He now lay connected to tubes for intravenous feeding. The whites of his soft, kind eyes were yellowed, a sure sign of a failing liver. I sat and held his hand, my throat swelling with emotion. I could see a faint smile in his tired eyes. I tried to cheer him up by recounting many of our long adventures together. When I left after our visit, Dikoh seemed worn out and resigned to his fate. It was only a matter of weeks after that hospital visit that Dikoh died, another victim of Sierra Leone's failing health system.

Isatu is trying to change that system. Given her many years of captivity by the rebels, her rise as a top medical student in Sierra Leone was stunning. It's hard to fathom that she had accomplished highest honors while never having the funds to buy and own a single one of her textbooks—she had borrowed them all from peers.

As I chatted with Isatu, I realized that she was working in the pediatric wards right next to the unit where I had last seen Dikoh. It was bittersweet to think of her trying to make a difference in that same under-resourced facility. However, it was in her nature to overcome adversity.

Isatu had come to meet me and Moses during a break between her shifts. I offered to buy her dinner, and she willingly agreed. She was tired and famished from the relentless pace of the hospital. We sat in the outside dining area of the Barmoi, by the small, deserted reflecting pool, and I found myself still struggling to replace the mental image of Isatu I had conjured after many years of reading her interview transcripts: a young, passionate student, her face stained with tears as she watched other reintegrated girls heading to school while she waited at the ICC. This was a strong contrast to the calm and polite woman sitting before me.

I had followed her life closely. Each year when Moses went back for field interviews, I would ask first for updates about both Sahr and Isatu. They captured the polar opposites of the themes of risk and resilience we studied. To sit with Isatu as a young woman now was to witness something really quite stunning. Here was someone whose personal traumas were so vast, they stretched beyond what most of us could imagine. Yet her personal perseverance, intelligence, and character had overcome every difficulty. She had broken down every possible barrier.

The list of individuals who had gone out of their way to give Isatu a leg up in life was also formidable. Even from her early days in RUF captivity, Isatu, her sister, and a few other children had arranged their own tutoring sessions to avoid falling behind in their studies. I remembered reading reports about this, so I asked Isatu to explain things a bit more now that she and I could finally chat.

Even the rebels valued education, she explained. I recalled reading the history of the war and speaking with many locals to learn that some of the early proponents of the rebel movement had been disgruntled young men from the provinces, angry about lack of educational opportunities. Quickly, the early motivations of the rebel movement became co-opted by outside forces. Charles Taylor, president of Liberia, and his cronies fomented the rebel movement, providing weapons and resources in a move to take control of the diamond-mining areas in Kono and other rural districts.[1]

The hunger for education was not forgotten, though, even during a very long war. Many rebel leaders had abducted young women and forced them into relationships as their "bush wives." These forced relationships bore children, and rebel leaders too wanted their children to have an education. Sometimes when a village raid captured an older or well-educated person, or a teacher, they would ask them to teach informal classes to the children.

As Isatu spoke, I recalled a poignant story she had recounted in an interview when she was still a young girl. It was in the early months after she was released from the RUF but still living in an interim care center. During that time, she recalled being visited by other formerly abducted girls who had been returned to their families or foster care. They had come to visit the ICC dressed in brightly colored, pressed school uniforms. Isatu's interview described her bitter tears once the girls left: "Our friends saw their parents and had started going to school while we stayed at home . . . that made me cry all day." She felt trapped and desperate—her desire to get back into school was overpowering.

Isatu's passion for learning propelled her relentlessly. As we finished our meal together, I learned other details on how she had beaten back barriers that might otherwise have delayed her educational progress. In most families, a range of household chores fall to children, especially young girls. When Isatu and her sister Amina were placed in foster care, the daily load of chores was enormous. Isatu knew she had it in her to succeed, but she needed the time to study and prepare her lessons. Rather organically, the two sisters worked out a system so that the many household chores expected of them would not detract from Isatu's intense focus on her education. Each school day, as the afternoon lunch break approached, Amina would sprint home from school to complete Isatu's chores so that her sister could log a few more hours of study.

Isatu's foster family soon noticed that she was unusually driven and gifted. Though normally families view paying secondary school fees as out of reach, especially for foster children and even more so for girls, Isatu's foster father could not deny her drive. He found himself shelling out the fees not only for his biological son, but for this serious and studious young girl who had entered their lives.

In truth, most people who come to know Isatu become compelled by her story. One of her most enduring supporters is a colleague, deeply grounded in his faith, whom I have known through his many years of work at UNICEF Sierra Leone. The two first met when Isatu was staying at the ICC. When he learned of Isatu's desire to go on to college and the limits that her foster family faced in finding the money, he started a funding drive. He would do this routinely each time the family fell short of resources. Isatu advanced quickly completing secondary school with top honors and getting a full scholarship to study further in Latin America. She was unstoppable.

When I told her more about our research and how we are hoping to learn what essential lessons can be taken from the experiences of someone like herself in order to help others, she chuckled softly and shrugged. She is humble, but she also seems proud of what she has accomplished. She credited her faith and the people around her, from her own biological mother and sister to her foster family. She is now very deeply involved in her church and feels a powerful sense of belonging and community there.

As I reflected on our conversation, I realized that sitting across from me in that dimly lit restaurant was a human example of the full resilience-promoting social ecology at work, interacting in a beautiful and powerful dance with her innate gifts and drive. When Isatu shrugged humbly about all she had accomplished, I thought about the title of Ann Masten's *Ordinary Magic.* Masten underscores that the truth of perseverance and resilience is not born of some unusual secret power—it comes from the basic interactions of personal agency and virtuous cycles of protection and support emanating from the family, the community, and even in some cases larger cultural or contextual forces.[2]

Without question, Isatu was born into this world with some degree of inherent intelligence and drive. In fact, she was well on her way along a normative track of development in her early years into primary school. She had been well loved and had found a passion for learning. The day her school was raided by rebels, that trajectory was thrown off course. Isatu had to contend with a frightening abduction and captivity fraught with family separation as well as constant fear and abuse. Yet the foundation that had been laid for her also was a source of strength and grounding.

In addition, she had the constant support of her sister Amina. Her character and desire to advance herself attracted the attention of others after she was released from captivity. She was loved. She was on a mission. She would transform her pain and her loss in order to be someone who could help others the way that people had gone out of their way to help her. And she, in turn, was committed to showing them how much their love and support meant.

Now a successful young doctor, Isatu wants to give back to others, to help in the way she was helped. I have no doubt that her perseverance and drive will ensure that she succeeds.

25

Coming of Age in the Aftermath of War

Coming of age is a time of momentous transition in any culture and context. In the backdrop of war, these moments become all the more fraught. In some cases, tribal affiliations and traditional secret societies play a role. I first learned of Sierra Leone's secret societies early in my fieldwork in the provinces. I have a vivid memory of an afternoon in Kono District when our staff returned sweaty and nervous after a day of fieldwork.

"The devil was out today," they gasped.

I didn't know what they meant, so I asked for an explanation. There was a raucous crowd moving about town linked to the Sande, they said, one of West Africa's largest traditional women's societies. At the center of this boisterous group who were chanting and singing was a dancing demon. The sowei, a kind of priestess in traditional dress decorated with dried grasses and cowrie shells, was dancing excitedly to the beat of a drum.

Sierra Leone has a range of tribes. The Sande society of women is found among the Kono, Mende, Limba, and Temne people, among others. The Poro society is the male counterpart. As the team explained, when the devil was out, the uninitiated could be taken to the bush for initiation rites. Moses further explained that, in some cases, this could involve circumcision rituals for both males and females. This risk was not one that anyone on the study team was ready to take.

Tribal identity and secret societies in West Africa are far more complicated than any account that could be given in this book. For some youth returning from war, to be initiated into a secret society was a marker of acceptance and belonging. For those who believe in its tenets, induction can herald the advent of adulthood and provide a sense of belonging to an intimate community and its concomitant political power. For others, secret societies can be a source of great mystery and even fear. What seemed to matter most was how the individual and community made meaning about what signaled acceptance and true belonging.

Our study was not the first to consider these dynamics. Some of the earliest research on child soldiers' reintegration was a study of thirty-nine boys conducted by Neil Boothby and his colleagues in Mozambique. The research documented the lives of these young men involved in Mozambique's civil conflict as either captured or escaped child soldiers.[1] Boothby and his team were interested in the factors shaping how these young men might fare as they grew into young adulthood. That research, begun in 1988, revealed dynamics similar to our findings in Sierra Leone— that most male former child soldiers were able to move on with their lives, develop relationships, get married, have children, and hold down jobs. However, Boothby also noted that these young men could not shake the traumatic memories of their past. Along with indicators of functioning, they continued to suffer from mental health consequences that included nightmares and traumatic memories of their time with fighting forces and the terrible violence that they had witnessed.[2]

The 1990s, shaped by the 1989 United Nations Convention on the Rights of the Child, gave more focused attention to "reintegrating" and "rehabilitating" former child soldiers. In that decade, the phrase "child soldiers" was seen as almost synonymous with a boy gripping a sawed-off machine gun; there was little thought to the girls whose lives had been equally shattered by the conflict. Today, both policy and programs have started to change, but the road to gender equity remains long and hard fought.

As discussed in Chapter 10, early understandings of rehabilitation and reintegration models underserved girls terribly. Dyan Mazurana researched and wrote about this state of affairs for girls and women in northern Uganda, where conditions for their reintegration process mirrored the conditions in Sierra Leone.[3] Mazurana's work, like our own, documented how many abducted young girls were traded as part of the spoils of war and given to top performing commanders, and the difficulties these young women faced in having children born of forced relationships.

I had first seen the devastating impact of such abuse on young mothers while doing research at interim care centers in northern Uganda. As a new mother myself, I was overwhelmed by the presence of very small babies who were crying out for affection, their eyes flocked with flies and streams of mucus running from their noses. The teen girls, many of them so traumatized they didn't speak, sometimes held the children distractedly. Most of the time the children toddled about, loosely attended, while their mothers stared despondently, their eyes unseeing. It was as if their maternal urge had been extinguished. These were girls forced into motherhood as the result of repeated sexual assault. These were babies the teen girls hadn't wanted. Motherhood had been violently forced upon them.

There are stories of how local practices were used to cleanse and reintegrate girls back into their communities. Lindsay Stark presented findings from interviews with girls and women from ages eight to thirty in four districts who had been abducted and subjected to horrible sexual violence. She also spoke with seventeen traditional healers and was invited to witness some of the traditional cleansing ceremonies, a rare glimpse into practices intended to chase away *noro,* or bad luck.[4]

Her findings argue for a broader view of reintegration, one which recognizes that psychological distress is grounded in social and cultural context. Accordingly, cleansing ceremonies led by local traditional healers represented an important transition for female former child soldiers who now would be received back into their community. One local healer described the process:

> The way I saw the girls, I knew I should cleanse them before their minds were set. I went to the ancestors and asked them how to help the girls. The ancestors instructed me in how to cleanse them. I went to the bush to fetch the herbs for the cleansing. I knew which herbs to pick because the ancestors had told me. I put the herbs in a pot and boiled them. I poured a libation on the ground and also drank some of it. After boiling the herbs, I steamed the girls under blankets and over the boiling pot for their bodies to become clean and their minds to become steady. After the steaming, we all slept in the house. The next morning we all went to the bush. In the bush, I gave them herbs to drink. We spent the day cooking, singing, eating, and telling stories. On the third day, I brought the girls to the waterside. I told them that they would not go back to town wearing the clothes that they had worn to the riverside. I washed the girls one by one with black soap and herbs. After the washing, they put on new clothing and we all came to town dancing and singing.[5]

Today, greater attention has been paid to community-oriented and gender-sensitive approaches to the reintegration of young women and young men. Gone are the days when a young person had to turn over a gun in order to indicate eligibility for services. The United Nations Security Council has now established a monitoring and reporting mechanism to keep track of six grave violations related to children in armed conflict including killing and maiming, recruiting or use of children by armed forces and armed groups, attacks on schools or hospitals, abduction, denial of humanitarian access, and rape and other forms of sexual violence.[6] Although not enforced with any real financial or military muscle, the monitoring and reporting mechanism allows for naming and shaming of governments that actively recruit children or fail to protect their recruitment by nonstate actors.[7]

Despite these important areas of progress, rehabilitation and reintegration efforts continue to focus on short-term stays in reintegration centers as the major feature of rehabilitation and the central cog in the machine designed for returning children home. Center-based approaches remain popular and draw in resources. Well-intentioned philanthropists are happy to post a sign with their name on such a building. Donors clamor to visit cleaned-up children, welcoming them with joyful singing and showing off art made with colored pens and paper—materials that would pay for months of school fees. But what about those real homes? As our study has documented, the return home is when the real work begins.

Not enough attention has been paid to providing resources, structuring a plan, and preparing the child and family before they are united, then working with them over the course of reunification, then following up with booster sessions, problem-solving, and check-ins to ensure that this vital placement into a home or family-based care holds. In our study, the young people who have struggled the most over time are those whose family and community relationships were too broken to shepherd them through the journey home.

We know from foster care research that permanency and a family who is dedicated to the child—committed to seeing them through thick or thin—is one of the best predictors of a young person able to navigate difficult circumstances over the course of their development. We have seen such dynamics in research ranging from children in poverty to those affected by HIV / AIDS. Groundbreaking work by Chuck Nelson and colleagues on children leaving Romanian orphanages and entering family-based care, mentioned in Chapter 8, has been a cornerstone of this research.[8]

Our findings speak to the power of social and family acceptance as an antidote to the harms of stigma. These remain critical ingredients of interventions to help former child soldiers adapt to post-conflict life. In addition to understanding the mental health conditions that may afflict former child soldiers, it is important to monitor their family and community relationships after the war. Although experiences of war-related violence and loss cannot be undone, three leverageable post-conflict factors—namely, family attachment, community acceptance, and stigma—appear to be related to adult outcomes, suggesting that campaigns to reduce stigma against former child soldiers may offer promising targets to improve mental health and life outcomes. Studies have identified the value of targeted interventions, such as group-based programs addressing the mental health needs of war-affected youth in post-conflict settings, and services to bolster protective opportunities, such as school and livelihood opportunities, which can improve social and family acceptance.

There is healing power in the relationships young people build within their families and communities. What these latest findings show is that as much attention should be paid to family and community relationships as to past traumatic events. Efforts to alleviate mental health problems and improve life outcomes for former child soldiers need to center on family and community relationships.

In order to achieve healthier pathways to reintegration, the field must rethink how we direct resources and where we place our attention to evidence-based practices. The time has come to develop and evaluate models that can work with the entire family system: in Sahr's case, to avoid the rejection of an uncle; to empower a loving mother to manifest her commitment to her child; to alleviate a mother's impairments due to depression and economic despair; to support a young man shadowed by trauma and difficulties in his social interactions with others; to teach him skills to navigate life and deepen his social support; to ensure he is prepared for the taunting and rejection that he will almost certainly face.

I had hopes for Sahr. In 2017, I couldn't wait for Moses to share what he had learned upon locating him again. Although I stayed back at the office to hear about the interview, I had a bad premonition as Moses approached. The look on his face spoke volumes. "I'm sorry, Theresa. He has died," Moses said. I burst into tears, something I have rarely done over the years.

The elder men had explained to Moses that Sahr had "died of snakebite" while working on the farm. But in truth, Sahr died of social isolation. With no friends or family nearby, no social support, there was no one to get him help when he needed it. Sahr's was a life cut far too short. Could Sahr have fared better if he had possessed the skills to present his best self, to de-escalate interpersonal situations, and to not be easily hijacked by his past trauma when others provoked him?

Sahr is just one of many who suffered upon their return, one whose lost potential resulted in lost life. I wonder what could have been done to help him build interpersonal skills to more successfully navigate relationships. I truly believe that with such efforts to promote his mental health and deepen connectedness to others around him, he might have been better positioned to present his best self to the world and to face his challenges rather than to retreat.

However, in conflict-affected settings like Sierra Leone, the truth is that spending on health alone is very low, and amounts spent on mental health are even more abysmal. In recent years, a much-needed effort at reforming the situation at the Sierra Leone Psychiatric and Teaching Hospital has been underway. Under the leadership of Dr. Abdul Jalloh and a successful partnership with the international NGO Partners in Health, new psychotropic medications have become available. For the first time ever, nearly every patient in the hospital has been freed from restraints. Under a new initiative between the hospital and Partners in Health, a cohort of eight psychiatric residents is now being trained. One dedicated psychiatry trainee, Dr. Elizabeth Allieu, has helped the hospital open a children's unit that offers family-engaged outpatient services for children, youth, and families. Times are slowly changing.

Nonetheless, expenditures on community-based mental health in Sierra Leone remain next to nothing. A 2021 report by Amnesty International, *They Are Forgetting about Us*, notes that "there is no dedicated budget line for mental health," according to systems-strengthening experts and government officials consulted for the report.[9]

Enriched and sustainable mental health and psychosocial support (MHPSS) do not happen by accident—they require leadership and intentionality. An enabling environment for systems strengthening must emanate from the top—from the Ministry of Health and associated technical assistance and vision, to the appropriate policies, financing, and human resource strategies needed to implement a true system of care. For individuals like the hard-working student Isatu, who became a doctor, the natural social ecology came together to help unlock her potential.

However, not everyone has the individual skills or social functioning to succeed without significant outside help, as we see in the case of Sahr, rejected by his influential uncle and socially withdrawn to the day that he died alone. Leadership and investments in mental health and social services systems in Sierra Leone, with greater outreach to the community, have the potential to help many more war-affected young people get back on track and unleash their own fledgling lives.

Michael Ungar, in writing about multisystemic resilience, defines resilience as "the capacity of both individuals and their environments to interact in ways that optimize developmental processes."[10] This is an important way to think about systems strengthening too. Certainly for individuals like Isatu, individual support from family and extended social networks have made all the difference, but such a richly resourced environment is not available to every young person.

In writing about traditional justice, Cedric de Coning wrote that "in the adaptive peacebuilding context, we can conceptualize resilience as the ability of a society to prevent, manage and recover from violent conflict in ways that maximize developmental processes."[11] The concept of maximizing developmental processes is part and parcel of making services and supports available to the most vulnerable young people to ensure that opportunities for resilient outcomes are not just limited to the few.

To enable others to unlock their natural potential and to have options to redirect a difficult past toward more resilient outcomes is a way to recognize and honor the reality of what these children, families, and communities all suffered. It's a sound investment in human capital, and it's also our best investment in a more peaceful future for many war-affected societies.

26

Trauma and Resilience across Generations

Despite the omnipresence of war and its aftermath, little is known about how parental trauma may impact the mental health and development of offspring. Might past trauma experienced by parents reverberate across generations? Violence and humanitarian crises are common in the lives of children around the world, particularly in low- and middle-income countries. Exposure to war-related violence is detrimental to the mental health of parents and children, but research exploring mechanisms by which emotional and behavioral disruptions are transmitted to subsequent generations remains nascent, especially in sub-Saharan Africa.

Until recently, most of our knowledge on the intergenerational impact of war came from studies of European Holocaust survivors and a handful of studies across generations of refugees from wars in Asia. For example, as mentioned in Chapter 3, the work of Natan Kellermann has unpacked differences in offspring dynamics by comparing adult children of Holocaust survivors to controls who were not exposed to Holocaust related trauma. Kellermann and his colleagues were interested in investigating the hypothesis that children who had been raised by Holocaust survivors may exhibit greater levels of anxiety and overprotectiveness. They created a measure of parenting styles among survivors of the Holocaust, drawing from the literature on intergenerational dynamics among survivors, and had the questions on the tool reviewed by psychotherapists working at a mental health clinic serving survivors and their families. Their analyses revealed four scales of parenting styles, including a transmission subscale with items such as "the past of my parents had an influence on my life." Affection subscale items included questions such as "when I was sad, I could get support from my parents," and a punishment subscale queried items such as "my parents punished me." A scale assessing overprotectiveness contained items such as "my parents warned me of various dangers that might happen."[1]

When comparing adults whose parents had lived through the Holocaust, Kellermann observed that both males and females in the survivor groups demonstrated higher levels of transmission-related dynamics. In addition, when comparing survivor fathers to controls, items on the punishing scale were also higher in the survivor fathers. In this manner, Kellermann found some evidence that the children of parents who survived the Holocaust experienced significant differences in experiences of transmission-related dynamics as well as punishing behaviors compared to those whose parents were not Holocaust survivors.

While work on Holocaust survivors remains the most studied area of intergenerational trauma research, there is now an emerging body of literature from sub-Saharan Africa, including families who lived through the 1994 Genocide against the Tutsi in Rwanda. Researchers such as Eugene Rutembesa in Rwanda have led a series of in-depth family histories unpacking both direct and indirect experiences of children of parents who survived the genocide.[2] In all studies of the mechanisms by which parental trauma may lead to effects on offspring, both behavioral and biological contributors must be explored. Rather than a simplistic equation whereby childhood behavior is a function of parental trauma, Kellermann and other theorists have emphasized that a more realistic understanding of these dynamics accounts for individual variation and context. Thus, a more appropriate question might ask which kinds of survivor parents influence "which kinds of children in which ways under which circumstances."[3]

Our research to date in Sierra Leone has documented how trauma shapes both the transition to adulthood and the foundations of parent-child relationships, which set the stage for how both biology and behavior might affect the next generation. As we observed the process of coming of age in our study across four waves of data, we documented how healthy transitions to adulthood were linked to engagement in prosocial behaviors and community involvement. In contrast, problems with hostility, poor emotion regulation, and social withdrawal all created barriers to achieving healthy and productive lives, including obstacles to becoming a loving and connected parent. These are not just individual processes, but instead result from interactions with the larger environment. For instance, community stigma and poor family acceptance further compounded barriers to healthy integration and social relationships.

Most recently, our study has branched out in new intergenerational directions. In our fourth wave of data collection in 2016–2017, we followed up with our index participants, but we also enrolled, where relevant, their intimate partners and biological offspring. This new addition to the data collection has allowed us to examine linkages between parental trauma exposure and both intimate partner and parent-child relationships. To better understand both the potential biological as well as behavioral mechanisms by which emotional and behavioral disruptions may be transmitted to subsequent generations, we have now added to our study biological measures of stress reactivity and self-regulation (autonomic nervous system reactivity, inflamma-tion, telomere length) in all index-participant parents, as well as their intimate partners and offspring.

Our data on the adult lives of our participants are beginning to illuminate how war-related experiences may influence child-rearing and parent-child relationships. Because of the large number of males in our sample, we have used the opportunity to dig more deeply into the experiences of both mothers and fathers. In a paper published in 2023, we used qualitative interviews to understand the experience of becoming a father in post-conflict Sierra Leone.[4] Fathers described the ways in which the war changed fatherhood in the country, such as by impacting the ability of fathers to provide housing for their families or by indi-rectly influencing the amount of time that parents had with their children. As one young man in our study explained it, the war still reverberated in the lives of parents today:

> The war affected so many children. Most children are not living with their parents because one way or the other they lost their mothers or their fathers during the war. All the houses were burned down, so for them to even have a good place to sleep, they have to work harder just to build, even if it is a single room, so that they can live there. All these things happened because of the war, so there is a very big link to the war.

Another father in a focus group interview talked about the community changes that have occurred since the war:

> Before the war, parents themselves raised their children. . . . The role of the mother at that time was to prepare food and manage the home while the father disciplined and provided clothing and food for the kids. However, the way parents

and caregivers raise their children has changed after the war. Now parents or caregivers no longer have time to raise their children properly [because they must earn a living]. For instance, most children now care for themselves and become street children.

Our quantitative data point to mechanisms that may be at play. In a paper using our data led by Binta Alleyne-Green, we found that a certain group of CAAFAG—those who had experienced higher levels of victimization by violence during the war—tended to exhibit more nurturing behaviors upon becoming parents, while parents who had a history of being involved in perpetration of violence at higher rates demonstrated lower levels of nurturing behaviors.[5]

Given the social-ecological nature of our longitudinal data, we have examined how post-conflict environmental factors such as poverty and stigma further compounded poor parent-child relationships. We have also begun to illuminate modifiable protective factors shaping both parental and offspring mental health, such as parental education, religiosity, community acceptance, collective efficacy, and social support. We can see some of these themes in operation in the life stories of young adults in our sample who have become parents.

Findings drawn from the four waves of data collection and analysis of our study indicate that a healthy transition to adulthood is linked to engagement in prosocial behavior and community involvement, while problems with hostility, poor emotion regulation, and social withdrawal create barriers to achieving healthy and productive lives.[6] Community stigma and poor family acceptance further compound these barriers.[7] As we move into future stages of our research, we will begin to unpack how social ecology—extending truly from neurons to neighborhoods—and biobehavioral mechanisms operate among war-affected parents to shape parenting and the mental health of subsequent generations.[8] We will link prior waves of behavioral assessments and observations of war-affected youth who became parents to data on their intimate partners and biological children added in at the fourth wave of our data collection in 2016–2017.

Our preliminary analyses of offspring of war-affected youth indicate that the perception of harsh paternal parenting was associated with their offspring's poor mental health. In addition, harsh or warm maternal parenting directly or indirectly predicted disruptions in emotion regulation and mental health in their offspring.[9] We anticipate such associations are linked to biological mechanisms, but research to date has been limited to cross-sectional data on the health and mental health of biological offspring. Our understanding of these relationships will include another follow-up time point in 2024, with a focus on potential biobehavioral mechanisms by which disruptions may travel across generations. In particular, we will examine processes such as dyadic relationships between both male and female caregivers and the social processes that may underlie self-regulation. By collecting and analyzing both behavioral data (parent-child interactions) and biological / physiological data, such as inflammatory markers, telomeres, and autonomic nervous system regulation and co-regulation between offspring and caregivers, we will deepen our understanding of mechanisms that may contribute to an increased risk of mental health difficulties in the offspring of war-affected youth.

As we investigate biobehavioral systems, we will continue to nest them within that broader social ecology of modifiable risk and protective factors across the social ecology at individual, family, and community levels. It is our hope that such explorations may assist us in identifying and prioritizing intervention targets for the purpose of addressing intergenerational risks to the mental health of offspring of war-affected parents and also of interrupting cycles of violence in conflict-affected regions.

PART V

Rebuilding the Future

27

The Next Generation

A growing body of evidence is emerging that documents how the threads of trauma stretch across generations. We have extended our research to follow this path as well. As the boys and girls in our sample have grown into adulthood and begun to start families of their own, we are deepening our understanding of what shapes more risky or resilient life outcomes by also looking to the next generation in our fifth wave of data collection. We often think of the young people in our study as "super survivors," knowing the reality of what they lived through. For any person to live through such horrors and emerge living a relatively "normal" day-to-day existence is truly a stunning accomplishment. To live and raise a family in post-conflict, post-Ebola Sierra Leone today means overcoming, or at least navigating, tremendous personal, community, and family challenges.

In our 2017 data collection, we were able to retain 67 percent of our original sample, and also expand the sample to include their intimate partners and biological offspring. Four hundred and seventeen young children had been born into the study by that time. Our assessments of the home environment and parenting style of each member of the sample show some worrisome associations between parental emotion dysregulation and harsh parenting as well as emotional and behavioral risks in offspring. As a result, we have also become squarely focused on the topic of family-based prevention.

In 2006, I had the great good fortune to collaborate with Partners in Health in Rwanda on a project to adapt an evidence-based parenting intervention for families affected by another form of hardship: HIV / AIDS. Our intervention development work continued between 2006 and 2010 with an important collaboration with William Beardslee, Professor Emeritus of Psychiatry at Children's Hospital in Boston, whose Family Talk intervention was discussed in Chapter 23. Family Talk was originally developed for the prevention of depression in the offspring of depressed caregivers. It has since been successfully adapted and implemented in a range of settings, including Costa Rica, Finland, and with Native American and low-income Head Start populations in the United States.

The intervention has a focus on improved family communication and information-sharing about chronic illness. It was a perfect family-based mental health intervention to support family functioning despite caregivers living with HIV / AIDS once the advent of antiretroviral treatment made living with HIV a lifelong illness that could be managed well, rather than the death sentence it had once been. Our early work to adapt Family Talk to Rwanda included critical community-based participatory research, like in Sierra Leone, with parental and youth advisory groups.[1]

Our pilot work on this new intervention adapted to sub-Saharan Africa indicated that it could be delivered successfully by lay workers—those without advanced professional degrees—if they received strong training and robust supervision. Soon after that experience, we were asked by the World Bank and the government of Rwanda to develop a more general version of the intervention—not focused on HIV, but instead addressing issues of violence and threats to child development in the context of extreme poverty. We leapt at this opportunity, given the strong political will and Rwanda's growing investment in early childhood development as a means of breaking cycles of poverty.

Soon, we had articulated a home-visiting model, delivered by nonspecialists, that was demonstrating great results in reducing family violence (both intimate partner violence and child maltreatment) as well as promoting responsive care, play, health, hygiene, and dietary diversity.[2] Because our research in post-conflict settings pointed to violence as a critical risk factor influencing the parent-child relationship, we designed the home-visiting model to focus on all family configurations and to always involve male caregivers engaged in the life of the child. In fact, we would go out of our way to include male caregivers if they were in the picture at all. We retooled our messaging to emphasize the very important role that fathers and male caregivers play. We highlighted their contribution to their child's success in addition to that of mothers and other female caregivers. By encouraging men to take on this proud mantle of fatherhood, we asked them to consider looking beyond the usual role of breadwinner to take joy in raising their young children, participating in their care and the joy of play.

Involving male caregivers in the care of young children was seen as something really quite new. Using this orientation, the home-visiting intervention *Sugira Muryango,* or "strengthen the family" in Kinyarwanda, was intended to both promote early childhood development and prevent violence against children and between intimate partners.[3] In this manner, our imagery shifted from cartoons of responsive mothers lovingly feeding their babies to coaching and playful depictions of both mothers *and* fathers getting at eye level and playing with their young child, making bathing, feeding, and even cleaning the house moments of joy, connection, and fun.

The father-engaged approach proved effective in helping to reduce harsh punishment of children and intimate partner violence. The approach also encouraged the use of nonviolent disciplinary practices in the home. Working with our collaborator at Brown University, Alethea Desrosiers, we have finished an adaptation of the home visiting intervention to the context and culture of Sierra Leone. The intervention was successfully piloted in Makeni District and delivered by Government of Sierra Leone community health workers while testing a digital tool for enhancing home visitor fidelity to each module and its content, as well as cross-cutting skills in family home visiting such as showing empathy, active listening, and coaching parent-child interactions in a way that engaged both male and female caregivers as relevant (competence). We anticipate that the findings of Wave 5 of our longitudinal study, currently planned for 2025, will lead to further refinements to this model and new opportunities to explore pathways to scaling the model in Sierra Leone to address the intergenerational consequences of violence.

A constant debate in the field of responding to the personal and societal impact of armed conflict in civilians is how to approach the topic of trauma. When speaking of children associated with armed forces and armed groups, one side of the argument points out that trauma in the lives of these youth is real and significant. It affects their daily lives as well as the community and larger social ecology around them. The other side of the argument holds that using trauma as the lens for understanding war-affected populations pathologizes them and closes out opportunities to engage in positive, community-level discussions about promoting strengths and opportunities for war-affected children, youth, and families. This is a false dichotomy. The truth is that both perspectives are true, and they need not be seen as mutually exclusive.

Over the years, it has been useful to approach this work through a lens that is trauma-informed. That may mean that when engaging with community actors or considering the needs of communities, we don't lead with trauma as the focal point, but we let it inform the work so that as other programs are initiated, that sensitivity is not lost. The use of such a trauma-informed lens has been well demonstrated in work such as the IRC's Learning in a Healing Classroom program, which helps teachers to both implement an evidence-based curriculum and also make the classroom a supportive place where emotional and behavioral concerns are addressed with sensitivity.[4] A similar trauma-informed lens is useful in everything from food programs to housing, legal support, and medical care with war-affected populations.

There has been important research by Kenneth Miller and Andrew Rasmussen underscoring how research with children, youth, and families in war-affected settings must not overlook the critical role of daily stressors.[5] In fact, when daily stressors such as housing and food insecurity are not addressed, they can actually serve to elevate mental distress, even aggravating trauma symptoms and making recovery more difficult. Daily stressors truly matter, as the realities of trauma may affect how individuals operate, even to meet their daily needs. The interrelated nature of trauma and daily functioning was also part of the genesis of our Youth Readiness Intervention. We observed that in conflict-affected settings, even when life opportunities to work or earn a livelihood presented themselves, not all young people were able to rise to the occasion and take advantage of such opportunities. In some cases, trauma had influenced their sense of trust and interpersonal relationships.

Similar research has demonstrated how parents with a significant trauma history may struggle to prioritize and solve such problems as arranging transport or childcare, or addressing other pressing needs while also caring for their young children.[6] For young adults with a serious trauma history, it can be hard to manage the flooding of executive functioning, to get beyond "live in the moment" thinking to sort and respond to many competing priorities. Bessel van der Kolk writes in *The Body Keeps the Score,*

> Ordinarily, the executive capacities of the prefrontal cortex enable people to observe what is going on, predict what will happen if they take a certain action, and make a conscious choice. Being able to hover calmly and objectively over our thoughts, feeling and emotions . . . and then take our time to respond allows the executive brain to inhibit, organize and modulate, the hardwired automatic reactions preprogrammed into the emotional brain . . . When that system breaks down, we become like conditioned animals: the moment we detect danger we automatically go into fight-or-flight mode.[7]

Van der Kolk writes, "in PTSD the critical balance between the amygdala . . . and the MPFC [medial prefrontal cortex] shifts radically, which makes it much harder to control emotions and impulses."[8] It can be difficult to shift the mindset of youth experiencing traumatic stress reactions or other mental health consequences of trauma toward appreciating that investments in activities that may not seem to provide a quick benefit, such as taking school seriously or becoming an apprentice, might have far greater long-term payoffs. What we know from neuroscience indicates that without interventions to focus on stabilization and skills to manage the consequences of trauma, shifting their mindsets to be more future oriented and to break problems down into manageable steps may be next to impossible for some war-affected youth.

Beyond such difficulties lies a harsh reality: the limited human resources for delivering mental health care in Sierra Leone. In 2023 in Cambridge, Massachusetts, where my family lives, we have some 2,303 psychiatrists for a population of 118,557.[9] Sierra Leone, in contrast, has three working psychiatrists and eight more in training for a population of over 8 million. That leads to a service gap that is unthinkable.

The good news is that recent innovation, such as that led by Vikram Patel and Sangath, his India-based NGO, supported by a range of published research in several settings, has demonstrated definitively that well-trained and supervised nonspecialists can provide high-quality frontline care for common mental disorders for a range of different populations.[10] In addition, such nonspecialists can be integrated into delivery platforms that reach the hard-to-reach, such as poverty reduction / social protection programs, educational initiatives, livelihoods and employment programs, and of course primary care.

In the context of trauma-informed care, we have demonstrated in our own work that nonspecialists / lay workers can do stabilization- and skills-based intervention. However, more training and clinical skill is often needed for PTSD-focused interventions, given the clinical sophistication of evidence-based treatments for the condition and iatrogenic effects, or risks of doing harm if done poorly. Frank Neuner and his colleagues behind the NET (Narrative Exposure Therapy) intervention, mentioned in Chapter 23, have demonstrated that community health workers could be trained to deliver the trauma-focused intervention with good effects. The study, however, was conducted under the highly structured conditions of a randomized controlled trial.[11]

As we begin to roll out trauma-informed and even trauma-focused interventions such as NET to real world settings, important questions arise: What interventions for trauma in children and adolescents show evidence of impact in low- and middle-income country settings? What safety parameters are needed in terms of training and supervision when trauma-informed interventions are delivered by nonspecialists? In terms of services and human resources for health initiatives, there is growing attention to topics such as if and how appropriate therapies for child maltreatment and child sexual abuse can be implemented under a task-sharing frame—all with less definitive results, but some promising signals.

For instance, in adapting trauma-focused cognitive behavioral therapy for survivors of sexual violence in Zambia, Laura Murray and her colleagues have demonstrated that a "cascade model," whereby mental health professionals train and supervise nonspecialist workers, can be both safe and effective in reducing mental health symptoms.[12] However, much of this work remains relegated to prevention and the detection of risks of sexual and physical violence, including in school environments.

We are not doing enough globally to develop systems of care that are evidence-based, ethical, sustainable, and adherent to "do no harm" principles, which entail that any intervention must be done in the context of standard best practices of MHPSS interventions, including confidentiality, therapeutic rapport, and continuity. To date, little attention has been given to how to bridge the gap between the focus and financing that occur during acute humanitarian responses and the longer road to stable mental health systems. Sustainable mental health and social services, those that can support children, youth, and families long after the acute crisis has subsided, need strengthening in conflict-affected regions. In such regions, MHPSS and social services should be part and parcel of efforts to build health systems that have reach, appropriate human resources, government and civil society engagement, and leadership to ensure the policy frameworks and financing that make such systems sustainable and high quality.[13]

Investments in health systems to strengthen mental health and social services must not essentialize the experiences of child soldiers above others also affected by war-related trauma and loss. The assaults on so many during Sierra Leone's conflict require strong and sustainable trauma-informed services that serve *all* of those affected, with investments in strengthening the health and social services sectors as a primary component of *building back better* after conflict.[14] In this manner, conflict-affected countries could lead the way in being more responsive to other types of trauma in the lives of children globally.

The research community remains very interested in the topic. As we have seen in the proliferation of research on adverse childhood experiences, the potential to deepen sensitivity exists in every topic, from community violence to manmade and natural disasters, which are only likely to be on the increase in the years ahead due to climate change.[15] Experiences such as these, as well as child sexual abuse, death of caregivers, and witnessing other forms of violence, occur daily in the lives of children, not only in war zones, but in the day-to-day life of those in insecure environments.

In this book I have reviewed many extant and emerging therapeutic interventions available now. Many share common elements in terms of their active ingredients and goals for therapeutic change.[16] We also now have the evidence that nonspecialists can administer high-quality and effective frontline MHPSS care and have an important role to play on care teams, including those working with populations affected by trauma.

Tremendous resources are now available, such as the immensely important WHO World Mental Health Gap materials, that indicate what is known about the contributions that nonspecialists can make to addressing the massive service gaps that exist in fragile and conflict-affected settings.[17] Any such guidance should also make mention of "do no harm" parameters. Any trauma-informed care, whether from nonspecialists or specialists, conducted without an ongoing therapeutic alliance and working relationship has the potential to be iatrogenic—to do harm if not done with strong training and supervision. We have seen this with "psychological debriefing" conducted in a one-shot manner. Quality must always lead. Poor quality care or harmful care is just as damaging as no care at all.

28

Ready to Learn, Ready to Work

It used to be the case that when we discussed our findings on youth mental health with government cabinet members and other policy officials, their eyes glazed over. Despite reams of data indicating how devastating the war's impact had been on its generation of youth, we were not seeing the investments in mental health and social services strengthening that were needed.

A first barrier to such investments was the tremendous stigma that existed about mental health. In Sierra Leone, the term *kraze* (crazy) was commonly used to refer to individuals with serious mental illnesses such as psychosis or schizophrenia. As discussed in Chapter 5, low-quality treatment of patients at the Kissy Psychiatric Hospital in the 1980s and 1990s further contributed to the stigma. At that time, to end up at Kissy was a death sentence. Patients at Kissy in those years often lived in squalor, many chained to their beds in an attempt to control unruly behavior. Advances in psychopharmaceuticals had largely skipped Sierra Leone, and the few drugs in stock—such as Haloperidol—were delivered in high doses, leaving those who received them in a constant stupor. In this light, the reforms to Kissy Psychiatric and Teaching Hospital seen in the post-EVD era have been a colossal step forward in reducing the stigma toward mental illness and introducing a more humane orientation toward treatment for serious mental illness in Sierra Leone.

With time, we began to see small glimmers of hope in other places too. The truth of Sierra Leone's war was that most people, including government officials, had been touched directly by the conflict. Even the "big men" in charge had experienced their own trauma. They had witnessed terrible things too. They had lost loved ones, and some had even been refugees or experienced internal displacement themselves. We had to get smart with our messaging.

Around the time that we began to consider intervention research, global political will was building on the topic of early childhood development and school readiness. We needed a corollary for young adults. The field of early child development was doing a great job in helping policymakers and donors understand that investments in early learning could ensure greater readiness of young children for school success. The work of Nobel Prize–winning economist James Heckman has been heavily influential, both regarding the importance of investment in early childhood development and the discussion around what he termed "noncognitive skills."[1]

Heckman used this broad term of noncognitive skills to refer to the ability to work in groups, maintain good interpersonal relations, control impulses, and demonstrate goal-directed behavior. His definition underscores the importance of such skills both for individual success and for the economic productivity of nations. However, the term "noncognitive" added confusion to the field by using language that implied that the interpersonal and self-regulation skills necessary to thrive in school or the workplace had little to do with the brain. Nothing could be further from the truth. In fact, as argued in a paper I co-wrote with Columbia University professor Pamela Scorza, brain processes are at the heart of the domains of self-regulation and executive function implicated in Heckman's work.[2] Heckman later wrote about such skills as "character skills"; others, including the World Bank and major nongovernmental organizations, went on to refer to them as life skills, twenty-first-century skills, socio-emotional skills, or soft skills.[3]

Regardless of the terminology used, many of these skills necessary for self-advancement in school and livelihoods fall under the more clearly defined umbrella of executive functions and self-regulatory processes rather than under the misleading term "noncognitive skills." These inherently brain-related processes allow us to flexibly regulate emotions, control anger or strong emotional reactions, and maintain calm under pressure, according to the demands of context. As Scorza explained:

> Executive function is an umbrella term that refers to the following mental processes: working memory or the capacity to hold and manipulate information over short periods of time, inhibitory control or the ability to master and filter thoughts and impulses and to pause and think before acting, and cognitive or mental flexibility such as the ability to shift attention between tasks. While executive functions refer to specific cognitive processes, they are intimately connected with emotions. . . . Studies from neurobiology to behavioral economics show that emotions affect a person's ability to self-regulate and that effortful regulation affects cognitive abilities and subsequent self-regulatory capacity.[4]

It is clear that self-regulation and executive functions, especially under stress, are critical to success in education as well as the workplace, and that trauma and its emotional consequences have a huge impact. Studies in a range of settings link these abilities, especially self-regulation, to a range of positive outcomes, from higher earnings to prevention of teen pregnancy.[5] *Readiness* was a word that woke up policymakers. We began to envision an intervention that could help war-affected youth become *ready* to learn, *ready* to work and, as a result, find success in education or livelihood opportunities.

Although our assessments of executive function were rudimentary, we began to demonstrate in our data a link between trauma, self-regulation, and interpersonal skills.[6] Our findings set the groundwork for intervention development.[7] Traditionally, research to address the mental health of war-affected youth had focused on classic elements of PTSD, such as avoidance and re-experiencing, and offered exposure-based PTSD treatment with a focus on reprocessing trauma memories. Less attention had been paid to emotion dysregulation—characterized by anger and interpersonal difficulties—that our study indicated was also a part of reactions to past trauma. These are the very same interactions documented so clearly in the neuroscience research laid out by Bessel van der Kolk in *The Body Keeps the Score*.[8] These emotional and behavioral disruptions are also a major threat to school and work success for war-affected youth.

Problems with emotion regulation and interpersonal relationships pose major barriers to achievement for war-affected youth in particular, both in education and economic self-sufficiency. As any teacher knows, the kids seen as unruly and disrespectful, no matter how bright they are, are far less likely to be given extra focus and attention to unleash their full potential. Similarly, it is very difficult to get hired or keep gainful employment if you lack the ability to get along with others or engage in healthy self-regulation, such as being on time and working with focus and high performance. Such dynamics apply to forms of work that range from harvesting crops and self-employment to office work.

For many war-affected youth, the aftereffects of loss and trauma led to paradoxical behaviors, such as young people squandering the opportunities given to them, as discussed in Chapter 3. For instance, in post-conflict Sierra Leone, low attendance in free youth employment and education programs was lamented by many NGO workers, baffled by the disinterest of youth who had so few opportunities. Why didn't these young people seem to care? These same staff were heartbroken to walk by local markets where they saw the materials they had provided free of charge in job training programs now being sold for a quick buck.

There has been a debate in the field of youth employment and entrepreneurship for some time about the effectiveness of such programs. We began to investigate the youth employment evidence base, but the literature was far from definitive. In fact, for many of the commonly used initiatives, such as youth training programs or entrepreneurship programs, the evidence was slim to nonexistent.

However, the literature on cash transfers was far more exciting. Both in the United States and globally, there was important evidence that young people in adversity benefit from financial capital.[9] Some of the most exciting work in conflict-affected areas had been carried out by economist Chris Blattman along with Suleiman Namara of the World Bank. In Uganda, they worked with government partners to develop an employment program that was structured as a simple, scalable model: troubled young men aged sixteen to thirty-five received unconditional cash transfers to develop proposals—with the assistance of a government or NGO "facilitator"—for training and funds to arrange start-up enterprises that would provide self-employment in a marketable trade.[10] In post-conflict Liberia, the team worked with the Network for Empowerment and Progressive Initiatives, an NGO, to develop and implement an initiative that combined cognitive behavioral therapy and a life-skills training program. The intervention for young men, called STYL, included modules on anger management, impulse control, future orientation, planning skills, and self-esteem promotion, among others. Using a randomized design, they assigned criminally involved adult males to either a no-intervention control, a cash transfer, or a cash transfer and the STYL intervention. Their research indicated that the program that combined evidence-based cognitive behavioral therapy with a cash transfer was both highly feasible and associated with reduced criminal involvement, increased self-control, anti-criminal values, and reduced antisocial behavior.[11]

A few factors became clear as we began to plan for bringing these ideas to Sierra Leone. First, we needed to adapt or develop models that did not require highly trained mental health professionals for delivery. In global health, as discussed earlier, a major innovation in recent years has been the increased involvement of nonspecialists in delivering evidence-based care. For mental health and other behavior-change interventions, task shifting or task sharing such models to nonspecialists has also demonstrated effectiveness.[12] In the use of nonspecialists to support mental health services for individuals exposed to significant trauma, defining best practices for training, supervision, and quality monitoring of nonspecialists takes on central importance. In addition, such services delivered by nonspecialists should be carefully linked to a continuum of care, so that more highly trained mental health professionals can be engaged whenever a higher level of care is indicated, especially when it comes to the consequences of trauma. Laying such groundwork can also provide the building blocks for "building back better" in conflict-affected settings, where major investments will ultimately be required in mental health, social services, and other elements of health, legal, education, and economic systems.[13]

In addition, as we did the legwork to prepare for the implementation, we realized that stand-alone mental health programs would not meet the need for life opportunities that youth were emphasizing when we interviewed them. It became clear that our mental health interventions needed to be deeply embedded into opportunities for advancement through education and employment. It was important for our programs to be trauma-informed and sensitive to content that could trigger memories of trauma or loss. At the same time, programs needed to offer skills for self-care, coping, and emotion regulation / stabilization. By focusing on stabilization and skills, we could give most youth a leg up and provide an entry point for identifying those with more serious chronic mental illness and link them to care providers. Lastly, we needed to attend to issues of scale and sustainment as well as quality in service delivery. We gave a lot of attention to how to identify and train the frontline providers, structures for ongoing supervision, and tools for monitoring both competence (cross-cutting skills) as well as fidelity (how accurately the facilitators conveyed the session-specific intervention content). Given a lack of MHPSS systems and a very weak health system, including for primary care, we identified many other opportunities to reach youth through alternate delivery platforms for war-affected young people, from schools to employment programs.

The backbone of what later became the Youth Readiness Intervention (YRI) began to emerge. In 2010, with support from a Harvard Clinical and Translational Science Award and the United States Institute of Peace, we conducted formative intervention development research building from our longitudinal study.[14] We set out to speak with young people themselves, mental health professionals, policy leaders, NGOs working with youth, and community leaders. Some of my favorite interviews were discussions that Adeyinka Akinsulure-Smith and I had with local youth workers about how to impart core concepts of the intervention through the use of local proverbs and language, such as the Krio phrase *Yu get pawa for chenje yu layf,* or "you have the power to change your life."

Founded on our formative research, we brought together a core set of evidence-based intervention ingredients, which we reviewed and refined with input from local stakeholders (e.g., community leaders, local youth). Through this process, we designed the YRI to address the multiple, co-occurring emotional and behavioral problems common in war-affected youth. With a focus on managing anger, problem-solving, building interpersonal skills, and daily functioning, the YRI was intended to ensure that young people could show up *ready* to maximize what employment and education programs had to offer. Extending beyond the work of Blattman and colleagues, we were always focused on both male and female youth in conflict-affected settings, and we designed the intervention to be safe and simple enough to be delivered by nonspecialists, including teachers or youth employment workers.

As we refined the content of the YRI, I reached out to experts in the field of trauma-informed treatment, including Judith Herman of the Cambridge Health Alliance, who kindly invited me to sit in on some of her group treatments for survivors of sexual violence. I was also impressed with the focus that Marylene Cloitre gave stabilization and skill in the early stages of her stepped-care intervention for PTSD, Skills Training in Affective and Interpersonal Regulation, or STAIR.[15] We developed the twelve-session YRI to be what Judith Herman defined as a Stage 1 trauma-informed intervention, intended to stabilize youth, ensure their safety, and build emotion regulation and skills for managing strong emotional reactions to triggering experiences.[16] In the literature on trauma and recovery, Stage 1 treatments target building emotion regulation skills, self-awareness, coping skills, immediate symptom alleviation, interpersonal abilities, and healthier day-to-day functioning. They can also serve as prerequisites for Stage 2 trauma-focused interventions for persistent conditions such as PTSD, which can then be addressed in stepped-care models carried out by well-trained mental health professionals once Stage 1 interventions are complete.[17]

The YRI integrates six evidence-based common practice elements drawing from cognitive behavioral therapy, interpersonal therapy, and mindfulness-based practices, which are empirically supported and shown to have transdiagnostic effectiveness across disorders ranging from major depressive disorder to PTSD and conduct disorders.[18] It represents an approach suitable for delivery by community mental health workers and nonspecialists with a basic level of formal mental health training if supported by robust training and supervision structures.[19]

Over the course of several pilots and eventual randomized controlled trials, we demonstrated that the YRI contributed to positive changes in mental health and functioning among male and female war-affected youth, including significantly greater improvements in emotion regulation skills, prosocial attitudes / behaviors, and social support, as well as reductions in functional impairment. These improvements in day-to-day functioning also had a knock-on effect on other areas of life, including school attendance. For example, in our trial of the YRI within educational settings, teachers, blinded to who was in the intervention or control groups, independently reported that YRI participants were better prepared and better behaved in the classroom. They were also six times more likely to persist in school, demonstrating significantly better attendance and academic performance.[20] A later trial in youth employment programs indicated not only improvements in anxiety and depression, but also reports by community leaders that YRI participants demonstrated better attitudes and efforts in the youth programs and in community interactions when compared to those who didn't receive the intervention.[21]

Another important aspect of the YRI development and implementation was our analysis of cost effectiveness. As a member of the team that carried out the YRI schools trial, Harvard doctoral student Ryan McBain—later Director of Economic Evaluation at Partners in Health—used our schools trial data for his doctoral dissertation research on the intervention's cost effectiveness. We collected data on all costs for implementation of the intervention in community settings and linked treatment outcomes to improvements in common health metrics of daily functioning used for evaluating other health conditions. Functional impairments were measured by the WHO Disability Assessment Scale, and scores were converted to quality-adjusted life years, or QALYs. We also estimated the financial and economic costs of doing the intervention, including the time young people spent in the sessions as opposed to being out doing other things to make money. Incremental cost-effectiveness ratios (ICERs) were expressed in terms of gains across dimensions of mental health and schooling. Secondary analyses explored whether intervention effects were largest among those worst off (youth scoring in the upper quartile of distress) at baseline. We found that the estimated economic cost of the intervention was $104 per participant. Functional impairment was lower among YRI recipients compared to controls following the intervention, but not at six-month follow-up, and yielded an ICER of $7,260 per QALY gained. At the eight-month follow-up, teacher interviews blind to group assignment indicated that YRI recipients had higher school enrollment, denoting a cost of $431 per additional school year gained, as well as better school attendance and performance. Secondary analyses indicated the intervention was cost effective among those worst off at baseline, yielding an ICER of $3,564 per QALY gained.

Importantly, our results indicate the YRI translated into a range of benefits, such as better school behavior and persistence, that are not captured by traditional cost-effectiveness analysis. We continue to explore questions of cost-benefit analysis in our work to help broaden how the public health field considers the economic impact of behavioral interventions in children and youth. But the truth is that we should not have to make an economic case for the value of such investments. The human rights case alone is justification enough.

Nonetheless, an enabling environment for reconciliation and moving forward is also one where there have been economic gains, and for Sierra Leone to better embrace its human capital agenda, shrewd consideration of the importance of investing in mental health and social services for economic advancement is important.

The YRI has been the centerpiece of our NIMH-funded multi-stakeholder regional hub for implementation science and mental health services research in west Africa, called Youth FORWARD. Our network of global implementation and dissemination partners see the potential of the YRI to meet the needs of vulnerable youth across a range of settings disrupted by violence, including Somalia, Syria, and Central America. We have also adapted the YRI to serve youth affected by war in Colombia and South Sudan.

In the literature on trauma and recovery, early-stage *stabilization* treatments like the YRI do best by targeting coping skills, immediate symptom alleviation, and healthier day-to-day functioning; they can also set the stage for more advanced trauma processing, such as exposure therapy, which has a strong evidence base for uprooting the trauma-related sequelae such as avoidance and re-experiencing that can haunt war survivors for years.[22] Although the six basic skills contained in the YRI draw largely from cognitive behavior therapy, the components meant to address interpersonal conflicts and the mindfulness-based practices in the intervention that help youth ground themselves in their physical bodies and explore practices of self-regulation remain very popular too. One of the favorites for both young men and young women is breath work, or deep belly breathing.[23]

The young women's and young men's groups have also proven to be a helpful way to get feedback on "putting your best self forward." We utilized the Krio proverb discussed in Chapter 14, *good wod pul good kola,* meaning that presenting well to others can be like bringing the kola nut, a sign of friendship and amiability traditional in Sierra Leone. Reflecting on the YRI development and all of our research on its impact, I am proud of how the team always prioritized the realities of culture and context. Although our research focused a great deal on the lives of former child soldiers, we also learned the lesson of social isolation and stigma. In this manner, we developed an intervention that could bring together youth from all backgrounds, including blending former child soldiers with general war-affected youth. Recognizing that all war-affected young people in Sierra Leone had missed a tremendous amount of school and oftentimes lacked basic literacy skills, we removed typical intervention practices of written homework and focused instead on imbuing the manual with local language and widely used proverbs uncovered in our formative research. As recommended by our experts and community advisory boards (CABs), these practices helped to imbue the YRI common elements with cultural content to ensure that key concepts were contextualized and culturally digestible. Each YRI session is now titled in the local Krio language, often using a well-known proverb, and reflects the skills to be practiced.

The groups are also used to help youth set out and pursue what are called S.M.A.R.T. goals, or targets that are "specific, relevant, achievable, realistic, and time-bound."[24] Setting such well-defined goals is a common practice element used in CBT. YRI sessions focus on a future orientation with monitoring and acknowledgment of progress through the intervention. Working in groups is responsive to the realities of limited resources for mental health, but group work also builds on the collectivist nature of the culture by capitalizing on the power of peer group support.[25] In Sierra Leone, where mental health professionals remain scarce, innovative ways of employing group work are essential to the program's success.

At the time of this writing, as mentioned earlier, Sierra Leone has a population of over 8.6 million people, but only three fully accredited psychiatrists (although Partners in Health has now launched a wonderful training program with eight up-and-coming psychiatrists in training), about twenty psychiatric nurses, and a handful of PhDs and masters-level health professionals. The very limited resources for mental health mean that Sierra Leone will need to remain creative to find ways to expand the reach of evidence-based mental health interventions, both through integration into new delivery settings like education and employment programs, as our research has demonstrated, but also through other platforms like health and social protection / poverty reduction programs. Limited mental health resources in the country make it all the more imperative that systems for ongoing supervision of and support to all mental health professionals, including growing networks of nonspecialists, also attend to fidelity to evidence-based practices and improve cross-cutting MHPSS competence skills over time. In the end, analyses of feasibility, acceptability, and effectiveness are essential for finding ways to transition evidence-based practices to scale while maintaining quality.[26]

Qualitative data collection and CAB meetings were used to identify important components of the intervention. The suggestions for a focus on addressing problems with self-regulation (including both anger and risk behavior) and improving interpersonal relationships was vetted in interviews with experts and the advisory boards, who provided feedback on a module layout sheet summarizing the suggested key elements.

Arthur Kleinman, Professor Emeritus in Anthropology at Harvard University, has written extensively about the expression of social suffering and mental health disorders across cultures. His work has helped to draw attention to the lived experience of suffering. Similar to what we have observed in the difficulty that community members have in understanding *mental* distress or suffering—but showing great compassion for *physical* scars or disability due to the war—Kleinman observed in his work in East Asia that shame and stigma associated with mental illness only served to exacerbate mental distress.[27]

Kleinman's work has also had a massive influence on understanding the lived experience of illness, including mental illness globally. Efforts to arrive at greater local understanding of the lived experience of suffering and distress have led to increased attention to understanding "idioms" of distress—local phenomenology of suffering and psychopathology in a given culture and context. When it comes to terminology, you can tell you are on the trail of such an "idiom" when the metaphor makes perfect sense in one culture and language but doesn't translate well into another. For example, in our YRI intervention, we have a session on the topic of staying focused to reach one's goal. The session is organized around a wonderful proverb from the Krio language: *If you tek tem kil anch yu go see em gut.*

Whenever I share that phrase in Krio in Sierra Leone, people are first shocked that a foreigner like myself would know this Krio saying, but soon after the bemusement fades, they often nod with solemn agreement and understanding. The phrase translates to "if you take time when killing an ant, you will get to see its guts." Most Westerners hearing this interpretation are left baffled: Why on earth would a person kill an ant in order to see its guts? This is the domain of the local idiom. To the Sierra Leoneans, the message is clear: *if you stay focused, you will achieve your goals.* This useful proverb drove home an important lesson in our intervention about setting goals and moving toward them one step at a time.

Other adaptations were necessary. For example, in many commonly used manuals in CBT pertaining to skills in mood monitoring, a young person may be asked to rate the intensity of a given emotion along the temperature lines of a thermometer. In Sierra Leone, however, few youth are familiar with thermometers, making the analogy difficult to transfer—the concept is too abstract.

In the early days of developing the YRI, I would sit with Yinka in our favorite room at the Hotel Barmoi. We would sit on the weathered wooden bed that served as our couch, eating white bread and cheese sandwiches and, with our local program manager, crowd around a common laptop to lay out each session, drawing from manuals we had used in the past and integrating the findings of our intervention development research.

We needed to find a new way to talk about mood monitoring. It was evident from our qualitative data that *vex,* or anger, was a key emotion that the youth in the sample struggled with, and that a pot of boiling water (reacting to increases and decreases in heat) or a radio (for which the volume can be turned up or down) would be more appropriate guiding metaphors. The clinical team tested these metaphors in group sessions, discussing how to watch for triggers for anger and implement self-regulation and mindfulness techniques as well as cognitive restructuring in a preventive fashion.

Ultimately, the metaphor of boiling water was seen as the most acceptable and effective means of communicating the concept and was retained in the manual. Youth using the intervention went on to develop this metaphor further. As they discussed how to visualize the pot of boiling water and their ability to control it, they would describe the maneuvers that worked for them as equivalent to pulling out a piece of wood beneath the pot to reduce the boil—a perfect metaphor for emotion regulation.

Additional changes were drawn from common elements of psychotherapeutic techniques used in cognitive behavioral therapy, group interpersonal therapy, and mindfulness-based therapies. We needed to ensure that these common practice elements could be imparted without reliance on writing, but also that there was still a mechanism for practicing and internalizing the skills learned in the group. Instead of written homework, participants were encouraged to practice skills learned in the group in their daily relationships with peers and family members between sessions. The results of their practice were then reviewed through discussion and verbal reports.

Of the mindfulness practices, deep belly (diaphragmatic) breathing was introduced and practiced as an emotion-regulation skill in our groups. Participants were instructed to practice it at least once during the intervening week when they encountered a stress-inducing situation. Participants then returned to the group to discuss their experiences using the technique. This approach, locally called *di belleh blo,* became so popular that our group facilitators would also provide gushing testimonials about how it had helped them calm themselves and avoid arguments with friends and loved ones at home.

Group interventions have particular potency in settings where few human resources for mental health exist. Groups can also encourage peer-to-peer learning and social connections that can contribute to sustainability of intervention impact by providing social support long after treatment ends.[28] YRI groups are always divided up to allow for discussion of content according to age and gender, with both a male and a female group for those under eighteen and a male and a female group for youth over eighteen, with separate male and female facilitators to create a safe space to discuss issues relevant to gender.

When we started the intergenerational study on war-affected youth back in 2002, the rationale was not just to conduct an interesting study, but also to help contribute to policies and programs to improve the lives of war-affected children, youth, and families. We have come far in our work on the YRI, but we have much further to go. Sierra Leone still struggles with very limited opportunities for young people. Even the promise of universal education access remains out of reach. Health systems continue to be weak, and the crisis of the Ebola outbreak unfortunately did little to strengthen them. However, unlike many war-affected countries, Sierra Leone has not fallen back into war. By investing in this generation of young innovators and dreamers, we can accompany the country on a path of steady growth, development, and opportunity.

29

Reaching the Hard to Reach

There are now a number of evidence-based interventions that have been tested in low-resource settings. In the decades ahead, we will need focus and determination to sustain these efforts. As I write this, there are thirty-two active conflicts underway, and one in five children around the globe live in a war zone. The war in Ukraine continues, as does the bloody Hamas-Israel conflict. Once again, civilians are caught in the cross fire. These are very troubled times. In trying to reach children, youth, and families with the highest-quality mental health and psychosocial support (MHPSS) in war-affected settings, we face new security threats and a massive problem of numbers. Reaching the hard to reach will require incredible creativity. The need for tools to scale and sustain high-quality MPHSS services in these regions is what drew me to the field of implementation science.

The discipline of implementation science grew out of this urgent need to ensure the integration of research findings and evidence into health-care policy and practice.[1] As the field of humanitarian response has developed more evidence-based behavioral interventions to support war-affected children and adolescents, the dynamic has shifted. There are now additional concerns about broadening the reach of such interventions while also retaining quality and helping to "build back better." We have a long way to go.

As I quickly realized in our early work on the YRI, it was not enough to just develop an intervention, conduct a randomized controlled trial, and present evidence that it was effective. We realized that to get services to the most vulnerable youth, we had to meet them where they were. In recent years, our team has shifted our research questions from "Does it work?" to "Now that we know this works, how can we get it to work at greater scale with quality and sustainment?" Putting on our implementation science hats, we began to test a series of strategies to reach youth most in need of MHPSS services and strategies for quality improvement, as well as sustainment of evidence-based practices. It was also important for us to remember that no single intervention can do everything in the way of building sustainable MHPSS and social services systems. Going back to the words of our beloved colleague and mentor, Paul Farmer—to truly build systems of respectful and sustainable health care, we need attention to the "staff, stuff, space, systems, and social support" necessary to get care to those who are in need.[2] A critical element of such system-building is also having the political will, technical vision, and leadership to pass the policies and associated budgets necessary for quality mental health and social services.

Unfunded mandates are common in post-conflict settings. In reading Sierra Leone's policies on child protection and education, one might think that they had encountered one of the most progressive societies on earth. But in reality, given their very limited budget and human resources, Sierra Leone's implementation of its ambitious policies to assist children, youth, and families remains limited.

Sierra Leone continues to have one of the highest rates of maternal mortality and child mortality globally—an indication of a very weak health system undermined by years of conflict and lack of investment.[3] Over the years, Sierra Leone has had some very promising policies such as the Free Child Health Care plan, which on paper provides free health care to pregnant and lactating mothers and their children under the age of five.[4] However, evaluations of the plan indicate that in practice, it often resulted in understaffed and understocked district hospitals and peripheral health units. Similarly, for the thousands who survived the historic outbreak of EVD, the government also promised free health care, but in practice, those promises were empty ones.

Health care in Sierra Leone today remains troubled—entirely lacking the space, staff, stuff, systems, and social support that Paul Farmer underscored as essential. In our efforts to reach war-affected youth with evidence-based MHPSS, it was clear that outreach through the EVD-ravaged health system would be a road to nowhere. Despite a veritable movement to integrate MHPSS evidence-based interventions into primary care, in a country where primary care itself was barely available that integration pathway was less feasible. It is exactly because of the weak health systems in Sierra Leone that much of our research to date has focused on the integration of mental health services into the alternate delivery systems of education, livelihoods, and entrepreneurship programs.

The Youth FORWARD scale-out study operated in three rural districts in eastern and northern Sierra Leone: Kailahun, Kono, and Koinadugu, where the government of Sierra Leone Ministry of Youth Affairs (MOYA) and the German development agency Deutsche Gesellschaft für Internationale Zusammenarbeit (GIZ) were delivering an Employment Promotion Program to ensure that young people had the skills necessary for successful employment, with particular attention to entrepreneurship. We negotiated with our partners to allow us to test the YRI as integrated into the employment promotion program. Central to the Youth FORWARD study was the use of a collaborative team approach in order to sustain the evidence-based practices once a new workforce of entrepreneurship workers were trained in the YRI. We used cross-site learning and quality improvement strategies to spread the YRI to over 764 youth across the three districts.

The best of our seasoned interventionists from our prior trials served as our expert "Seed Team," training the entrepreneurship program staff selected to deliver the YRI. This meant that we had to work with our Seed Team to build their skills as both trainers and supervisors who would monitor and provide feedback to new YRI interventionists. Our original vision for cross-site learning involved plans for regional meetups and exchange, but after our cell phones fell silent in hilly forests that lacked network connections, we realized that relying on telecommunications was a nonstarter. Instead, our intrepid Seed Team members would temporarily relocate to the rural districts where new YRI groups were being facilitated.

Unisa Jalloh, Aunty Chris, and Alimamy Kamara would bump along rutted roads for hours, negotiate a space to stay with a local family for weeks on end, and then diligently sit in and observe their newly trained YRI facilitators—employees of the agency that was also providing entrepreneurship training—hard at work. As our Seed Team experts, they were trained to provide targeted feedback to help the new facilitators improve their practice.

The Youth FORWARD implementation science initiative brought together "ideas and experiences to enhance capacity building; increase mental health promotion; improve efficiency and sustainability; and foster cross-site sharing of information, evidence, and research," Seed Team leader Alimamy Kamara explained. Using the collaborative team approach as a scale-out strategy for integrating the YRI into the entrepreneurship delivery platform was singularly innovative. We hypothesized that this approach would benefit youth mental health and also attendance, engagement, and performance of youth during the employment promotion project and even afterward, encouraging greater socioeconomic self-sufficiency.

As paraprofessionals working in MHPSS in Sierra Leone for many years, our Seed Team members were all too familiar with the barriers to mental health care access in Sierra Leone. The broader vision of the Youth FORWARD project gave them a sense of hope. Each of them had personally witnessed the positive impact of the intervention on the lives of participants.

Alimamy had observed this firsthand in his work with young people. He recounted how his experiences had led him to witness previously distressed war-affected youth "use positive thinking, deep breathing, and their imagination to find inner peace during times of discomfort." He felt that the Youth FORWARD initiative was successful with war-affected eighteen- to thirty-year-olds as well as out-of-school youth, helping all to understand that in times of struggle "feelings and emotions such as anger, withdrawal, sadness, and fear are normal reactions to trauma and are okay."

As a Seed Team leader, Alimamy described the transformation he saw in the groups. "A sense of belonging, purpose, and meaning in life had been restored in these young women and men," he said. Looking back, he was happy with how things had gone in integrating YRI into the employment promotion project. When asked what had helped, he felt it was due to the personalized training, supervision, and coaching from the experienced Seed Team. They could draw from their own experience to help facilitators problem-solve on implementation barriers, such as when young parents could not find childcare, or village leaders wanted to combine the boys' groups and girls' groups due to lack of space for group meetings. Each time, with collaborative problem solving, they had been able to negotiate a solution, such as arranging for a local grandmother to babysit, or speaking with village leaders to get access to the school building in the evenings for group meetings, allowing boys' groups and girls' groups to maintain their own sense of privacy with same-gender peers.

The supervision model, Alimamy explained, allowed him to effectively support new YRI delivery through "building their strengths and addressing their weaknesses, and promoting their growth and development through teaching." He felt that the monitoring and on-site support of the Seed Team had helped the new facilitators by empowering them "to solve problems and achieve goals."

In 2019, I visited a member of the Seed Team, Unisa, at his site in Kailahun District. Protocol required that I first go and meet the village chief. Having read countless tales of famous Sierra Leonean chiefs like Bai Bureh or Mami Yoko, I was prepared to see an ornate home and beautiful handwoven garments adorned with cowrie shells. Instead, I was caught a bit off guard by the stocky young man in Nike plastic slides, long yellow athletic shorts, and a dark blue sports tank. This young guy, barely in his thirties, was the village leader.

However, once he welcomed me to his home and told us about his village, I could see why he had been elected. He was passionate and concerned about the tremendous level of youth underemployment in the area. He was grateful for the employment program, which was training young people in the basics of developing an idea from an early concept, "planting" an entrepreneurship "seed" and "watering" it over time. He was also thrilled to meet Unisa and the team and learn of the additional "readiness" skills that were the focus of the YRI program. He mentioned that issues with aggression and hopelessness had been a big issue in young people since the end of the war.

Bringing together both the technical and the interpersonal skills to succeed in livelihoods really hadn't been considered much. In his experience as an expert Seed Team trainer, as Alimamy explained, the combined program was is an innovation that addressing multiple needs at once: "It helps sustain the healing process by enabling young people to gain the basic knowledge and skills to manage resources and develop sustainable livelihoods."

Most recently, follow-up interviews of YRI participants completed in 2023 following the global COVID-19 pandemic indicate that even four years after the intervention had been delivered, youth participants retained many of the skills they had learned both in the entrepreneurship program and in the YRI. As a twenty-three-year-old woman from Koinadugu District explained:

> Well now that the YRI has ended I am still practicing the things we were taught and some of the factors which have helped me remember them after all of these years is the fact that I have been doing them regularly, so it is now becoming a normal routine for me, especially the aspects that have to deal with becoming a better person, teamwork and even managing my emotions better and not allowing anything to weigh me down, no matter the situation in which I find myself.

A thirty-four-year-old father in a nearby community extolled the benefits of YRI both for himself and also for his family. It shaped his family interactions, he said:

> Well, since I started the YRI sessions, my life has changed so far as I can now do the problem-solving skills to analyze the problems in my life and then try to get solutions. Also, I can now take care of my family better and now am a changed man. I no longer allow stress or any issues to hold me down. In addition to that, they have also motivated me to improve on myself in terms of education.

In fact, several of the youth served by the program had moved from being in trouble with local leaders due to fighting to becoming local "role models," teaching others how to use the emotion regulation and problem-solving skills they had learned. One young man, Bailah, had been named youth chairman after local leaders noticed his transformation. He explained:

My participation in the YRI has made a huge difference in my life . . . my family and friends now listen to me based on the advice that I give them and how I carry myself . . . I now share with my wife on issues in the home and we make decisions together . . . and also in the community, I listen to other youth's problems and I explain what we were taught at the sessions so they can also easily learn.

Other young people mentioned becoming peacemakers in their community. As a twenty-eight-year-old man stated:

So far all I can say is that I am happy I was allowed to take part in these sessions as all that I have learned has been very good and helpful to my life. I am now a peacemaker in my community and I try as much as possible to be always advising my fellow youth on what needs to be done and how to avoid quarrels and do the problem-solving skills approach.

Our future hopes for the YRI include scaling out across fifty schools in Freetown and the Western Area and a youth-led version of the program that can be delivered from one peer to another.[5] Our experiences with intervention prove time and time again that young people in Sierra Leone remain eager to jump at any opportunity to manifest their full potential.

Epilogue

In February 2023, I returned to Sierra Leone for the first time since the social and economic consequences of the COVID-19 pandemic and Russia's war in Ukraine threw the country into a tailspin. Fuel prices had skyrocketed since my last visit, as had the cost of rice and other essential foods. In the summer of that same year, after my trip, political rhetoric stirred by social media posts following the elections in Sierra Leone led to riots and even some deaths, but the country did not collapse back into mass violence. That February, as I picked my way through the streets of Freetown, there were many signs of progress.

The first delightful surprise was the paved road from the airport in Lungi to the Sea Coach terminal. Gone are the days of ancient helicopters flown by aged Russian pilots with noses reddened by gin blossoms. Gone now too is the swaying, bumpy ride up the pitted road to cross the waters to Freetown by boat. As the road rolled smoothly by, even though our bus was well-worn, I heard a fellow passenger remark, "this is the first thing that anyone who comes to this country sees—it's about time that they improved it!"

So many small things around Freetown could be seen through that same lens. Most of the main roads were paved, with freshly painted white lines denoting the raised sidewalks. The Hotel Barmoi, my home away from home in Freetown, was a source of comfort and so many fond memories—all the staff remembered me. I was thrilled to see them all well and thriving after so many years. With some negotiation I returned to my favorite lower-level balcony room with a view of the twinkling sea.

A new airport terminal opened in March 2023, just after my visit; it's three times the size of the old terminal, and the first fully green airport terminal in West Africa, powered by a bank of solar panels.[1] There is talk of a bridge across the expanse of water that separates Lungi Airport from Freetown. The Salem family, who endowed my professorship at Boston College, have helped their director of logistics to open a school in Lungi, in his father's ancestral Temne village. It is the first school in the history of that area.

In addition to the new Radisson Blu, where we held our big Youth FORWARD launch, a Hilton hotel will soon adorn the point in Aberdeen. We enjoyed Lebanese mezze at a hotel that also took credit cards. Freetown now has a keke tour—a mode of transportation similar to that of a covered motorcycle—of the city led by Mustapha, a charming young university student. Shockingly, just as when I travel to London or Paris, my AT&T cell phone plan had the same coverage in Freetown.

Of the many things we have learned in our study, the most crucial is that just like the slow progress to paving that bumpy road to the ferry terminal, healing takes time. While we may wish that we could simply undo the traumas of the past, their ugly truth lingers. Too often we forget that in the journey of healing, there is a lot we still can do about the post-conflict environment. When the COVID-19 outbreak spread through Sierra Leone, for example, the nation was ready. It repurposed many of its prior protocols of screening, containment, and care—lessons learned from the EVD crisis—for those affected by the illness.[2]

These elements of Sierra Leone's rebirth remain the aim of the work ahead. The country is currently battling a deadly scourge of addiction to a substance called Kush—a mix of marijuana and other synthetic drugs and additives—which is being sold cheaply in the streets of Freetown.[3] What was once the Ministry of Social Welfare and Gender has now been split into two ministries, one on Gender and one on Social Welfare and Children's Affairs. Though progress is being made, these ministries continue to have the smallest budgets available. Clearly, there is still work to be done.

Many groundbreaking policies are now on the books in Sierra Leone, but they remain unfunded mandates. Since the time that President Julius Maada Bio declared rape a national emergency early in his term, a law was passed that at least 30 percent of parliamentarians must be female. In Rwanda, in comparison, a record 61 percent of lawmakers are female.[4] Maada Bio's reelection in July 2023 formed a cabinet that has already exceeded the goal of 30 percent female participation. However, the immensely successful Rainbo centers, which provide legal and psychosocial support to survivors of sexual and gender-based violence, remain limited to just five districts.[5] Intergenerational violence continues at concerning rates. Although an increasing number of sexual assaults are prosecuted, forensic labs are still not available to provide necessary biological evidence to hold offenders responsible. Girls and young women still experience staggering rates of sexual violence, and trafficking of women and girls remains an enduring issue.[6]

That outer layer of Sierra Leone's social ecology is not yet the enabling environment needed to support robust healing at the community level. As discussed throughout this book, it is far more valid to think of resilience as a process, rather than some unique trait of certain individuals. With the right social ecology around a child who has experienced trauma, healing can be fostered in ways that are astounding. In addition to the great strides we see exemplified in Isatu, one of our male study participants is now a parliamentarian. It's hard for the team to interview him these days as he is just so busy.

The career of our dear family friend David Sengeh, once Minister of Basic and Primary Education, has had a meteoric rise. After being awarded "Best Minister" out of a field of global competitors in 2023, he was appointed Chief Minister in the cabinet.[7] Under his watch, education grew to 22 percent of Sierra Leone's budget. His book, *Radical Inclusion,* was released to much acclaim, documenting the policies his leadership ensured so that never again would a girl be pushed out of school because of pregnancy, or a child with a disability not accommodated.[8] As chief minister, there is hope that his talent can spread beyond education to help several weak and unrealized elements of policy in Sierra Leone, health and mental health central among them.

Though these changes are monumental steps forward, the legacy of intergenerational violence cannot be ignored. During that same trip, we deepened collaborations with Kenema General Hospital and Tulane University to expand our understanding of intergenerational trauma. Our study will now include elements of both physical and mental health as well as parent–child relationships. In addition to stress biology, we will dig deeper into the lives of children formerly involved in armed forces and armed groups, both as mothers and as fathers, and investigate how the forces around them enable their potential or undermine their ambitions.

Other vestiges of intergenerational violence were revealed to us during the trip. As we bumped along Freetown on the keke tour, we were brought to the top of the city to see where the European colonizers had lived, far from the malaria-ridden low-lying areas. We visited the new engineering buildings of the University of Sierra Leone. The well-kept cemetery for those who perished in World War I and II stood in strong contrast to the neglected and weed-covered cemetery where those who died during the EVD outbreak were buried.

After the sadness of the latter cemetery, the final stop on the keke tour took us to a set of steps just a few meters from the big market. Our guide asked us to follow him. He parked the keke at the side of the main road and guided us down what he explained were the "Portuguese Steps," set widely toward the top of the street with elegant banisters and crumbling red-brown painted stairs that wound down toward two parallel rock walls. The walls were thick slabs of stone stretching toward a trash-filled shoreline.

The area had wooden stalls, which likely served local fish hawkers. At this time of day, they were filled with listless sleeping young men. We were guided by an energetic local with spiky dreadlocks and a loosely fitting black tank top and shorts. He pointed to a sickening piece of history: European slavers had installed a series of brass rings in rows on each side of a narrow stone wall. Our guide explained that humans in shackles were chained there before being loaded onto boats bound for the Americas.

Enslaved people who were deemed unruly were forced into small stone compartments that could barely fit a crouching person. We were told they were stuffed with as many as four people at a time. Captives held there had carved symbols into the stone. Moses, a linguist, explained that this was *Kaka kwi,* an almost-extinct form of written Mende. Later, Father Peter explained to me that humans had been sold at the big market long before anything else.

The dark truths of the horrors wrought on West Africa to build the economic power of the West have received little reckoning. In the United States today, even public school curricula teaching the truths about our long history of slavery and racism are being challenged.[9] We still have many rivers to cross.

Long-term engagement and commitment to change is a part of this path forward. A theme that arises frequently in our research is the role played by collectivity, our deep sense of connection and obligation to one another. We see its healing power in the powerful unleashing of Isatu's full potential. We see our failures in the social rejection that Sahr experienced, which left him to die in isolation.

Today, our commitment to long-term engagement and social justice means that we are writing very different types of grants in addition to our current research. One of these new projects is ACHIEVE, a collaboration with several major US and African universities and faculty working in sub-Saharan Africa, led by scholars from the region committed to training the next generation of African scholars equipped to carry out global research focused on child and family mental health.

As our longitudinal research reveals mechanisms that can be successful targets for intervention, we have an obligation to move our science beyond the simple question of whether it works to larger questions of how MHPSS and social services systems can work at scale and be sustained with quality. Naturally, such questions lead to working much more closely with governments and key stakeholders on creative strategies to extend the reach of evidence-based interventions and to ensure the technical leadership and political will necessary to enshrine services in budgets and policy.

Just as individuals may be affected by virtuous cycles, virtuous cycles can also occur at the level of policy. As a result of Maada Bio's delivery on his promises and Chief Minister Sengeh's achievements, donors have begun to reinvest in Sierra Leone's education system. As we look at the years ahead, Sierra Leone is in a hopeful place. The near future will reveal if this collective effort can pull the country toward a place of greater equity and progress.

In the end, Sierra Leone has given me much more than I have ever been able to contribute. We have had the honor of watching a place that has slowly emerged from trauma and loss grow to a place of stability and even leadership. There is still so much progress that can be made; the path forward is a long one. However, if twenty-two years of work in the region has taught me anything, it is that determination pays off. And so, Sierra Leone sits on a precipice. With its current government elected to a second term despite a growing economic crisis, the nation looks ahead to new things, and as always, its people will persevere.

Notes

1. War's Children

1. Theresa S. Betancourt, Katrina Keegan, Jordan Farrar, and Robert T. Brennan, "The Intergenerational Impact of War on Mental Health and Psychosocial Wellbeing: Lessons from the Longitudinal Study of War-Affected Youth in Sierra Leone," *Conflict and Health* 14, no. 1 (2020), https://doi.org/10.1186/s13031-020-00308-7.

2. Theresa S. Betancourt, Robert T. Brennan, Julia Rubin-Smith, Garrett M. Fitzmaurice, and Stephen E. Gilman, "Sierra Leone's Former Child Soldiers: A Longitudinal Study of Risk, Protective Factors, and Mental Health," *Journal of the American Academy of Child & Adolescent Psychiatry* 49, no. 6 (2010): 606–615, https://doi.org/10.1016/j.jaac.2010.03.008.

2. The Global Face of Conflict

1. Gabriella Waaijman, "2024: A Tough Year Ahead for Children Living in an Increasingly Hostile World," Save the Children International, 2024, https://www.savethechildren.net/blog/2024-tough-year-ahead-children-living-increasingly-hostile-world.

2. "More Than Half of Ukraine's Children Displaced after One Month of War," UNICEF press release, March 24, 2022, https://www.unicef.org/press-releases/more-half-ukraines-children-displaced-after-one-month-war.

3. "Onslaught of Violence against Women and Children in Gaza Unacceptable: UN Experts," United Nations Human Rights Office of the High Commissioner, May 6, 2024, https://www.ohchr.org/en/press-re leases/2024/05/onslaught-violence-against-women-and-children-gaza -unacceptable-un-experts.

4. Artemis Christodoulou, "Appendix 5: Amputations in the Sierra Leone Conflict," in *Witness to Truth: Report of the Sierra Leone Truth and Reconciliation Commission,* 2004, available at http://www.sierra-leone.org /Other-Conflict/APPENDICES/Appendix%205%20%20Amputations. pdf; Edward Conteh and Maria Berghs, "'Mi at Don Poil': A Report on Reparations in Sierra Leone for Amputee and War-Wounded People," Amputee and War-Wounded Association, Freetown, Sierra Leone, 2014, https://www.researchgate.net/publication/263931738_'Mi_At_Don _Poil'_A_Report_on_Reparations_in_Sierra_Leone_for_Amputee_and _War-_Wounded_People.

5. Susan McKay and Dyan E. Mazurana, "Where Are the Girls? Girls in Fighting Forces in Northern Uganda, Sierra Leone and Mozambique: Their Lives during and after War," Rights and Democracy (International Centre for Human Rights and Democratic Development), Montreal, 2004, https://numerique.banq.qc.ca/patrimoine/details/52327/2160400.

6. John Williamson, "Reintegration of Child Soldiers in Sierra Leone," USAID, 2005, https://pdf.usaid.gov/pdf_docs/PDACH599.pdf.

7. Ilene Cohn and Guy S. Goodwin-Gill, *Child Soldiers: The Role of Children in Armed Conflicts* (Oxford: Clarendon Press, 1994).

8. Peter W. Singer, "Talk Is Cheap: Getting Serious about Preventing Child Soldiers," *Cornell International Law Journal* 37, no. 3 (2004): 561–586, https://www.brookings.edu/articles/talk-is-cheap-getting-serious-about -preventing-child-soldiers/.

9. Ishmael Beah, *A Long Way Gone: Memoirs of a Boy Soldier* (New York: Sarah Crichton Books, 2007).

3. Children, War, and Trauma

1. Rachel Yehuda and Amy Lehrner, "Intergenerational Transmission of Trauma Effects: Putative Role of Epigenetic Mechanisms," *World Psychiatry* 17, no. 3 (2018): 243–257, https://doi.org/10.1002/wps.20568;

Ciara Downes, Elaine Harrison, David Curran, and Michele Kavanagh, "The Trauma Still Goes On . . . : The Multigenerational Legacy of Northern Ireland's Conflict," *Clinical Child Psychology and Psychiatry* 18, no. 4 (2012): 583–603, https://doi.org/10.1177/1359104512462548.

2. Theresa Betancourt, "400 Million Children Beset by War Is a Global Public Health Crisis," *Boston Globe,* December 26, 2023.

3. Patricia Dashorst, Trudy M. Mooren, Rolf J. Kleber, Peter J. de Jong, and Rafaele J. C. Huntjens, "Intergenerational Consequences of the Holocaust on Offspring Mental Health: A Systematic Review of Associated Factors and Mechanisms," *European Journal of Psychotraumatology* 10, no. 1 (2019): 1654065, https://doi.org/10.1080/20008198.2019.1654065.

4. N. P. Kellermann, "Perceived Parental Rearing Behavior in Children of Holocaust Survivors," *Israel Journal of Psychiatry and Related Sciences* 38, no. 1 (2001): 58–68.

5. Kellermann, "Perceived Parental Rearing Behavior."

6. Albert Bandura, "The Role of Imitation in Personality Development," *Journal of Nursery Education* 18, no. 3 (1963): 207–215, https://www.jstor.org/stable/42717645.

7. Regarding lower levels of cortisol, see Rachel Yehuda, Linda M. Bierer, James Schmeidler, et al., "Low Cortisol and Risk for PTSD in Adult Offspring of Holocaust Survivors," *American Journal of Psychiatry* 15, no. 8 (2000): 1252–9, doi: 10.1176/appi.ajp.157.8.125. Regarding changes in the glucocorticoid receptor gene, see Rachel Yehuda, Janine D. Flory, Linda M. Bierer, et al., "Lower Methylation of Glucocorticoid Receptor Gene Promoter 1F in Peripheral Blood of Veterans with Posttraumatic Stress Disorder," *Biological Psychiatry* 77, no. 4 (2015): 356–364, https://doi.org/10.1016/j.biopsych.2014.02.006.

8. Yael Danieli, Fran H. Norris, and Brian Engdahl, "Multigenerational Legacies of Trauma: Modeling the What and How of Transmission," *American Journal of Orthopsychiatry* 86, no. 6 (2016): 639–651, https://doi.org/10.1037/ort0000145.

9. Kellermann, "Perceived Parental Rearing Behavior."

10. Nigel P. Field, Sophear Muong, and Vannavuth Sochanvimean, "Parental Styles in the Intergenerational Transmission of Trauma Stemming from the Khmer Rouge Regime in Cambodia," *American Journal of Orthopsychiatry* 83, no. 4 (2013): 483–494, https://doi.org/10.1111/ajop.12057.

11. Danieli, Norris, and Engdahl, "Multigenerational Legacies of Trauma."

12. Heide Rieder and Thomas Elbert, "Rwanda—Lasting Imprints of a Genocide: Trauma, Mental Health and Psychosocial Conditions in Survivors, Former Prisoners, and Their Children," *Conflict and Health* 7, no. 1 (2013), https://doi.org/10.1186/1752-1505-7-6.

13. Celestin Mutuyimana, Vincent Sezibera, and Cindi Cassady, "Determinants of Intergenerational Trauma Transmission: A Case of the Survivors of the 1994 Genocide against Tutsi in Rwanda," in *Child Behavioral Health in Sub-Saharan Africa,* ed. Fred M. Ssewamala, Ozge Sensoy Bahar, and Mary M. McKay, 213–233 (Cham: Springer, 2021), https://doi.org /10.1007/978-3-030-83707-5_11.

14. UNHCR, "Global Report 2020," 217–233, https://reporting .unhcr.org/sites/default/files/gr2020/pdf/GR2020_English_Full_lowres .pdf.

15. Kathryn C. Monahan, Kevin M. King, Elizabeth P. Shulman, Elizabeth Cauffman, and Laurie Chassin, "The Effects of Violence Exposure on the Development of Impulse Control and Future Orientation across Adolescence and Early Adulthood: Time-Specific and Generalized Effects in a Sample of Juvenile Offenders," *Development and Psychopathology* 27, no. 4, pt. 1 (2015): 1267–1283, https://doi.org/10.1017/s0954579414001394.

16. E. S. Mezzacappa, R. M. Kelsey, E. S. Katkin, and R. P. Sloan, "Vagal Rebound and Recovery from Psychological Stress," *Psychosomatic Medicine* 63, no. 4 (2001): 650–657, https://doi.org/10.1097/00006842 -200107000-00018.

17. Ann S. Masten, *Ordinary Magic: Resilience in Development* (New York: Guilford Press, 2015).

18. Masten, *Ordinary Magic,* 6.

19. Glen H. Elder, *Children of the Great Depression* (Boulder, CO: Westview Press, 1999).

20. Elder, *Children of the Great Depression.*

21. UNHCR, "Global Report 2020."

22. Franklin D. Roosevelt, "One Third of a Nation," January 1937, https://historymatters.gmu.edu/d/5105/.

23. R. D. Conger, X. Ge, G. H. Elder, F. O. Lorenz, and R. L. Simons, "Economic Stress, Coercive Family Process, and Developmental Problems

of Adolescents," *Child Development* 65, no. 2 (1994): 541–561, https://doi .org/10.2307/1131401.

24. William Schneider, Jane Waldfogel, and Jeanne Brooks-Gunn, "The Great Recession and Risk for Child Abuse and Neglect," *Children and Youth Services Review* 72 (January 2017): 71–81, https://doi.org/10.1016/j .childyouth.2016.10.016; Melissa Hidrobo and Lia Fernald, "Cash Transfers and Domestic Violence," *Journal of Health Economics* 32, no. 1 (2013): 304–319, https://doi.org/10.1016/j.jhealeco.2012.11.002.

25. Lydie A. Lebrun-Harris, Reem M. Ghandour, Michael D. Kogan, and Michael D. Warren, "Five-Year Trends in US Children's Health and Well-Being, 2016–2020," *JAMA Pediatrics* 176, no. 7 (2022), https://doi .org/10.1001/jamapediatrics.2022.0056; Nicole Racine, Brae Anne McArthur, Jessica E. Cooke, Rachel Eirich, Jenney Zhu, and Sheri Madigan, "Global Prevalence of Depressive and Anxiety Symptoms in Children and Adolescents during COVID-19," *JAMA Pediatrics* 175, no. 11 (2021): 1142–1150, https://doi.org/10.1001/jamapediatrics.2021 .2482.

26. Vivek Murthy, "Protecting Youth Mental Health," U.S. Surgeon General's Advisory, 2021, https://www.hhs.gov/sites/default/files/surgeon -general-youth-mental-health-advisory.pdf.

4. Jellybeans in Darkness

1. "Convention on the Rights of the Child," United Nations General Assembly Resolution 44/25, adopted November 20, 1989, Part I, Article I, https://www.ohchr.org/en/instruments-mechanisms/instruments/con vention-rights-child.

5. Swit Salone

1. Ivana Elbl, "The Volume of the Early Atlantic Slave Trade, 1450–1521," *Journal of African History* 38, no. 1 (1997): 31–75, https://doi.org/10 .1017/S0021853796006810.

2. Kip D. Zimmerman, Theodore G. Schurr, Wei-Min Chen, et al., "Genetic Landscape of Gullah African Americans," *American Journal of Physical Anthropology* 175 no. 4 (2021): 905–919, https://doi.org/10.1002/ajpa .24333.

3. Marcus Rediker, *The Amistad Rebellion: An Atlantic Odyssey of Slavery and Freedom* (New York: Penguin, 2012).

4. *United States v. The Amistad*, 1841, 518, Taney Court.

5. "The Amistad Case," Educator Resources, National Archives, August 15, 2016, https://www.archives.gov/education/lessons/amistad.

6. Paul Farmer, *Fevers, Feuds, and Diamonds: Ebola and the Ravages of History* (Sierra Leone: Picador, 2021).

7. Tom Collins, "'Patients Were Chained to Walls and Beds': Freetown's Psychiatric Hospital Released from the Past," *The Guardian,* January 17, 2023.

8. Cooper Inveen, "Ebola Survivors Sue Government of Sierra Leone over Missing Millions," *The Guardian,* January 5, 2018, https://www.theguardian.com/global-development/2018/jan/05/ebola-survivors-sue-sierra-leone-government-over-missing-ebola-millions.

9. Susan Shepler, "The Rites of the Child: Global Discourses of Youth and Reintegrating Child Soldiers in Sierra Leone," *Journal of Human Rights* 4, no. 2 (2005): 197–211, 197, https://doi.org/10.1080/14754830590952143.

6. The Embodiment of War

1. Charles A. Nelson, Zulfiqar A. Bhutta, Nadine Burke Harris, Andrea Danese, and Muthanna Samara, "Adversity in Childhood Is Linked to Mental and Physical Health throughout Life," *BMJ* 371 (2020), art. 3048, https://doi.org/10.1136/bmj.m3048.

2. National Scientific Council on the Developing Child, "Excessive Stress Disrupts the Architecture of the Developing Brain," Harvard University Center on the Developing Child, Working Paper 3, 2005, updated January 2014, https://developingchild.harvard.edu/wp-content/uploads/2005/05/Stress_Disrupts_Architecture_Developing_Brain-1.pdf.

3. National Scientific Council on the Developing Child, "Excessive Stress Disrupts the Architecture."

4. Susan Shepler, "The Rites of the Child: Global Discourses of Youth and Reintegrating Child Soldiers in Sierra Leone," *Journal of Human Rights* 4, no. 2 (2005): 197–211, https://doi.org/10.1080/14754830590952143.

5. Urie Bronfenbrenner, *The Ecology of Human Development: Experiments by Nature and Design* (Cambridge, MA: Harvard University Press, 1979).

6. Urie Bronfenbrenner, "Interacting Systems in Human Development: Research Paradigms: Present and Future," in *Persons in Context: Developmental Processes,* ed. Niall Bolger et al. (Cambridge: Cambridge University Press, 1988).

7. Bronfenbrenner, *Ecology of Human Development.*

8. Larry Brendtro, "The Vision of Urie Bronfenbrenner: Adults Who Are Crazy about Kids," *Reclaiming Children and Youth* 15, no. 3 (2006): 162–166, 163, https://www.researchgate.net/publication/234721190_The _Vision_of_Urie_Bronfenbrenner_Adults_Who_Are_Crazy_about_Kids.

9. Stevan Hobfoll, "Resource Caravans and Resource Caravan Passageways: A New Paradigm for Trauma Responding," *Intervention* 12, no. 4 (2014): 21–32, https://doi.org/10.1097/WTF.0000000000000067.

10. Hobfoll, "Resource Caravans."

11. Albert Schweitzer, *Out of My Life and Thought: An Autobiography,* trans. A. B. Lemke, rev. ed. (New York: Henry Holt, 1990).

7. Without Family

1. Brett T. Litz and Matt J. Gray, "Emotional Numbing in Post-Traumatic Stress Disorder: Current and Future Research Directions," *Australian and New Zealand Journal of Psychiatry* 36, no. 2 (2002): 198–204, https://doi.org/10.1046/j.1440-1614.2002.01002.x.

2. Judith Lewis Herman, *Trauma and Recovery: The Aftermath of Violence—from Domestic Abuse to Political Terror* (New York: Basic Books, 2015).

8. Touchstones

1. Charles H. Zeanah, Kathryn L. Humphreys, Nathan A. Fox, and Charles A. Nelson, "Alternatives for Abandoned Children: Insights from the Bucharest Early Intervention Project," *Current Opinion in Psychology* 15 (June 2017): 182–188, https://doi.org/10.1016/j.copsyc.2017.02.024.

2. Charles A. Nelson, Kathleen M. Thomas, and Michelle de Haan, "Neural Bases of Cognitive Development," *Handbook of Child Psychology* 2 (June 2007), https://doi.org/10.1002/9780470147658.chpsy0201.

3. John Bowlby, "Maternal Care and Mental Health," *Bulletin of the World Health Organization* 3, no. 3 (1951): 355–533, https://pubmed.ncbi .nlm.nlih.gov/14821768/.

4. Diane Benoit, "Infant-Parent Attachment: Definition, Types, Antecedents, Measurement and Outcome," *Paediatrics & Child Health* 9, no. 8 (2004): 541–545, https://www.ncbi.nlm.nih.gov/pmc/articles /PMC2724160/.

5. M. D. Ainsworth, "Patterns of Infant-Mother Attachments: Antecedents and Effects on Development," *Bulletin of the New York Academy of Medicine* 61, no. 9 (1985): 771–791, 774.

6. Ainsworth, "Patterns of Infant-Mother Attachments," 774.

7. Ainsworth, "Patterns of Infant-Mother Attachments," 774.

8. Ainsworth, "Patterns of Infant-Mother Attachments," 774.

9. Judith Lewis Herman, *Trauma and Recovery: Aftermath of Violence from Domestic Abuse to Political Terror* (New York: Basic Books, 1992).

10. Bessel van der Kolk, *The Body Keeps the Score: Mind, Brain and Body in the Transformation of Trauma* (London: Penguin Books, 2015).

11. Judith L. Herman, "Recovery from Psychological Trauma," *Psychiatry and Clinical Neurosciences* 52, S1 (1998): S98–103, https://doi.org/10 .1046/j.1440-1819.1998.0520s5s145.x.

12. Herman, "Recovery from Psychological Trauma."

13. W. Thomas Boyce, *The Orchid and the Dandelion* (New York: Knopf, 2019).

14. Tim Allen, Jackline Atingo, Dorothy Atim, et al., "What Happened to Children Who Returned from the Lord's Resistance Army in Uganda?" *Journal of Refugee Studies* 33, no. 4 (2020): 663–683, https://doi.org/10 .1093/jrs/fez116.

15. R. M. Penzerro and L. Lein, "Burning Their Bridges: Disordered Attachment and Foster Care Discharge," *Child Welfare* 74, no. 2 (1995): 351–366, https://pubmed.ncbi.nlm.nih.gov/7705170/.

16. Theresa Stichick Betancourt, Ivelina Ivanova Borisova, Timothy Philip Williams, et al., "Sierra Leone's Former Child Soldiers: A Follow-Up Study of Psychosocial Adjustment and Community Reintegration," *Child Development* 81, no. 4 (2010), https://doi.org/10.1111/j.1467-8624 .2010.01455.x.

17. Charles A. Nelson, Nathan A. Fox, and Charles H. Zeanah, *Romania's Abandoned Children: Deprivation, Brain Development, and the Struggle for Recovery* (Cambridge, MA: Harvard University Press, 2014).

9. Finding the Way Home

1. American Psychiatric Association, *Diagnostic and Statistical Manual of Mental Disorders, DSM-5,* 5th ed. (Saint Louis, MO: American Psychiatric Association, 2022).

2. Willy Oppenheim and Amy Stambach, "Global Norm Making as Lens and Mirror: Comparative Education and Gender Mainstreaming in Northern Pakistan," *Comparative Education Review* 58, no. 3 (2014): 377–400, https://doi.org/10.1086/676016.

10. Post-traumatic Growth

1. Lawrence G. Calhoun, Richard G. Tedeschi, and Marianne Amir, *Handbook of Posttraumatic Growth: Research and Practice* (New York: Psychology Press, 2014).

2. All quotations from Eranda Jayawickreme in this chapter can be found at "Healing 2.0: What We Gain from Pain," *Hidden Brain,* podcast, host Shankar Vedantam, National Public Radio, 2022, https://hiddenbrain .org/podcast/what-we-gain-from-pain/.

13. The Helpers

1. "Sierra Leone," United Nations Development Programme, 2002, https://www.undp.org/sierra-leone.

2. Anna Freud and Dorothy Burlingham, *War and Children* (New York: Ernst Willard, 1943).

14. The Sting of Rejection

1. Carol S. Aneshensel, "Social Stress: Theory and Research," *Annual Review of Sociology* 18, no. 1 (1992): 15–38, https://doi.org/10.1146/annu rev.so.18.080192.000311.

2. Theresa S. Betancourt, Jessica Agnew-Blais, Stephen E. Gilman, David R. Williams, and B. Heidi Ellis, "Past Horrors, Present Struggles: The Role of Stigma in the Association between War Experiences and Psychosocial Adjustment among Former Child Soldiers in Sierra Leone," *Social Science and Medicine* 70, no. 1 (2010): 17–26, https://doi.org/10.1016/j.socscimed.2009.09.038.

3. Jeannie Annan, Christopher Blattman, and Roger Horton, "The State of Youth and Youth Protection in Northern Uganda: Findings from the Survey for War Affected Youth," UNICEF Uganda, 2006, https://chrisblattman.com/documents/policy/sway/SWAY.Phase1.FinalReport.pdf.

4. Verena Ertl, Anett Pfeiffer, Elisabeth Schauer-Kaiser, Thomas Elbert, and Frank Neuner, "The Challenge of Living On: Psychopathology and Its Mediating Influence on the Readjustment of Former Child Soldiers," edited by Linda Chao, *PLOS One* 9, no. 7 (2014): e102786, https://doi.org/10.1371/journal.pone.0102786.

5. Kennedy Amone-P'Olak, Jan Stochl, Emilio Ovuga, et al., "Postwar Environment and Long-Term Mental Health Problems in Former Child Soldiers in Northern Uganda: The WAYS Study," *Journal of Epidemiology and Community Health* 68, no. 5 (2014): 425–430, https://doi.org/10.1136/jech-2013-203042.

6. Amone-P'Olak et al., "Postwar Environment and Long-Term Mental Health Problems"; Kennedy Amone-P'Olak, Tlholego Molemane Lekhutlile, Emilio Ovuga, et al., "Sexual Violence and General Functioning among Formerly Abducted Girls in Northern Uganda: The Mediating Roles of Stigma and Community Relations—the WAYS Study," *BMC Public Health* 16, no. 1 (2016), https://doi.org/10.1186/s12889-016-2735-4.

7. Myriam Denov and Atim Angela Lakor, "When War Is Better Than Peace: The Post-Conflict Realities of Children Born of Wartime Rape in Northern Uganda," *Child Abuse & Neglect* 65 (March 2017): 255–265, https://doi.org/10.1016/j.chiabu.2017.02.014.

15. Social Ties

1. Mike Wessells, "What Are We Learning about Community-Based Child Protection Mechanisms? An Inter-Agency Review of the Evidence

from Humanitarian and Development Settings," Save the Children International, 2009, https://resourcecentre.savethechildren.net/a088b28/.

2. Jacobus Cilliers, Oeindrila Dube, and Bilal Siddiqi, "Reconciling after Civil Conflict Increases Social Capital but Decreases Individual Well-Being," *Science* 352, no. 6287 (2016): 787–794, https://doi.org/10.1126/science.aad9682.

3. Cilliers, Dube, and Siddiqi, "Reconciling after Civil Conflict."

16. The Puzzle of Girls' Resilience

1. Manasi Sharma, Shoshanna L. Fine, Robert T. Brennan, and Theresa S. Betancourt, "Coping and Mental Health Outcomes among Sierra Leonean War-Affected Youth: Results from a Longitudinal Study," *Development and Psychopathology* 29, no. 1 (2016): 11–23, https://doi.org/10.1017/s0954579416001073.

2. Kristen E. McLean, "Fatherhood and Futurity: Youth, Masculinity, and Contingency in Post-Crisis Sierra Leone" (PhD diss., Yale University, 2019), https://www.proquest.com/docview/2394855012.

3. John Williamson, "The Disarmament, Demobilization, and Reintegration of Child Soldiers: Social and Psychological Transformation in Sierra Leone," *Intervention* 4, no. 3 (2006): 185–205, 188, https://doi.org/10.1097/wtf.0b013e328011a7fb.

4. Chris Coulter, *Bush Wives and Girl Soldiers: Women's Lives through War and Peace in Sierra Leone* (Ithaca, NY: Cornell University Press, 2009).

5. Opiyo Oloya, *Child to Soldier: Stories from Joseph Kony's Lord's Resistance Army* (Toronto: University of Toronto Press, 2013).

6. World Bank, "Sierra Leone—Rapid Damage and Loss Assessment of August 14th, 2017 Landslides and Floods in the Western Area," Working Paper 121120, November 1, 2017, https://documents.worldbank.org/en/publication/documents-reports/documentdetail/523671510297364577/sierra-leone-rapid-damage-and-loss-assessment-of-august-14th-2017-landslides-and-floods-in-the-western-area.

17. Reverberations of Violence against Girls and Women

1. Theresa S. Betancourt, Ivelina I. Borisova, Marie de la Soudière, and John Williamson, "Sierra Leone's Child Soldiers: War Exposures and

Mental Health Problems by Gender," *Journal of Adolescent Health* 49, no. 1 (2011): 21–28, https://doi.org/10.1016/j.jadohealth.2010.00.021.

2. "Sierra Leone Faces a Culture of Rape," AfricaNews, updated September 12, 2019, https://www.africanews.com/2019/01/14/sierra-leone -faces-a-culture-of-rape/; "Sierra Leone: Rape and Murder of Child Must Be Catalyst for Real Change," Amnesty International, June 23, 2020, https://www.amnesty.org/en/latest/news/2020/06/sierra-leone-rape-and -murder-of-child-must-be-catalyst-for-real-change/.

3. Statistics Sierra Leone and ICF, *Sierra Leone Demographic and Health Survey* (Freetown, SL: Stats SL; Rockville, MD: ICF, 2019), https://dhs program.com/publications/publication-FR365-DHS-Final-Reports.cfm.

4. Daniel F. H. Kettor, "Quarterly Newsletter," *Rainbo Initiative,* January–March 2021, https://rainboinitiative.org/wp-content/uploads /2021/04/Rainbo-Newsletter_January-March_2021.pdf.

5. UNFPA-UNICEF Global Programme to End Child Marriage, "Sierra Leone Country Report," 2019, https://www.unicef.org/media /88841/file/Child-marriage-Sierra-Leone-profile-2019.pdf; State House of Sierra Leone Media and Communications Unit, "President Julius Maada Bio Declares Rape and Sexual Violence as a National Emergency in Sierra Leone," State House of Sierra Leone, February 7, 2019, https://statehouse .gov.sl/president-julius-maada-bio-declares-rape-and-sexual-violence-as -a-national-emergency-in-sierra-leone/.

6. Statistics Sierra Leone and ICF, *Sierra Leone Demographic and Health Survey.*

7. Sunita Kishor and Kiersten Johnson, *Profiling Domestic Violence: A Multi-Country Study* (Calverton, MD: MEASURE DHS+, ORC Macro, June 2004), https://dhsprogram.com/pubs/pdf/od31/od31.pdf; Michelle J. Hindin, "Adolescent Childbearing and Women's Attitudes towards Wife Beating in 25 Sub-Saharan African Countries," *Maternal and Child Health Journal* 18, no. 6 (2013): 1488–1495, https://doi.org/10.1007/s10995-013 -1389-4.

8. Stephanie Simmons Zuilkowski, Elyse Joan Thulin, Kristen McLean, Tia McGill Rogers, Adeyinka M. Akinsulure-Smith, and Theresa S. Betancourt, "Parenting and Discipline in Post-Conflict Sierra Leone," *Child Abuse & Neglect* 97 (November 2019): 104–138, https://doi.org/10.1016 /j.chiabu.2019.104138.

9. "Sierra Leone Bans Corporal Punishment in Schools," *Politico SL,* October 28, 2021, https://www.politicosl.com/articles/sierra-leone-bans -corporal-punishment-schools.

10. Zuilkowski et al., "Parenting and Discipline in Post-Conflict Sierra Leone."

11. "Corporal Punishment Is Fading Away in Schools," *Awoko Newspaper,* December 21, 2022, https://awokonewspaper.sl/corporal-punish ment-is-fading-away-in-schools/.

12. Heather F. McClintock, Marsha L. Trego, and Evangeline M. Wang, "Controlling Behavior and Lifetime Physical, Sexual, and Emotional Violence in Sub-Saharan Africa," *Journal of Interpersonal Violence* 36, nos. 15–16 (2019): 088626051983587, https://doi.org/10.1177/088626 0519835878.

13. Harriet Mason, "A Second Chance at Schooling for Pregnant Teenagers in Ebola-Affected Sierra Leone," UNICEF, April 28, 2016, https://www.unicef.org/stories/second-chance-schooling-pregnant -teenagers-sierra-leone.

14. Randa Grob-Zakhary and David Moinina Sengeh, "Lessons from Sierra Leone: How to Get Girls Back to School," Al Jazeera, December 15, 2022, https://www.aljazeera.com/opinions/2022/12/15/sierra-leone-can -teach-the-world-how-to-get-girls-back-to-school.

15. Emmanuel Akinwotu, "Sierra Leone Backs Bill to Legalise Abortion and End Colonial-Era Law," *The Guardian,* July 6, 2022.

16. Kingsley Ighobor, "How We Are Moving the Gender Agenda Forward in Sierra Leone," *Africa Renewal,* March 14, 2023, https://www.un .org/africarenewal/magazine/february-2023/how-we-are-moving -gender-agenda-forward-sierra-leone.

17. "Sierra Leone," Girls Not Brides, https://www.girlsnotbrides.org /learning-resources/child-marriage-atlas/regions-and-countries/sierra -leone/, accessed May 28, 2024.

18. "Sierra Leone: Government and Donors Must Prioritize Mental Health to Address Legacy of War and Ebola Epidemic—New Report," Amnesty International, May 25, 2021, https://www.amnesty.org/en/latest /news/2021/05/sierra-leone-government-and-donors-must-prioritize -mental-health-to-address-legacy-of-war-and-ebola-epidemic-new -report.

19. "Management and Functional Review of the Ministry of Gender and Children's Affairs," Government of Sierra Leone Public Sector Reform Unit, January 2021, https://archive.psru.gov.sl/content/management-and -functional-review-ministry-gender-and-children%E2%80%99s-affair -final-report-january.

20. "Sierra Leone Human Rights Report," Country Reports on Human Rights Practices for 2021, United States Department of State, Bureau of Democracy, Human Rights, and Labor, 2021, https://www.state.gov/wp -content/uploads/2022/02/313615_SIERRA-LEONE-2021-HUMAN -RIGHTS-REPORT.pdf.

21. UNESCO IIEP Dakar Africa Office and United Nations Children's Fund, *Republic of Sierra Leone Education Sector Analysis: Assessing the Enabling Environment for Gender Equality* (Dakar: UNESCO, 2020).

22. Sierra Leone: Foreign Direct Investment and Percent of GDP, The Global Economy.com, data accessed November 2023, https://www .theglobaleconomy.com/Sierra-Leone/Foreign_Direct_Investment/.

23. "Sierra Leone: Overview," World Bank, March 30, 2023, https:// www.worldbank.org/en/country/sierraleone/overview.

24. Luisa T. Schneider, "Why Sierra Leonean Women Don't Feel Pro-tected by Domestic Violence Laws," *The Conversation,* January 9, 2019, https://theconversation.com/why-sierra-leonean-women-dont-feel -protected-by-domestic-violence-laws-109436.

19. Meaning Making and Transformation

1. Helen Berents, "No Child's Play: Recognising the Agency of Former Child Soldiers in Peace Building Processes," *Dialogue E-Journal* 6, no. 2 (2009): 1–35, https://eprints.qut.edu.au/217204/.

20. Adversity upon Adversity

1. "Ebola Virus Disease," World Health Organization, April 20, 2023, https://www.who.int/en/news-room/fact-sheets/detail/ebola-virus -disease.

2. Silas Gbandia, "Ebola Spreads to Sierra Leone Capital of Freetown as Deaths Rise," Bloomberg, July 12, 2014, https://www.bloomberg.com

/news/articles/2014-07-12/ebola-spreads-to-sierra-leone-capital-of
-freetown-as-deaths-rise.

3. "Ebola Situation Report," World Health Organization, March 16, 2016, https://web.archive.org/web/20160318125119/http://apps.who.int
/ebola/current-situation/ebola-situation-report-16-march-2016.

4. Paul Farmer, *Fevers, Feuds, and Diamonds: Ebola and the Ravages of History* (Sierra Leone: Picador, 2021).

5. Jonah Lipton, "Care and Burial Practices in Urban Sierra Leone," Ebola Response Anthropology Platform, October 14, 2021, http://www
.ebola-anthropology.net/wp-content/uploads/2014/11/care-and-burial
-practice.pdf.

6. Farmer, *Fevers, Feuds, and Diamonds*.

7. Theresa S. Betancourt, Robert T. Brennan, Patrick Vinck, et al., "Associations between Mental Health and Ebola-Related Health Behaviors: A Regionally Representative Cross-Sectional Survey in Post-Conflict Sierra Leone," edited by Phillipa J. Hay, *PLOS Medicine* 13, no. 8 (2016): e1002073, https://doi.org/10.1371/journal.pmed.1002073.

8. Betancourt et al., "Associations between Mental Health and Ebola-Related Health Behaviors."

9. Thomas M. Crea, K. Megan Collier, Elizabeth K. Klein, et al., "Social Distancing, Community Stigma, and Implications for Psychological Distress in the Aftermath of Ebola Virus Disease," *PLOS One* 17, no. 11 (2022): e0276790, https://doi.org/10.1371/journal.pone.0276790.

10. Crea et al., "Social Distancing."

21. Write on the World

1. "Convention on the Rights of the Child," United Nations General Assembly Resolution 44/25, adopted November 20, 1989, Part I, Article I, https://www.ohchr.org/en/instruments-mechanisms/instruments/con
vention-rights-child.

2. "Convention on the Rights of the Child," United Nations General Assembly Resolution 44/25, adopted November 20, 1989, Part I, Articles 12–15, https://www.ohchr.org/en/instruments-mechanisms/instruments
/convention-rights-child.

3. "Convention on the Rights of the Child," Part I, Articles 12–15.

4. Helen Berents, "No Child's Play: Recognizing the Agency of Former Child Soldiers in Peace Building Processes," *Dialogue E-Journal* 6, no. 2 (2009): 1–35, https://eprints.qut.edu.au/217204/.

22. The Education Gap

1. "What Do Children Want in Times of Emergency and Crisis? They Want an Education," Save the Children UK, 2015, https://resourcecentre .savethechildren.net/document/what-do-children-want-times-emergency -and-crisis-they-want-education/.

2. Myriam Denov and Andi Buccitelli, "Navigating Crisis and Chronicity in the Everyday: Former Child Soldiers in Urban Sierra Leone," *Stability: International Journal of Security & Development* 2, no. 2 (2013): art. 45, https://doi.org/10.5334/sta.ce.

3. Jeannie Annan, Christopher Blattman, and Roger Horton, *The State of Youth and Youth Protection in Northern Uganda: Findings from the Survey for War Affected Youth,* UNICEF Uganda, 2006, https://chrisblattman.com /documents/policy/sway/SWAY.Phase1.FinalReport.pdf.

4. Peter Moyi, "An Examination of Primary School Attendance and Completion among Secondary School Age Adolescents in Post-Conflict Sierra Leone," *Research in Comparative and International Education* 8, no. 4 (2013): 524–539, 525, https://doi.org/10.2304/rcie.2013.8.4.524.

5. UNESCO Institute for Statistics, "Literacy Rate, Adult Total (% of People Ages 15 and Above)—Sierra Leone," World Bank, accessed 2022, https://data.worldbank.org/indicator/SE.ADT.LITR.ZS?locations=SL.

6. Denov and Buccitelli, "Navigating Crisis and Chronicity in the Everyday."

7. Theresa S. Betancourt, Stephanie Simmons, Ivelina Borisova, Stephanie E. Brewer, Uzo Iweala, and Marie de la Soudière, "High Hopes, Grim Reality: Reintegration and the Education of Former Child Soldiers in Sierra Leone," *Comparative Education Review* 52, no. 4 (2008): 565–587, https://doi.org/10.1086/591298.

8. Myriam Denov and Atim Angela Lakor, "When War Is Better Than Peace: The Post-Conflict Realities of Children Born of Wartime Rape in Northern Uganda," *Child Abuse & Neglect* 65 (March 2017): 255–265, https://doi.org/10.1016/j.chiabu.2017.02.014.

9. Michelle V. Porche, Lisa R. Fortuna, Julia Lin, and Margarita Alegria, "Childhood Trauma and Psychiatric Disorders as Correlates of School Dropout in a National Sample of Young Adults," *Child Development* 82, no. 3 (2011): 982–998, https://doi.org/10.1111/j.1467-8624.2010.01534.x.

10. Betancourt et al., "High Hopes, Grim Reality."

11. Jackie Kirk and Rebecca Winthrop, "Promoting Quality Education in Refugee Contexts: Supporting Teacher Development in Northern Ethiopia," *International Review of Education* 53, no. 5–6 (2007): 715–723, https://doi.org/10.1007/s11159-007-9061-0.

12. Nazish Imran, Atif Rahman, Nakhshab Chaudhry, and Aftab Asif, "Effectiveness of a School-Based Mental Health Intervention for School Teachers in Urban Pakistan: A Randomized Controlled Trial," *Child and Adolescent Psychiatry and Mental Health* 16, no. 1 (2022), https://doi.org/10.1186/s13034-022-00470-1.

13. Betancourt et al., "High Hopes, Grim Reality."

14. Denov and Lakor, "When War Is Better Than Peace."

15. David Moinina Sengeh, *Radical Inclusion: Seven Steps to Help You Create a More Just Workplace, Home, and World* (New York: Flatiron Books, 2023).

16. Graça Machel, *The Impact of War on Children* (London: Hurst, 2001).

17. Annan, Blattman, and Horton, "State of Youth and Youth Protection in Northern Uganda."

18. Beth Verhey, "Child Soldiers—Lessons Learned on Prevention, Demobilization, and Reintegration," report 207, Africa Region, World Bank, May 2002, https://openknowledge.worldbank.org/server/api/core/bitstreams/d13c2061-3c19-5fd8-bbe4-35f5231a48b9/content.

23. Narrative Healing

1. Paul L. Geltman, Wanda Grant-Knight, Supriya D. Mehta, et al., "The 'Lost Boys of Sudan': Functional and Behavioral Health of Unaccompanied Refugee Minors Resettled in the United States," *Archives of Pediatrics & Adolescent Medicine* 159, no. 6 (June 1, 2005): 585, https://doi.org/10.1001/archpedi.159.6.585.

2. "Narrative Exposure Therapy (NET)," American Psychological Association, *APA,* May 2017, https://www.apa.org/ptsd-guideline/treatments/narrative-exposure-therapy.

3. Verena Ertl, Anett Pfeiffer, Elisabeth Schauer, Thomas Elbert, and Frank Neuner, "Community-Implemented Trauma Therapy for Former Child Soldiers in Northern Uganda," *JAMA Network* 306, no. 5 (August 3, 2011), https://doi.org/10.1001/jama.2011.1060.

4. Theresa J.Hoeft, John C. Fortney, Vikram Patel, and Jürgen Unützer, "Task-Sharing Approaches to Improve Mental Health Care in Rural and Other Low-Resource Settings: A Systematic Review," *Journal of Rural Health* 34, no. 1 (2017): 48–62, https://doi.org/10.1111/jrh.12229.

5. Sayed Jafar Ahmadi, Laura Jobson, Arul Earnest, et al., "Prevalence of Poor Mental Health among Adolescents in Kabul, Afghanistan, as of November 2021," *JAMA Network Open* 5, no. 6 (2022): e2218981, https://doi.org/10.1001/jamanetworkopen.2022.18981.

6. William R. Beardslee, Tytti Solantaus, Bradley S. Morgan, Tracy R. Gladstone, and Nicholas M. Kowalenko, "Preventive Interventions for Children of Parents with Depression: International Perspectives," *Medical Journal of Australia* 1, Suppl 1 (April 16, 2012): 23–25, https://doi.org/10.5694/mjao11.11289.

7. William R. Beardslee, *Out of the Darkened Room* (Little, Brown, 2009).

24. Adult Lives

1. Marianne Ducasse-Rogier, "The Sierra Leonean Conflict: Resolving Intractable Conflicts in Africa," Working paper 31, Clingendael Institute, September 2004, https://www.clingendael.org/sites/default/files/pdfs/20040900_cru_working_paper_31.pdf.

2. Ann S. Masten, *Ordinary Magic: Resilience in Development* (New York: Guilford Press, 2015).

25. Coming of Age in the Aftermath of War

1. Neil Boothby, "What Happens When Child Soldiers Grow Up? The Mozambique Case Study," *Intervention* 4, no. 3 (2006): 244–259, https://doi.org/10.1097/wtf.0b013e32801181ab.

2. Neil Boothby, J. Crawford, and J. Halperin, "Mozambique Child Soldier Life Outcome Study: Lessons Learned in Rehabilitation and Re-

integration Efforts," *Global Public Health* 1, no. 1 (2006): 87–107, https://doi .org/10.1080/17441690500324347.

3. Dyan E. Mazurana, Susan A. McKay, Khristopher C. Carlson, and Janel C. Kasper, "Girls in Fighting Forces and Groups: Their Recruitment, Participation, Demobilization, and Reintegration," *Peace and Conflict: Journal of Peace Psychology* 8, no. 2 (2002): 97–123, https://doi.org/10.1207/s1532 7949pac0802_01.

4. Lindsay Stark, "Cleansing the Wounds of War: An Examination of Traditional Healing, Psychosocial Health and Reintegration in Sierra Leone," *Intervention* 4, no. 3 (2006): 206–218, https://doi.org/10.1097/wtf .0b013e328011a7d2.

5. Stark, "Cleansing the Wounds of War."

6. UN Office of the Special Representative of the Secretary-General for Children and Armed Conflict, "The Gender Dimensions of Grave Violations against Children in Armed Conflict," United Nations, 2022, https://childrenandarmedconflict.un.org/wp-content/uploads/2022/04 /220426-Concept-Note-Gender-Paper-Launch.pdf.

7. "Monitoring and Reporting on Grave Violations," Office of the Special Representative of the Secretary-General for Children and Armed Conflict, United Nations, n.d., https://childrenandarmedconflict.un.org /tools-for-action/monitoring-and-reporting/.

8. Charles H. Zeanah, Kathryn L. Humphreys, Nathan A. Fox, and Charles A. Nelson, "Alternatives for Abandoned Children: Insights from the Bucharest Early Intervention Project," *Current Opinion in Psychology* 15 (June 2017): 182–188, https://doi.org/10.1016/j.copsyc.2017.02.024.

9. "'They Are Forgetting about Us': The Long-Term Mental Health Impact of War and Ebola in Sierra Leone," Amnesty International, 2021, https://www.amnesty.org/en/documents/afr51/4095/2021/en/.

10. Michael Ungar, Linda Theron, Kathleen Murphy, and Philip Jefferies, "Researching Multisystemic Resilience: A Sample Methodology," *Frontiers in Psychology* 11 (2021), https://doi.org/10.3389/fpsyg.2020.607994.

11. Cedric de Coning, "Fitting the Pieces Together: Implications for Resilience, Adaptive Peacebuilding and Transitional Justice," in *Resilience, Adaptive Peacebuilding and Transitional Justice: How Societies Recover after Collective Violence,* edited by Janine Natalya Clark and Michael Ungar,

257–275, 262 (Cambridge: Cambridge University Press, 2021), https://doi .org/10.1017/9781108919500.012.

26. Trauma and Resilience across Generations

1. N. P. Kellermann, "Perceived Parental Rearing Behavior in Children of Holocaust Survivors," *Israel Journal of Psychiatry and Related Sciences* 38, no. 1 (2001): 58–68.

2. Clarisse Musanabaganwa, Stephan Jansen, Agaz Wani, et al., "Community Engagement in Epigenomic and Neurocognitive Research on Post-Traumatic Stress Disorder in Rwandans Exposed to the 1994 Genocide against the Tutsi: Lessons Learned," *Epigenomics* 14, no. 15 (2022): 887–895, https://doi.org/10.2217/epi-2022-0079.

3. Kellermann, "Perceived Parental Rearing Behavior in Children of Holocaust Survivors."

4. Elizabeth K. Klein, Laura Bond, Kristen E. McLean, Mahmoud Feika, Abdulia Jawo Bah, and Theresa S. Betancourt, "Navigating the Tension between Fatherhood Ideals and Realities of a Post-Conflict Setting: A Phenomenological Study of Former Child Soldiers in Sierra Leone," *SSM—Qualitative Research in Health* 3 (January 2023): 100227, https://doi .org/10.1016/j.ssmqr.2023.100227.

5. Binta Alleyne-Green, Alex Kulick, Sara Matsuzaka, and Theresa S. Betancourt, "War Violence Exposure, Reintegration Experiences, and Intimate Partner Violence among a Sample of War-Affected Females in Sierra Leone," *Global Social Welfare* 6, no. 2 (2018): 97–106, https://doi .org/10.1007/s40609-018-0125-9.

6. Theresa S. Betancourt, Ryan McBain, Elizabeth A. Newnham, and Robert T. Brennan, "Context Matters: Community Characteristics and Mental Health among War-Affected Youth in Sierra Leone," *Journal of Child Psychology and Psychiatry* 55, no. 3 (2013): 217–226, https://doi.org /10.1111/jcpp.12131; Theresa S. Betancourt, Elizabeth A. Newnham, Ryan McBain, and Robert T. Brennan, "Post-Traumatic Stress Symptoms among Former Child Soldiers in Sierra Leone: Follow-Up Study," *British Journal of Psychiatry* 203, no. 3 (2013): 196–202, https://doi.org/10.1192 /bjp.bp.112.113514; Shaobing Su, Rochelle L. Frounfelker, Alethea Desrosiers, Robert T. Brennan, Jordan Farrar, and Theresa S. Betancourt,

"Classifying Childhood War Trauma Exposure: Latent Profile Analyses of Sierra Leone's Former Child Soldiers," *Journal of Child Psychology and Psychiatry* 62, no. 6 (2020), https://doi.org/10.1111/jcpp.13312.

7. Theresa S. Betancourt, Jessica Agnew-Blais, Stephen E. Gilman, David R. Williams, and B. Heidi Ellis, "Past Horrors, Present Struggles: The Role of Stigma in the Association between War Experiences and Psychosocial Adjustment among Former Child Soldiers in Sierra Leone," *Social Science and Medicine* 70, no. 1 (2010): 17–26, https://doi.org/10.1016/j.socscimed.2009.09.038; Theresa Stichick Betancourt, Ivelina Ivanova Borisova, Timothy Philip Williams, et al., "Sierra Leone's Former Child Soldiers: A Follow-Up Study of Psychosocial Adjustment and Community Reintegration," *Child Development* 81, no. 4 (2010), https://doi.org/10.1111/j.1467-8624.2010.01455.x.

8. National Research Council (US) and Institute of Medicine (US) Committee on Integrating the Science of Early Childhood Development, *From Neurons to Neighborhoods,* ed. Jack P. Shonkoff and Deborah A. Phillips (Washington, DC: National Academies Press, 2000), https://doi.org/10.17226/9824.

9. Sarah K. G. Jensen, Vincent Sezibera, Shauna M. Murray, Robert T. Brennan, and Theresa S. Betancourt, "Intergenerational Impacts of Trauma and Hardship through Parenting," *Journal of Child Psychology and Psychiatry* 62, no. 8 (2020), https://doi.org/10.1111/jcpp.13359.

27. The Next Generation

1. Theresa S. Betancourt, Sarah E. Meyers-Ohki, Anne Stevenson, et al., "Using Mixed-Methods Research to Adapt and Evaluate a Family Strengthening Intervention in Rwanda." *African Journal of Traumatic Stress* 2, no. 1 (2011): 32–45, https://www.ncbi.nlm.nih.gov/pmc/articles/PMC4189126/.

2. Theresa S. Betancourt, Sarah K. G. Jensen, Dale A. Barnhart, et al., "Promoting Parent-Child Relationships and Preventing Violence via Home-Visiting: A Pre-Post Cluster Randomised Trial among Rwandan Families Linked to Social Protection Programmes." *BMC Public Health* 20, no. 1 (2020), https://doi.org/10.1186/s12889-020-08693-7.

3. Betancourt et al., "Promoting Parent-Child Relationships."

4. Carly Tubbs Dolan and Jamie Weiss-Yagoda, "IRC *Healing Class-rooms* Retention Support Programming improves Syrian Refugee Children's Learning in Lebanon," 3EA Impact Report 1.1, International Rescue Committee, updated March 14, 2018, https://www.rescue.org/sites/default /files/document/5467/3ea-impactreport11updated31418.pdf.

5. Kenneth E. Miller and Andrew Rasmussen, "War Exposure, Daily Stressors, and Mental Health in Conflict and Post-Conflict Settings: Bridging the Divide between Trauma-Focused and Psychosocial Frameworks," *Social Science and Medicine* 70, no. 1 (2010): 7–16, https://doi.org /10.1016/j.socscimed.2009.09.029.

6. Elisabeth Babcock, "Using Brain Science to Create New Pathways out of Poverty," presentation at Crittenton Women's Union, Boston, October 9, 2014, https://www.cwda.org/sites/main/files/file-attachments /using-brain-science_beth-babcock.pdf.

7. Bessel van der Kolk, *The Body Keeps the Score: Mind, Brain and Body in the Transformation of Trauma* (London: Penguin, 2015), 74–75.

8. van der Kolk, *Body Keeps the Score,* 75.

9. Healthline, FindCare, Cambridge, Massachusetts, accessed May 6, 2024, https://care.healthline.com/find-care/specialty/psychology/ma/ cambridge; World Population Review, Cambridge, Massachusetts, 2024, https://worldpopulationreview.com/us-cities/cambridge-ma-population.

10. Vikram Patel, Helen A. Weiss, Neerja Chowdhary, et al., "Effectiveness of an Intervention Led by Lay Health Counsellors for Depressive and Anxiety Disorders in Primary Care in Goa, India (MANAS): A Cluster Randomised Controlled Trial," *The Lancet* 376, no. 9758 (2010): 2086–2095, https://doi.org/10.1016/s0140-6736(10)61508-5.

11. Verena Ertl, Anett Pfeiffer, Elisabeth Schauer, Thomas Elbert, and Frank Neuner, "Community-Implemented Trauma Therapy for Former Child Soldiers in Northern Uganda," *JAMA Network* 306, no. 5 (August 3, 2011), https://doi.org/10.1001/jama.2011.1060.

12. Laura K. Murray, Stephanie Skavenski, Jeremy C. Kane, et al., "Effectiveness of Trauma-Focused Cognitive Behavioral Therapy among Trauma-Affected Children in Lusaka, Zambia," *JAMA Pediatrics* 169, no. 8 (2015): 761–769, 761, https://doi.org/10.1001/jamapediatrics.2015.0580.

13. Margaret E. Kruk and Muhammad Pate, "*The Lancet Global Health* Commission on High Quality Health Systems 1 Year On: Progress on a

Global Imperative," *The Lancet Global Health* 8, no. 1 (2020): e30–32, https://doi.org/10.1016/s2214-109x(19)30485-1.

14. World Health Organization (WHO), "Building Back Better: Sustainable Mental Health Care after Emergencies," February 28, 2013, https://www.who.int/publications/i/item/9789241564571.

15. Zulfiqar A. Bhutta, Supriya Bhavnani, Theresa S. Betancourt, Mark Tomlinson, and Vikram Patel, "Adverse Childhood Experiences and Lifelong Health," *Nature Medicine* 29, no. 7 (2023): 1639–1648, https://doi.org /10.1038/s41591-023-02426-0.

16. Felicity L. Brown, Anne M. de Graaff, Jeannie Annan, and Theresa S. Betancourt, "Annual Research Review: Breaking Cycles of Violence—A Systematic Review and Common Practice Elements Analysis of Psychosocial Interventions for Children and Youth Affected by Armed Conflict," *Journal of Child Psychology and Psychiatry* 58, no. 4 (2016): 507–524, https://doi.org/10.1111/jcpp.12671; Marianna Purgatto, Alden L. Gross, Theresa S. Betancourt, et al., "Focused Psychosocial Interventions for Children in Low-Resource Humanitarian Settings: A Systematic Review and Individual Participant Data Meta-Analysis," *The Lancet Global Health* 6, no. 4 (2018): e390–400, https://doi.org/10.1016/s2214-109x (18)30046-9.

17. World Health Organization, *MhGAP Intervention Guide for Mental, Neurological, and Substance-Use Disorders in Non-Specialized Health Settings,* 2nd ed. (Geneva: World Health Organization, 2019).

28. Ready to Learn, Ready to Work

1. James J. Heckman, Jora Stixrud, and Sergio Urzua, "The Effects of Cognitive and Noncognitive Abilities on Labor Market Outcomes and Social Behavior," *Journal of Labor Economics* 24, no. 3 (2006): 411–482, https://doi.org/10.1086/504455.

2. Pamela Scorza, Ricardo Araya, Alice J. Wuermli, and Theresa S. Betancourt, "Towards Clarity in Research on 'Non-Cognitive' Skills: Linking Executive Functions, Self-Regulation, and Economic Development to Advance Life Outcomes for Children, Adolescents and Youth Globally," *Human Development* 58, no. 6 (2015): 313–317, https://doi.org /10.1159/000443711.

3. James J. Heckman and Tim Kautz, "Hard Evidence on Soft Skills," *Labour Economics* 19, no. 4 (2012). 431–464, https://doi.org/10.1016/j .labeco.2012.05.014; Merrell Tuck-Primdahl, "Heckman and the Case for Soft Skills," *World Bank Blogs,* December 16, 2011, https://blogs.worldbank .org/developmenttalk/heckman-and-the-case-for-soft-skills; Raja Ben-taouet Kattan, "Non-Cognitive Skills: What Are They and Why Should We Care?" *World Bank Blogs,* May 8, 2017, https://blogs.worldbank.org /education/non-cognitive-skills-what-are-they-and-why-should-we-care.

4. Scorza et al., "Towards Clarity in Research on 'Non-Cognitive' Skills," 2.

5. Mengying Li, Jenna L. Riis, Sharon R. Ghazarian, and Sara B. Johnson, "Income, Family Context, and Self-Regulation in 5-Year-Old Children," *Journal of Developmental & Behavioral Pediatrics* 38, no. 2 (217): 99–108, https://doi.org/10.1097/dbp.0000000000000380; Hye Kyung Kim, Jeff Niederdeppe, Meredith Graham, Christine Olson, and Geri Gay, "Effects of Online Self-Regulation Activities on Physical Activity among Pregnant and Early Postpartum Women," *Journal of Health Communication* 20, no. 10 (2015): 1115–1124, https://doi.org/10.1080/10810730.2015 .1018639.

6. Theresa S. Betancourt, Dana L. Thomson, Robert T. Brennan, Cara M. Antonaccio, Stephen E. Gilman, and Tyler J. VanderWeele, "Stigma and Acceptance of Sierra Leone's Child Soldiers: A Prospective Longitudinal Study of Adult Mental Health and Social Functioning," *Journal of the American Academy of Child & Adolescent Psychiatry* 59, no. 6 (2019): 715–726, https://doi.org/10.1016/j.jaac.2019.05.026.

7. Theresa S. Betancourt, Ivelina I. Borisova, Timothy P. Williams, et al., "Sierra Leone's Former Child Soldiers: A Follow-Up Study of Psychosocial Adjustment and Community Reintegration," *Child Development* 81, no. 4 (2011): 1077–1095, https://doi.org/10.1111/j.1467-8624.2010 .01455.x.

8. Bessel van der Kolk, *The Body Keeps the Score: Mind, Brain and Body in the Transformation of Trauma* (London: Penguin, 2015).

9. Annie Zimmerman, Emily Garman, Mauricio Avendano-Pabon, et al., "The Impact of Cash Transfers on Mental Health in Children and Young People in Low-Income and Middle-Income Countries: A Systematic Review and Meta-Analysis," *BMJ Global Health* 6, no. 4 (2021): e004661,

https://doi.org/10.1136/bmjgh-2020-004661; Francesca Bastagli, Jessica Hagen-Zanker, Luke Harman, et al., "Cash Transfers: What Does the Evidence Say? A Rigorous Review of Programme Impact and of the Role of Design and Implementation Features," Overseas Development Institute, London, July 27, 2016, https://odi.cdn.ngo/media/documents/11316.pdf.

10. Christopher Blattman, Nathan Fiala, and Sebastian Martinez, "Generating Skilled Self-Employment in Developing Countries: Experimental Evidence from Uganda," *Quarterly Journal of Economics* 129, no. 2 (2014): 697–752, https://doi.org/10.1093/qje/qjt057.

11. Christopher Blattman, Julian C. Jamison, and Margaret Sheridan, "Reducing Crime and Violence: Experimental Evidence from Cognitive Behavioral Therapy in Liberia," *American Economic Review* 107, no. 4 (2017): 1165–1206, https://doi.org/10.1257/aer.20150503.

12. Vikram Patel, Shekhar Saxena, Crick Lund, et al., "The Lancet Commission on Global Mental Health and Sustainable Development." *The Lancet* 392, no. 10157 (2018): 1553–1598, https://doi.org/10.1016/s0140 -6736(18)31612-x.

13. Neha S. Singh, Anushka Ataullahjan, Khadidiatou Ndiaye, et al., "Delivering Health Interventions to Women, Children, and Adolescents in Conflict Settings: What Have We Learned from Ten Country Case Studies?" *The Lancet* 397, no. 10273 (2021): 533–542, https://doi.org/10.1016/s0140 -6736(21)00132-x.

14. Elizabeth A. Newnham, Ryan K. McBain, Katrina Hann, et al., "The Youth Readiness Intervention for War-Affected Youth," *Journal of Adolescent Health* 56, no. 6 (2015): 606–611, https://doi.org/10.1016/j .jadohealth.2015.01.020.

15. Marylene Cloitre, Lisa R. Cohen, Kile M. Ortigo, Christie Jackson, and Karestan C. Koenen, *Treating Survivors of Childhood Abuse and Interpersonal Trauma,* 2nd ed. (New York: Guilford Press, 2020).

16. Judith L. Herman, *Trauma and Recovery* (New York: Basic Books, 1992).

17. Judith Lewis Herman, *Truth and Repair: How Trauma Survivors Envision Justice* (New York: Basic Books, 2023).

18. Bruce F. Chorpita, Eric L. Daleiden, and John R. Weisz, "Identifying and Selecting the Common Elements of Evidence-Based Interventions: A Distillation and Matching Model," *Mental Health Services Research* 7,

no. 1 (2005): 5–20, https://doi.org/10.1007/s11020-005-1962-6; Marylene Cloitre, Karestan C. Koenen, Lisa R. Cohen, and Hyemee Han, "Skills Training in Affective and Interpersonal Regulation Followed by Exposure: A Phase-Based Treatment for PTSD Related to Childhood Abuse," *Journal of Consulting and Clinical Psychology* 70, no. 5 (2002): 1067–1074, https://doi .org/10.1037/0022-006x.70.5.1067.

19. Theresa S. Betancourt, Ryan McBain, Elizabeth A. Newnham, et al., "A Behavioral Intervention for War-Affected Youth in Sierra Leone: A Randomized Controlled Trial," *Journal of the American Academy of Child & Adolescent Psychiatry* 53, no. 12 (2014): 1288–1297, https://doi.org/10 .1016/j.jaac.2014.09.011.

20. Betancourt et al., "Behavioral Intervention."

21. Jordan Freeman, Jordan Farrar, Matías Placencio-Castro, et al., "Integrating Youth Readiness Intervention and Entrepreneurship in Sierra Leone: A Hybrid Type II Cluster Randomized Trial," *Journal of the American Academy of Child and Adolescent Psychiatry* (2024; in press), https://doi .org/10.1016/j.jaac.2023.09.552.

22. Herman, *Trauma and Recovery*.

23. Betancourt et al., "Behavioral Intervention"; Paul Bolton, Judith Bass, Theresa Betancourt, et al., "Interventions for Depression Symptoms among Adolescent Survivors of War and Displacement in Northern Uganda: A Randomized Controlled Trial," *JAMA* 298, no. 5 (2007): 519–527, https://doi.org/10.1001/jama.298.5.519; Susan I. Hopper, Sherrie L. Murray, Lucille R. Ferrara, and Joanne K. Singleton, "Effectiveness of Diaphragmatic Breathing for Reducing Physiological and Psychological Stress in Adults," *JBI Database of Systematic Reviews and Implementation Reports* 17, no. 9 (2019): 1855–1876, https://doi.org/10.11124 /jbisrir-2017-003848.

24. Alice J. Cairns, David J. Kavanagh, Frances Dark, and Steven M. McPhail, "Goal Setting Improves Retention in Youth Mental Health: A Cross-Sectional Analysis," *Child and Adolescent Psychiatry and Mental Health* 13, no. 1 (2019): art. 31, https://doi.org/10.1186/s13034-019 -0288-x.

25. John R. Weisz, Kristin M. Hawley, and Amanda Jensen Doss, "Empirically Tested Psychotherapies for Youth Internalizing and Externalizing Problems and Disorders," *Child and Adolescent Psychiatric Clinics*

of North America 13, no. 4 (2004): 729–815, https://doi.org/10.1016/j.chc
.2004.05.006.

26. Laura Asher, Rahel Birhane, Solomon Teferra, et al., "'Like a Doctor, Like a Brother': Achieving Competence amongst Lay Health Workers Delivering Community-Based Rehabilitation for People with Schizophrenia in Ethiopia," edited by Danuta Wasserman, *PLoS One* 16, no. 2 (2021): e0246158, https://doi.org/10.1371/journal.pone.0246158.

27. Lawrence Hsin Yang, Arthur Kleinman, Bruce G. Link, Jo C. Phelan, Sing Lee, and Byron Good, "Culture and Stigma: Adding Moral Experience to Stigma Theory," *Social Science & Medicine* 64, no. 7 (2007): 1524–1535, https://doi.org/10.1016/j.socscimed.2006.11.013.

28. Judith Bass, Richard Neugebauer, Kathleen F. Clougherty, et al., "Group Interpersonal Psychotherapy for Depression in Rural Uganda: 6-Month Outcomes," *British Journal of Psychiatry* 188, no. 6 (2006): 567–573, https://doi.org/10.1192/bjp.188.6.567.

29. Reaching the Hard to Reach

1. Russell E. Glasgow, Erin T. Eckstein, and M. Khair ElZarrad, "Implementation Science Perspectives and Opportunities for HIV / AIDS Research: Integrating Science, Practice, and Policy," *JAIDS Journal of Acquired Immune Deficiency Syndromes* 63 (June 2013): S26, https://doi.org /10.1097/QAI.0b013e3182920286.

2. "PIH's Five S's: Essential Elements for Strong Health Systems," Partners in Health, June 30, 2021, https://www.pih.org/article/pihs-five -ss-essential-elements-strong-health-systems.

3. "Maternal, Neonatal, and Child Health," UNICEF, 2018, https://www.unicef.org/sierraleone/maternal-neonatal-and-child-health.

4. Amy Maxmen, "Sierra Leone's Free Healthcare Initiative: A Work in Progress," *The Lancet* 38, no. 9862 (2013): 191–192, https://doi.org/10 .1016/s0140-6736(13)60074-4.

5. Jordan A. Freeman, Alethea Desrosiers, Carolyn Schafer, et al., "The Adaptation of a Youth Mental Health Intervention to a Peer-Delivery Model Utilizing CBPR Methods and the ADAPT-ITT Framework in Sierra Leone," *Transcultural Psychiatry* 61, no. 1 (2023), https://doi.org/10 .1177/13634615231202091.

Epilogue

1. "Freetown's New Terminal Makes History in Sierra Leone," *Airport World,* March 6, 2023, https://airport-world.com/freetowns-new-terminal-makes-history-in-sierra-leone/.

2. Tracey Elizabeth Claire Jones-Konneh, Angella Isata Kaikai, Ibrahim Borbor Bah, Daisuke Nonaka, Rie Takeuchi, and Jun Kobayashi, "Impact of Health Systems Reform on COVID-19 Control in Sierra Leone: A Case Study," *Tropical Medicine and Health* 51, no. 1 (2023), https://doi.org/10.1186/s41182-023-00521-z.

3. Tommy Trenchard, "Cheap, Plentiful and Devastating: The Synthetic Drug Kush Is Walloping Sierra Leone," National Public Radio, February 10, 2024, https://www.npr.org/sections/goatsandsoda/2024/02/10/1229662975/kush-synthetic-drug-sierra-leone.

4. Julius Maada Bio, *The Gender Equality and Women's Empowerment Act,* 2022, https://www.un.org/sites/www.un.org.africarenewal/files/ACT%20MOGCA.pdf; Kartikeya Sharma, "Rwandan Revolution: World's Highest Women's Participation in Parliament," *Sunday Guardian Live,* https://sundayguardianlive.com/news/rwandan-revolution-worlds-highest-womens-participation-parliament.

5. "Rainbo Initiative (RI)," Purposeful, 2021, https://wearepurposeful.org/meet-our-community/rainbo-initiative-ri/.

6. Sally Hayden, "What Can Other Countries Learn from Sierra Leone's Sexual Violence State of Emergency?" *Irish Times,* May 21, 2023, https://www.irishtimes.com/world/africa/2023/05/20/hands-off-our-girls-sierra-leones-fight-against-sexual-violence/.

7. "World Government Summit: Dr. David Sengeh of Sierra Leone Best Education Minister," *Patriotic Vanguard,* February 14, 2023, http://thepatrioticvanguard.com/world-government-summit-dr-david-sengeh-of-sierra-best-education-minister.

8. "World Government Summit."

9. Rashawn Ray and Alexandra Gibbons, "Why Are States Banning Critical Race Theory?" Brookings, November 2021, https://www.brookings.edu/articles/why-are-states-banning-critical-race-theory/.

Acknowledgments

It has taken over twenty-two years for *Shadows into Light* to come into being. As a result of this study, I have forged some of the most meaningful and lasting friendships of my life and a deep respect for the people and culture of Sierra Leone. This book has truly been a labor of love for a place that I cherish and a journey enriched by so many people—too many to name!—who have helped all along the way.

To Moses Zombo, my good friend and storyteller extraordinaire, who helped me get this study off the ground and served as one of the principal interviewers of the children and families involved. Moses has given these pages life through his words, and is largely responsible for all of the fieldwork that made telling these stories possible.

This book is a result of research funded by several major foundations and the following NIH grants: Intergenerational Impact of War: A Prospective Longitudinal Study (R01HD073349); Youth FORWARD: Capacity Building in Alternate Delivery Platforms and Implementation Models for Bringing Evidence-Based Behavioral Interventions to Scale for Youth Facing Adversity in West Africa (U19MH109989); Expanding the Reach of

Evidence-Based Mental Health Treatment; Diffusion and Spillover of Mental Health Benefits Among Peer Networks and Caregivers of Youth Facing Compounded Adversity in Sierra Leone (R01MH117359); and Social and Biological Mechanisms Driving the Intergenerational Impact of War on Child Mental Health: Implications for Developing Family-Based Interventions (R01MH128928). To our funders—a heartfelt thank you for your support and collaboration.

To Marie de la Soudière for her innovative efforts in family tracing and emphatic encouragement of something that had never been achieved before in following the lives of both young men and young women returning home. To my friends and colleagues Catherine Wiesner, Jeannie Annan, and Wendy Wheaton for helping me forge wonderful partnerships with the International Rescue Committee and for sharing their expertise and insights with me over many years of collaboration. To Paul Farmer, Maggie Alegria, Greg Aarons, Henry Louis Gates, Jr., Aiah Gbakima, Rebecca Esliker, Joel Marrant, Linda Olds, Judy Herman, Tony Earls, Steve Buka, and so many others for giving me feedback on culturally grounded and ethical research and interventions approaches.

To Father Peter Konteh, Father Joseph Bangura, and Ishmael Alfred Charles of Caritas Freetown, as well as the local leaders and community members in the districts where we have worked over the years, who have always given their time and input, and welcomed us to share key messages coming from study findings. Thank you for your collaboration, innovation, and support of a project that has grown in ways I could have never imagined when this all began. To Musu Moigua, Mahmoud Feika, and Mama G, for their dedication to improving our ethical and data management practices over our many years together as well as their oversight of our local research team. Without this team, all these years of research would not have been possible. Thank you for lending your voices, your expertise, and your professionalism.

To Paul, Elizabeth, and Dr. David Sengeh—a changemaker and visionary, as well as a friend—and to Kate and the girls, for always being so supportive.

To my dear friend and collaborator, Dr. Adeyinka Akinsulure-Smith, for all those hours brainstorming on a balcony in Freetown and for reading this book cover to cover. Another heartfelt thank you to her entire family, for helping me learn in depth about Sierra Leone's language, culture, and traditions. To Vikram Patel, Arthur Kleinman, and Alan Brandt for wonderful input on the book prospectus, and to Martha Minow for reading everything I sent and providing such thoughtful insights, chapter by chapter.

To the Harvard University Press team, specifically to Grigory Tovbis, Kate Brick, and former Press editor Andrew Kinney: thank you for seeing the value in these stories and allowing me the space to tell them. Thank you also to the UNICEF Innocenti Office of Research and Foresight for hosting me while I took a sabbatical to finish this book.

To my friends, family, and co-workers at the Research Program on Children and Adversity, especially Rachel Stram and Jamison O'Sullivan, who have tolerated my many late-night emails and the logistics of complicated fieldwork. To the Boston College School of Social Work, for giving this research a home.

To my own children, A and Joey, who traveled so willingly to Sierra Leone with me to learn and also to give back. To Rohn, for being an amazing and patient partner, despite my endless travel. To my parents, Michael and Norma Stichick, who taught me the value of truly listening and honoring culture and the values of social justice while raising our family in Alaska's Yukon-Kuskokwim Delta. It is this same spirit that I have endeavored to carry forward.

To those Sierra Leoneans who let my team inside of their homes and their lives year after year, or supported our work in any way: *tenki* for being a part of this work, for sharing your stories, and for letting me tell them. I can only hope to do them justice.

And finally, to the readers: thank you. I hope that this book was able to impart even a fraction of what I have felt and learned in my years of working in *Swit Salone.*

Index

Index

Bucharest Early Intervention Program
    (BEIP), 59–60
Burlingham, Dorothy, 117
"bush wives," 208

Calhoun, Lawrence, 89, 90
camp for internally displaced people, 98,
    108–111, 157
caregivers: children, attachment to, 40,
    42; interviews with, 78; relationships
    between, 220; as resource for healing,
    58, 81, 82–84; support of the former
    child soldiers by, 87–88
Caritas interim care center, 146–148
"cascade model" in mental health care,
    230
Ceaușescu, Nicolae, 59
character skills, 235
check point stop, 34–36
Child Behavior Checklist, 71
child development: attachment and, 71;
    caregivers' role in, 42; environment
    and, 42; father-engaged approach in,
    225–226; as field of study, 58–59, 234;
    resources for, 43; services, 225, 226;
    systems of, 42–43
Child Protective Services, 23
children: abducted by armed groups,
    3–4, 6–7, 8–9, 40, 77; access to digital
    tools, 23; anxiety and depression rates,
    25; armed conflicts and, 8, 15–16,
    117, 190, 249, 250; attachment of,
    40, 73; born of rape, 145, 208; climate
    change and, 25; definition of, 30,
    173–174; with disabilities, 108, 109,
    110–111; economic hardship of, 23–24,
    41; exposure to toxic stress, 21; global
    humanitarian crisis and, 15; mental
    health needs, 25; readiness for
    schooling, 234, 235–236; resilience of,
    16; rights of, 150, 153–155, 156, 174,
    260; six grave violations related to, 210
children associated with armed forces
    and armed groups (CAAFAG), 9, 11,
    12–13, 219. See also child soldiers
children's agency, 173, 174

Child Rights Act, 154
child soldiers: artwork of, 48; behavioral
    problems, 69, 79, 80, 82, 122; careers
    of, 94; community relationships, 54–55,
    57, 69, 79–80, 85, 86, 94, 118–119,
    165, 177; crimes committed by, 10;
    data collection about, 163; depression
    and anxiety of, 131, 141; discrimina-
    tion of, 120–121; disrupted attach-
    ments, 68, 69, 70–71; drug and alcohol
    problems, 79; education gap, 44–45,
    180, 186–187, 188, 190, 244; escape
    from captivity, 102; family reunions,
    53–54, 55, 73, 77–78, 81–82, 84–85,
    101–103, 105–107, 177; foster families
    of, 44–45, 60; fulfillment of human
    potential, 95–96; injuries of, 53,
    162–164; in interim care centers,
    11–12, 44, 47–48; leadership skills,
    165–166, 175, 178; life in captivity,
    49, 50, 52–53, 72; mental health prob-
    lems, 82–83, 94, 120, 122, 139–141,
    211–212; mortality rate of, 93–94,
    212; nicknames of, 72; nonbiological
    caregivers of, 81, 82–84, 87–88; par-
    ents' relationships with, 72–73, 74,
    119–120; partners and biological off-
    spring of, 56, 223; personal agency of,
    96, 166, 175, 178; rebel commanders
    and, 4–5, 10, 124, 145–146, 175–177;
    reintegration and rehabilitation of, 12,
    30, 73–74, 140, 207–208; rejection of,
    43–44, 118–119, 120; released from
    fighting forces, 11, 44; resilience of, 5,
    14, 48–49; schooling of, 55, 69, 79,
    86, 115, 157, 163, 177–178, 179–182,
    185–186, 187; self-care skills, 114,
    171, 239; self-image of, 187; sense of
    compassion, 94–95; sense of faith, 95;
    sense of identity, 142–143; separation
    from families, 49–50, 51–52; social
    isolation of, 74, 93, 119, 212–213;
    stereotypes of, 207–208; stigmatization
    of, 43, 121–122, 125, 183, 211; struggle
    with intrusive memories, 95; success
    stories, 56–57; toxic stress of, 39–40;

298

Index

Mandela, Nelson, 190
Masten, Ann: *Ordinary Magic,* 21, 204
Mazzurana, Dyan, 200
McBain, Ryan, 242
McLean, Kristen, 142
Médecins Sans Frontières, 113
memory-processing interventions, 95, 194
Memory Training for Recovery, 194
mental health: gender and, 139, 141; global crisis, 25; limited human resources for, 229, 233; medication, 82–83; stigmatization of, 125, 183–184, 211, 246; studies of, 139–140, 243, 246; war-related violence and, 215
MHPSS (mental health and psychosocial support) interventions: best practices of, 230, 245, 254–255; collaborative efforts, 224; common elements, 231; in conflict zones, 250; effectiveness of, 263; evidence-based components of, 37, 245–246, 250–251; family-based approach, 195–196; father-engaged approach, 226; frontline providers, 229, 239, 253–254; group-based programs, 211; home-visiting approach, 225, 226; identification of targets of, 220; integration with other programs, 199; investments in, 231–232, 245; limited resources for, 230–232, 239, 251; in Makeni District, 226; opportunities for advancement, 238–239; primary health care and, 252; trauma-informed approach to, 229, 230, 231, 240
Miller, Kenneth, 227
Ministry of Gender and Children's Affairs, 154
Ministry of Youth Affairs (MOYA), 252
Moigua, Musu, 56–57, 163, 168–169
Momoh, Joseph, 9
mothers of child soldiers: as caregivers, 104, 105; clothing deprivation, 51; courage of, 105; discrimination and stigmatization of, 123; in Guinea refugee camp, 105; relationships with children, 51–52, 53–54, 55, 104,

105–107; traumatic experience of, 49–50, 52
Mozambique: child soldiers in, 207
Murray, Laura, 230
Murthy, Vivek, 25
Mutuyimana, Celestin, 19

Namara, Suleiman, 237
Narrative Exposure Therapy (NET), 193, 194, 229
National Committee for Disarmament, Demobilization, and Reintegration, 10, 129–130
National Institute of Mental Health (NIMH), 198, 243
National Male Involvement Strategy for the Prevention of Sexual and Gender-Based Violence, 154
National Workshop Camp, 157–158
Nelson, Chuck, 59, 211
Network for Empowerment and Progressive Initiatives, 237
Neuner, Frank, 193, 229
Nigeria: child soldiers in, 9
9 / 11 terrorist attack, 91
noncognitive skills, 234–235
nongovernmental organizations (NGOs), 20, 34, 155, 186, 237, 252
numbing, 52–53

"orchid" children, 64
overprotective parenting, 18, 215, 216

Pakistan: education initiatives in, 184
parents: biobehavioral mechanisms of war-affected, 219–220; children and, 17, 220; depression, 195–196; hypervigilance, 18; negative practices, 24; studies of, 18, 58; trauma of, 17, 215–217, 227–228. *See also* fatherhood; mothers of child soldiers
Partners in Health, 213, 224, 242, 245
Pasteur, Louis, 171
Patel, Vikram, 229
Patricia (abducted girl): abduction of, 118, 123; community relationships,